Schizophrenia

The idea of 'schizophrenia' as a disease is now so influential that those who criticise it are apt to be dismissed as being ignorant of the latest research or indifferent to the fate of the 'mentally ill'. This book challenges such ideas by offering an original and detailed critique of the origins, development and maintenance of the concept and diagnosis of schizophrenia, and of the arguments used to support them.

Mary Boyle shows how such diagnoses, and research based on them, are characterised by conceptual confusion, and how research, particularly genetic research, has been misleadingly presented. She questions the scientific status of the concept of schizophrenia but emphasises that this is not to deny the existence of bizarre behaviour or the distress it may cause. She offers alternative interpretations of such behaviour and points out the need to ask searching questions about the labelling of some behaviour as symptomatic of mental illness.

By focusing not on 'schizophrenics' but on those who diagnose 'schizophrenia', this book will undoubtedly attract some criticism and debate. Yet the approach allows the reader to question traditional interpretations of bizarre behaviour and to place them in their social and ethical context.

Schizophrenia – a scientific delusion? is aimed at psychologists, psychiatrists, historians of medicine and psychiatry, as well as students of the sociology of knowledge.

The author

Mary Boyle has worked as an NHS clinical psychologist and, since 1983, has been head of clinical psychology training at the Polytechnic of East London.

Schizophrenia
A scientific delusion?

Mary Boyle

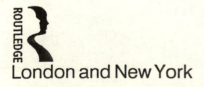

London and New York

First published 1990
by Routledge
11 New Fetter Lane, London EC4P 4EE

Simultaneously published in the USA and Canada
by Routledge
a division of Routledge, Chapman and Hall, Inc.
29 West 35th Street, New York, NY 10001

© 1990 Mary Boyle

Typeset by NWL Editorial Services,
Langport, Somerset TA10 9DG

Printed and bound in Great Britain by
Billings & Sons Ltd, Worcester.

British Library Cataloguing in Publication Data
Boyle, Mary, *1949–*
    Schizophrenia – a scientific delusion?
    1. Man. Schizophrenia
    I. Title
    616.89'82

Library of Congress Cataloging in Publication Data
Boyle, Mary.
    Schizophrenia – a scientific delusion? / Mary Boyle.
    p.   cm.
    Includes bibliographical references.
    1. Schizophrenia—Diagnosis—History. I. Title.
    RC514.B65   1990   89–70179
    616.89'82075—dc20   CIP

ISBN 0–415–04096–5

Contents

Figures and tables

Preface

It is now almost a hundred years since Kraepelin introduced his concept of dementia praecox, the direct forerunner of Bleuler's and the modern concepts of schizophrenia. Criticising these concepts has been a popular sport for almost the same length of time, although the criticism has perhaps become more pointed, and more radical, over the last twenty years. A variety of responses has been made to the critics, with one of the most popular recent themes being 'We're getting there': given enough time and complex measuring equipment, diagnosis will be made more rigorous and the causes of schizophrenia will be better understood. There seems, too, to be little doubt amongst supporters of the concept that the route to progress will be via the laboratories of neurochemists, geneticists and molecular biologists. (See, for example, the Medical Research Council's 1987 Report on 'Research into Schizophrenia'.)

The major aim of this book is to show that such answers will simply not do, because they ignore fundamental problems of the concept of schizophrenia and of variants such as the 'schizophrenia spectrum'. The book has four more specific aims. The first is to set out the claims made for 'schizophrenia' and, more importantly, what must be achieved for these to be accepted. It is my impression that this latter question is often glossed over, if not misrepresented, in much of the literature, so that it is difficult for readers to assess the strength of the claims. The second aim is to evaluate the extent to which the claims made for 'schizophrenia' are justified and the third (having concluded that they are not) is to discuss alternatives to the concept, both in terms of research design and theories of bizarre behaviour. Finally, by setting out in some detail the story of the introduction, development and use of 'schizophrenia' as well as some of the fallacious arguments used to support it, I hope to make understandable some of the reasons for the chaos and controversy which have so often surrounded the concept, for its persistence in spite of these, and to make clear why no amount of tinkering with it will bestow scientific respectability.

If the book can be said to adopt an approach, it is that of Social Constructionism. It has been ironically said of this approach that it has the "annoying feature of turning attention away from a problem and onto those who are trying to deal with the problem" (Heise, 1988). This book certainly has that feature: it concentrates not on 'schizophrenics' but on those who diagnose schizophrenia. It will, therefore, probably annoy many people. I hope, however, that for others it will be thought-provoking, and will encourage them seriously to question traditional interpretations of bizarre behaviour and to make more central the social and ethical issues involved both in theorising about, and responding to, such behaviour.

Acknowledgements

Although I have to take full responsibility for the opinions and arguments put forward in this book, I owe a special debt to three people who, in various ways, have helped and encouraged me to develop them: Peter Slade, Clive Gabriel, and Ted Sarbin.

I have also benefited greatly from discussions with Dick Hallam (to whom thanks also for the title!), John Radford, and Ernie Govier. And thanks, too, to Colin Berry for his meticulous translations of German manuscripts.

Mary Boyle
January 1990

Chapter one

Evaluating the validity of 'schizophrenia'

Two major claims have been made about the concept of schizophrenia – that it is a scientific concept or, at least, that those who use it work within a scientific framework (for example, Wing, 1978b; Arieti, 1979; Clare, 1980; Neale and Oltmanns, 1980; Gottesman and Shields, 1982); and that the term refers to a particular kind of medical pattern known as a syndrome (Kendell, 1975b; APA, 1980; Neale and Oltmanns, 1980; Strauss and Carpenter, 1981; Gottesman and Shields, 1982). These claims imply that the concept has been developed and is used in a manner similar to that of other concepts which claim scientific status and that the phenomena to which it refers are similar in form to those usually denoted by the medical term, syndrome. This chapter will describe in detail what is meant by these claims, so as to compare the development and use of 'schizophrenia' with them.

'Schizophrenia' as a scientific concept

As Medawar (1984) has pointed out, attempts to define 'science', to give the term some absolute meaning, have always ended in failure. Thus, all that will be attempted here is a description of some of the ways in which those who call themselves scientists tend to proceed.

The search for patterns and attempts to describe relationships between phenomena are central to scientific activity. They are central, too, to much non-scientific activity; of particular interest here is that they are central to lay or everyday attempts to understand behaviour and other events. What perhaps distinguishes the two is the scientist's persistent demand for the provision of certain types of evidence that a pattern has been observed and the imposition of various publicly demonstrable criteria for evaluating it. This demand for evidence, and its public evaluation, is crucial in view of our apparent propensity to claim that certain events 'go together', in the absence of any direct evidence that this is the case (see, for example, Mischel, 1968; Shweder, 1977).

Observables and unobservables in scientific theory

Although the term observable may give the misleading impression of pertaining to some outside reality, it will be used here simply to mean readily agreed statements about sense data with a minimum of interpretation. From simple statements about putative relationships between observables (when certain metals are brought close together, one moves towards the other), unobservables (magnetic force) may be inferred and, as will be seen, used to aid the construction of more elaborate statements.

It is readily agreed that 'schizophrenia' is an unobservable, an abstract concept inferred from overt behaviour or from verbal reports of behaviour and experience (for example, Kendell, 1975b; APA, 1980; Neale and Oltmanns, 1980). Scientific theories, however, may contain different types of unobservable and it is important to distinguish them in assessing the validity of 'schizophrenia'. Beck (1953) has distinguished two by applying the concepts of *systemic* and *real* 'existence' and the language of logic to differentiate them. The first, he says, is that "mode of existence of an (unobserved) entity all descriptions of which are analytical within a system of propositions", while real existence "is the mode of existence attributed to an entity if there is any true synthetic proposition that can be made about it" (369). Thus, statements about an unobservable said to have real existence will contain words which are not reducible to the empirical relationships from which it is inferred and will imply hypotheses about their antecedents.

Benjamin (1937) has made the same distinction by contrasting what he calls abstractive and hypothetical methods in scientific activity. In the abstractive method, phenomena are grouped by a restrictive set of properties into classes whose relationship can be discovered empirically; nothing is added to what is observed. The hypothetical method relates observations by "inventing a fictitious substance or process or idea in terms of which the experiences can be expressed. It correlates observations by adding something to them." (184) Constructs formed by Benjamin's abstractive method (for example, solubility, resistance, temperature, habit strength, hunger as X hours food deprivation, and so on) would be said by Beck to have systemic existence while those formed by the hypothetical method (electricity, proton, intelligence, diabetes) would be said to have real existence. MacCorquodale and Meehl (1948) have suggested the terms intervening variables and hypothetical constructs to distinguish these two types of unobservable, and these terms will be adopted here. Other names have, however, been suggested: Beck uses constructions and inferred entities while Carnap (1937) uses the term dispositional concepts rather than intervening variables. Although all hypothetical concepts refer to unobservables, it is worth noting a distinction between two different types. The first is that which becomes, in Beck's phrase, an 'object of search' and which is postulated to show certain characteristics. The constructs of atom or proton are examples of this type; although unobserved, they are postulated to exist as a result of certain observations and mathematical calculations. The second type remains for ever an abstraction, which cannot be postulated to exist except in the most abstract sense. 'Intelligence', 'memory' and 'diabetes' are examples of this type of hypothetical construct.

Which kind of concept is 'schizophrenia'? Kraepelin clearly did not see his concept of dementia praecox, from which the modern concept of schizophrenia is derived, as being reducible to a statement about correlations between behaviours. Instead, he postulated a 'metabolic disorder' to *account for* the putative correlations. Similarly, statements made today about the concept contain terms not reducible to statements about behavioural correlations. 'Schizophrenia' is said to be an illness; a biochemical disorder; a genetic disorder. What is implied by such statements is not always specified but it is clear that something is being added to a statement about behavioural correlations. 'Schizophrenia' therefore functions as a hypothetical construct rather than as an intervening variable; and as an abstraction from observables, rather than an 'entity' postulated to exist as a result of observations, it also functions as one of the second type of hypothetical construct. It must be emphasised that this status has nothing to do with the present lack of a clear relationship between biochemical events and behaviour said to be symptomatic of schizophrenia. Even if such events were to be observed, the construct would remain an abstraction, because there is no identity between it and any biological, genetic or behavioural event, any more than there is identity between the concept of diabetes and a specific biological event.

The most important distinction between hypothetical constructs (of both types) and intervening variables lies in the predictive function of hypothetical constructs (Benjamin, 1937; MacCorquodale and Meehl, 1948; Beck, 1953; Carnap, 1974). They have, or should have, the power to generate predictions about events which have not yet been observed. This power derives in part from the fact that hypothetical constructs, unlike intervening variables, are not reducible to statements about what has already been observed, but imply hypotheses about antecedents. This distinction has important implications for evaluating the validity of the two types of construct. The validity of an intervening variable can be questioned only by denying the observations from which it was originally inferred, i.e. by claiming that such and such did not actually happen. The concept of solubility, for example, requires only that substances be observed to dissolve at different rates and to different extents in water or other liquids; it implies nothing about the variables which control this. Thus, these observations are said to be both *necessary* and *sufficient* conditions for asserting the validity of the concept. For a hypothetical construct, the actual occurrence of the empirical relationships from which it was inferred is, of course, a necessary condition for asserting its validity but it is not sufficient. The demonstration of predictive power is central to assertions of the validity of hypothetical constructs and is the sufficient condition for inferring them.

The correspondence rules of hypothetical constructs

To say that a construct has predictive power is to say that it is capable of predicting events which, though observable in principle, have not yet been observed. Thus, the construct of intelligence may be capable of predicting performance differences in a laboratory task. It is possible to use unobservables to make and investigate statements about observables because of what are variously called correspondence rules (Carnap, 1974), operational rules (Bridgman, 1927) and The Dictionary (Campbell, 1920; cited in Carnap, 1974). These rules, which may be very simple or highly complex, specify what must be observed before a construct can be inferred and may specify quantitatively the relationship between variation in what is observed and variation in the inferred construct. The correspondence rules for the construct of intelligence, for example, specify the relationship between observable responses to items on a standardised test and 'amounts' of the unobservable construct intelligence. Any investigation of the predictive power of a hypothetical construct therefore involves examining the relationship between two sets of observables.

The process of change of correspondence rules

It is usual for inferred constructs to start as relatively vague concepts associated with certain observations. It is then discovered, by empirical investigation, that these observations vary systematically with another observation which can be more reliably made and is more strongly correlated with relevant experimental changes. The concept of temperature, for example, was originally associated with global, subjective judgements of hot and cold. It was later shown that these judgements and a range of other phenomena were reliably correlated with measurable changes in the height of a mercury column. Similarly, the concept of intelligence was originally associated with subjective judgements of cleverness and dullness. The correspondence rules for inferred constructs, i.e. what must be observed before the construct is inferred, therefore change over time as a result of increasing specification and elaboration of events which can be shown to be associated with the original set of observations from which the construct was inferred. That correspondence rules do change in this way may, of course, be a demonstration of a construct's predictive power.

This process of change in correspondence rules is well illustrated by the development of the medical concept of diabetes mellitus. The construct of diabetes was originally inferred by the Greeks from observations of the co-occurrence of inordinate thirst and urine production, lethargy and emaciation. These observations therefore constituted the first set of correspondence rules for the hypothetical construct of diabetes. In the seventeenth century it was noted that this cluster was frequently and reliably associated with sweet-tasting urine. Thus, a new correspondence rule could be set up between an observable event and the unobservable 'diabetes'. Later, it was discovered that sweet-tasting urine contained glucose which could be detected independently of the original observation of inordinate thirst, and so on or judgements about the sweetness of urine. Yet another set of correspondence rules could be set up. These, in turn, were superseded by rules specifying that diabetes mellitus was to be inferred when a certain relationship between intake of glucose and its level in the blood at certain time intervals was observed. (The 'division' of the concept of diabetes into mellitus and insipidus was necessitated by the observations that inordinate thirst and urine production were not always associated with sweet-tasting urine and, later, that they could be associated with low levels of anti-diuretic hormone.)

Every attempt to examine the fate of predictions from a hypothetical construct involves the use of its correspondence rules. Thus, each attempt to show that the *sufficient* conditions for inferring the construct are fulfilled involves invoking the necessary conditions for inferring its existence. In the very early stages of a construct's development, the necessary conditions – the putative regularities from which the construct was originally inferred – will also be the correspondence rules. Later, the necessary conditions will be invoked indirectly as the correspondence rules change. But it would be quite wrong to depict this process of change in correspondence rules as one of finding out what a hypothetical construct 'is'. Young (1951) and Carnap (1974) have noted how often the question, 'What is X?', where X is a hypothetical construct, is put to scientists by lay people. They point out that the question is unanswerable and is based on a misunderstanding of the function of hypothetical constructs, which can be described only in terms of the observed events from which they are inferred and the predictions which have been made from them, in terms, that is, of the theoretical network in which they are embedded. The question 'What is diabetes?' would be answered (and attempts, however misguided, are often made to answer such questions) very differently in classical Greece and in the twentieth-century western world and will, no doubt, be answered very differently again in the twenty-first century as the theoretical network is further elaborated. Each answer is 'true' but misleading; to pose the question at all is to reify the construct and to imply that there is a final, concrete answer.

Deriving predictions from hypothetical constructs

The correspondence rules which tie an unobservable to observable events provide the general means for examining predictions from a construct. The *content* of these predictions can be specified only by examining the whole theoretical network which surrounds the concept, the assumptions on which it is based, indeed, everything that is asserted about it (Cronbach and Meehl, 1955). The statements which make up this network may relate observables to

5

each other, unobservables to observables, and/or unobservables to one another. It is, however, axiomatic that any construct which claims scientific status be embedded in a network at least some of whose statements contain observables. The ease with which predictions may be derived from this network, and investigated, depends not on its simplicity but on its specificity. One obvious result of a lack of specificity is disagreement over the content of predictions; another is disagreement over the results of attempts to test an agreed prediction. There is no question of a construct's validity depending on a particular number of the predictions derived from it being upheld; there is certainly no quantitative answer to the question, 'How valid is construct X?' Rather, validity is usually assessed from a utilitarian stance by asking in what ways and for what purposes the construct has proved useful. Thus, the term utility is often substituted for validity to reflect the fact that, as a rule, a hypothetical construct has no claim to validity unless it can be used to predict events which, without the construct, would probably have gone undetected. If the same events are predicted by different constructs, then that which carries fewest assumptions is usually preferred.

It may happen, however, that research fails to detect events predicted from a construct. The question then arises as to whether the 'fault' lies with the construct, and its theoretical network, or with the method of enquiry. As will be seen in Chapter 2, the nineteenth-century medical profession sought to retain the concept of mental disease even though they were unable to detect the predicted differences between the brains of those from whose behaviour the construct had been inferred and those from whose it had not. It was argued that existing methods of measuring brain function were not sufficiently advanced to detect the postulated differences. This may well have been true, but such a *post hoc* argument could be used indefinitely to justify the continued use of a construct, one of whose major predictions had no empirical support. It can be argued that, if a construct has already led to the detection of hitherto unobserved events and is the source of predictions to specific events observable in principle but thought to be undetectable by existing methods, then the failure to detect such an event might well indicate that a more sophisticated methodology is required and not that the construct is invalid. But if a construct is in the early stages of development, if it lacks a history of 'successful' predictions or is embedded in a loose theoretical network which cannot be used to predict specific events, then the 'failure' of a major prediction should direct attention to the construct itself. In particular, we may ask whether the necessary conditions for inferring it are fulfilled (i.e. was a set of regularities originally observed?) as these are invoked, directly or indirectly, each time a prediction is 'tested'. This question – of whether or not the necessary conditions for inferring schizophrenia have been fulfilled – will be central to this book.

Lay and scientific concepts

These methods of developing and investigating constructs may be compared with the development and use of what are usually called 'lay' or 'folk' concepts. Our language is rich in terms, particularly those referring to people, which are superficially similar to hypothetical constructs. Some of them (deep; hard) are obviously metaphorical and others (anxious; normal) less obviously so. There are some major differences between these concepts and those whose claims to scientific status are rarely disputed; two of these are of particular interest here. The first is that the correspondence rules of lay concepts are often many and varied, and vary from user to user. They tend also to change in idiosycratic ways over time: the referents of the concept 'nice', for example, used to be very similar, when applied to women, to those of more modern concepts like 'fast'. The second difference is that, although these terms may appear to be derived from patterns of behaviour, no systematic attempts are usually made to check this; or, when they have been made (for example, Chapman and Chapman, 1967; Mischel, 1968; Shweder, 1977) the apparent patterns have been shown to be more closely related to cultural beliefs about 'what goes with what' than to reliable observations. It must be emphasised that attempts to demonstrate that lay concepts are not necessarily 'messy' (for example, Cantor and Mischel, 1977; Cantor *et al.*, 1980) do not affect their status as lay constructs but at most can be said to demonstrate the orderliness of cultural beliefs and stereotypes.

None of this is intended as criticism of lay concepts or as a demonstration of their inferiority. They are not intended to serve the functions of scientific concepts but to be used in day-to-day discourse. It would place an intolerable burden on our interaction if we had to assess the reliability and validity of every concept before we could use it. Problems arise only when lay concepts are used *as if* they had been derived in a way quite different from how they actually were (see, for example, Sarbin's 1968 discussion of 'anxiety' and Warburton's 1985 discussion of 'addiction'). These points are made in some detail here because, as will be seen, they may be important in understanding some of the problems encountered by 'schizophrenia'.

'Schizophrenia' as a syndrome

The claim that 'schizophrenia' is a scientific concept implies that it was derived from the observation of a pattern of regularities. The claim that the term refers to a syndrome implies that it was derived from, and now refers to, a particular type of pattern. This pattern, and the ways in which it differs from that originally envisaged by Kraepelin, can perhaps best be clarified by describing some of the historical background to modern medical ideas about pattern description.

In medicine, ideas about pattern identification, about the grouping of phenomena, are inseparable from ideas about the concept of disease. Engle (1963) has described two important and contrasting views on diseases which can be traced to classical Greece. The Platonic tradition taught that reality was universal and unchanging, unlike perceptions received through the senses, which were relative and imperfect. Applied to medicine, these ideas led to a search for unvarying universals – individual diseases 'out there' and separable from the person. The Aristotelian tradition, by contrast, did not scorn sense data and encouraged the detailed study, for its own sake, of what were assumed to be the manifestations of disease in individuals, rather than the search for abstract (or metaphysical?) universals.

In practice, of course, it was not always an easy matter to distinguish those who claimed adherence to one school or the other. The theories were expressed in a way which made less than clear exactly what behaviour should follow and, in any case, adherents to the Platonic school, their distrust of the senses notwithstanding, were forced to work with phenomena as they presented to the senses. They did this to such an extent that it seemed that every phenomenon they observed was classified as a disease – skin rashes, swellings, fevers, and so on. Indeed, de Sauvages was able, in 1763, to list 2,400 diseases, most of which would now be considered to be individual symptoms (Zilboorg, 1941). It would therefore be naive to expect the Platonic and Aristotelian views to be clearly distinguishable in the actual activities of medical men (as distinct from what they said they were doing); nevertheless, two distinct themes, roughly corresponding to the two ancient traditions, can be discerned in the writings of philosophers and physicians on 'disease'. These have been variously characterised as ontological (disease-entity) versus biographical; qualitative versus quantitative; discontinuous versus continuous (Kendell, 1975b). Thomas Sydenham was one of the most articulate proponents of the ontological view of disease. Writing at the end of the seventeenth century, he reiterated the belief in the existence of natural and unvarying disease entities, separable from the person, and whose presentation was uniform across sufferers. These entities, he maintained, must be separated because each required a different treatment.

Sydenham's ideas, which were heavily influenced by the classification systems of botanists and by the 'disease' of malaria, were extremely popular because, as Kräupl-Taylor (1979) suggests, they encouraged medical men to participate fully, via clinical observations, in the search for clinical data on which to base a classificatory system. Indeed, this was done with such enthusiasm that for almost every physician, there was a classificatory system. These efforts were considerably hampered not only by tenuous acquaintance with the principles of classification (Zilboorg, 1941) but also by the fact that observations were subjective and limited to what could be observed 'at the bedside'.

Sydenham's ontological theories were strongly challenged in the late eighteenth and early nineteenth centuries. In particular, critics attacked his view of disease entities as having a separate existence and suggested that disease was a quantitative and not a qualitative deviation from the norm, and that the course might vary from individual to individual. In 1847, Virchow declared that "Diseases have no independent or isolated existence; they are not autonomous organisms, nor beings invading a body, nor parasites growing on it; they are only the manifestations of life process under altered conditions." (Kräupl-Taylor, 1979: 11) But later in the century, Virchow was to alter his views to the extent that he was able, in 1895, to call himself a "thoroughgoing ontologist". His concept of disease entity was, however, very different from Sydenham's. The introduction of the microscope and the practice of histology in the late nineteenth century allowed the detailed investigation of the various bodily derangements which accompanied overt symptoms. For Virchow, a disease entity was a particular pathological abnormality. A disease entity therefore became an altered body part, a significant change which avoided the metaphysical overtones of Sydenham's theory. Classification consisted of descriptions of the various types of change which could be observed in different body organs; diagnosis, in the matching of these to the changes observed in a particular patient.

Virchow's views in turn were challenged by bacteriologists at the end of the nineteenth century. The nature of their dispute is clearly illustrated by an example given by Kräupl-Taylor (1979). Virchow began from the premiss that a pathological abnormality constituted a disease entity and that the diagnosis had to name the abnormality, no matter how it was caused. Diphtheria, for example, would be diagnosed whenever surface necrosis and membrane formation were observed in an organ. That these changes could have causes other than the presence of the diphtheria bacilli was not important to Virchow. To the bacteriologists, diagnosis consisted in identifying the kind of organism which had invaded the body, regardless of the nature of the pathological changes it might produce in any individual. The bacteriologists' views won the day because they proved more useful than those of Virchow. But the debate between them and Virchow was between one kind of ontological theory and another; there is no doubt that the bacteriologists' findings served to strengthen the already popular ontological theories to an extent never achieved by Sydenham and his many followers. Once again, a disease entity had become a discrete and separate unit, with its own distinctive cause, symptoms, course and outcome.

It is interesting to note the strength of ontological theories in lay discourse about physical ailments. As Kräupl-Taylor (1979) has pointed out, much of the language surrounding disease implies an ontological theory – we talk of 'catching' or 'getting rid of a disease'; we are 'attacked by diseases'; we 'carry diseases' which we 'pass on' to our children or to others. It is notable also that ontological theories seem to offer a reassuringly simple solution to the apparent chaos of physical suffering: a number of seemingly disparate phenomena can be accounted for and perhaps abolished by reference to one underlying cause.

From disease-entity to syndrome

As Kendell (1975b) has pointed out, Kraepelin's ideas about the phenomena with which he was confronted in asylums were derived from a Platonic view of the world. His belief in natural disease entities with an independent existence was, of course, strengthened by the finding that single micro-organisms, with an independent existence, were responsible for certain clusters of phenomena with their own, apparently natural, course and outcome. Kraepelin accepted unquestioningly that the behaviour of asylum inmates was a manifestation of biological events, just as were the fevers, rashes and, at times, odd behaviours of those infected with various micro-organisms. He therefore assumed that the inmates' behaviour would be found to fall into natural clusters, representing qualitative deviations from whatever he thought of as normality and that each cluster would have its own distinct antecedent, both necessary and sufficient to produce the cluster.

But, as was noted earlier, there were conflicting views as to the nature of these entities. Some said the entity was the observed cluster; others that it was the antecedent of the cluster and still others that it was the anatomical pathology which accompanied the overt cluster. Indeed, as Kräupl-Taylor (1982) has pointed out, Sydenham himself appears to have used the term in two quite different ways – to refer both to an independent, God-given species and to the body's reaction to invasion by external agents. Kraepelin was well aware of the fact that any attempt to postulate antecedents for putative clusters of behaviour was pure speculation; similarly, it made no sense to suggest that the term disease entity be applied to morbid anatomy when none could be found in many asylum inmates. However, as Jaspers (1963) has remarked, Kraepelin "embarked on a new approach which hoped to arrive at disease entities in spite of everything" (566). This approach consisted in observing inmates' behaviour in an attempt to discover similarities amongst the most frequently appearing behaviours and similarities in the ways they changed over time. Charting behaviour changes over time (called 'the whole course of the illness') presented considerable problems as asylum doctors had direct access to inmates' behaviour only from the time of their incarceration. Attempts were to be made, however, to reconstruct the past from discussion with inmates or their relatives. Strictly speaking, Kraepelin's approach was not new; followers of both the Platonic and the Aristotelian traditions had stressed the importance of careful observation of morbid manifestations, although attempts to describe similarities amongst these phenomena in different individuals and the view that a disease-entity accounted for them, was largely confined to the Platonic school. The novelty of Kraepelin's approach lay in its emphasis on investigating the 'whole course of the illness' in an attempt to discover natural groupings. Kraepelin believed that the behavioural clusters he hoped to discover would be found to have distinctive biological antecedents and cerebral pathology as well as course and outcome. The totality of this pattern would be called a natural disease entity.

It is well documented that Kraepelin's hopes of finding such patterns were never realised, either by him or by any of his successors (Jaspers, 1963; Kendell, 1975b; Wing, 1978a; Gottesman and Shields, 1982). Instead, as was pointed out earlier, it is now claimed that the term schizophrenia refers to a syndrome, which is usually described as a clustering of symptoms and signs (Morris, 1978). More generally, the term syndrome refers to the fact that certain phenomena appear to cluster at greater than chance level. It is not assumed that the clusters of events denoted by the syndrome name are distinctive natural groupings. There may, for example, be considerable variability across people displaying the cluster in the way it changes over time. The antecedents of the cluster are generally unknown.

Most syndrome names (for example, rheumatoid arthritis) refer to hypothetical constructs and should therefore fulfil the functions of summarising a pattern of observations and of allowing predictions to as yet unobserved events. Syndrome names are thus theoretical abstractions which are thought to be useful in research but which may be abandoned if and when they cease to fulfil this function. The construct of Down's Syndrome, for example, has proved extremely useful in that it allowed predictions to hitherto unobserved features of chromosomes. The idea of a syndrome, unlike that of a disease-entity, can encompass both qualitative and quantitative deviations from a norm: there is no reason to suppose that the possession of certain characteristics which represent a quantitative deviation from some standard might not have implications which are different in important ways from those associated with the possession of a standard set of characteristics.

The identification of syndrome patterns

One function of the construct denoted by a syndrome name is to summarise a meaningful cluster of phenomena, i.e. a cluster unlikely to have occurred by chance and therefore likely to signify other, as yet unknown, events. It is easy to imagine that certain occurrences form a pattern (Shweder, 1977; Chapman and Chapman, 1982); it is much more difficult to determine whether a pattern actually has been observed. The method favoured by Kraepelin – that of charting the progress of a postulated cluster – has a number of problems associated with it, whether or not it involves ideas about disease entities. The use of the term outcome in this context implies, erroneously, that a specific end-point can be identified. In practice, however, the term usually refers to a complex series of events or processes with no obvious end-point. Given the problems of deciding which variables to measure and when to end the process, and the finding that most of the clusters which are the source of syndrome names show considerable variability over time, it would be unproductive to rely on outcome as a criterion of meaningfulness for any postulated cluster. The problem is compounded by the fact that identification of possible new instances of the cluster (diagnosis) is impossible until their progress is charted, to check that it matches that of the earlier instances. A reliance on 'outcome' is apt to lead to *post hoc* diagnosis (and, as will be shown, Kraepelin himself fell into this trap) where a diagnostic label may be changed several times, depending on the progress of the phenomena from which it was inferred.

A more productive method of judging whether a postulated cluster is meaningful is to search for an independently and reliably measurable phenomenon which is reliably associated with the cluster and which can be demonstrated, or reasonably suggested to be an antecedent. This phenomenon may, in turn, be found to be associated with another reliably and independently measurable event, and so on along an assumed 'causal' chain. This process is, of course, one by which correspondence rules for an unobservable may become more reliable and more specific and its theoretical network more elaborate; it was described earlier for the construct of diabetes mellitus.

In medicine, those phenomena which made up the cluster from which unobservables were originally inferred were often those most easily and directly perceptible to an observer or to the person themselves, for example pallor, sweating, rashes, vomiting, pain, and so on. Such phenomena are usually called symptoms and share a number of characteristics. First, they are often not directly observable to an onlooker (for example, nausea) but are made available by verbal report. Second, the reliability with which they can be observed may be unsatisfactorily low. Third, they are overdetermined in that each may have many antecedents. The clustering of any of these events in an individual might therefore be a chance occurrence; indeed, if the reliability of reports of their occurrence is low, then reports of their co-occurrence may be false. It is therefore unwise to assume that any reported co-occurrence of such events is meaningful or to infer from it the existence of an unobserved process. Instead, it is necessary to demonstrate that any supposed cluster of symptoms is reliably associated with another independently measurable event. In medicine, such events are called signs and they differ from events designated as symptoms in a number of important ways. First, they can be observed with a much higher degree of reliability. Second, they are directly available to an observer, rather than being available only through introspection and verbal report or by inference from, for example, shaking or moaning. Third, although signs are also overdetermined, it is assumed that the number of antecedents is fewer than for symptoms. The frequency of occurrence of signs in an unselected population will therefore be less than that of symptoms. Fourth, there should exist plausible, even if speculative, theoretical links between those signs and symptoms whose co-occurrence is said to be meaningful, to justify the assumption that the signs are antecedents of the symptoms.

In order to clarify the distinction between signs and symptoms in medicine, Kräupl-Taylor (1979) uses the example of glucose in the urine. This is designated as a sign because it can be reliably measured by an external observer, its frequency of occurrence is less than is the individual frequency of events with which it may be associated (excess urine production, thirst, tiredness, and so on) and because there are plausible grounds for assuming that it is not a consequence of these. The term sign suggests that an event signifies, or is indicative of, another event which can be independently observed. The presence of glucose in the urine may signify hyperglycaemia (itself an overdetermined event) or diminished glucose reabsorption in the renal tubes. Because hyperglycaemia fulfils the criteria listed above, it too is designated a sign. Signs are often mistakenly said to be indicative of a syndrome name as, for example, when high blood glucose levels are said to be a sign of diabetes. Such statements are obviously tautological because the syndrome name does not refer to an observable event which can be measured independently of the sign.

People to whom the same syndrome name is applied as a diagnostic label will usually be homogeneous for at least one sign in the cluster from which the syndrome name is inferred. They will, however, be heterogeneous for symptoms because the same sign may be associated with a variety of symptoms. This heterogeneity suggests that unknown mediating variables are operating in the chain from sign to symptoms. Similarly, because signs are overdetermined, people who show the same sign may be given different diagnostic labels to reflect the fact that the antecedents of the sign they share – probably unknown in the case of those given the syndrome name as a diagnostic label – appear to be different. These people are also likely to share a number of symptoms. But even those who do not share signs may share symptoms because different signs are associated with the same symptoms (for example, nausea, abdominal pain, fever, and so on).

In spite of the heterogeneity amongst those given the same diagnostic label and the overlap amongst those given different labels, it is thought to be useful to maintain the separation between some groups who share signs and symptoms because they do not share antecedents. Only some of those who show glucose in the urine, for example, will show hyperglycaemia and those who do will, in turn, show a variety of pancreatic abnormalities. It is therefore assumed that different processes led to the appearance of the signs in the various groups. This assumption may be supported by the observations that between-group variability in progress over time is considerably greater than within-group variance; that the groups, without intervention, reach obviously different end-points, for example early death versus average life-span, or that response to the same intervention is quite different between groups. Taken together, these differences provide good grounds for separating the groups for research purposes. Even if such differences are not observed, the separation of the groups, for the present, may be justified if the proximal antecedents of the sign they share seem to be different.

Implications for the validity of 'schizophrenia'

The necessary conditions

It has been noted that the necessary condition for inferring a hypothetical construct is the observation of a pattern of regularities. The original inference of dementia praecox and then of schizophrenia therefore implies that such a pattern was observed in the behaviour of asylum inmates. It has also been noted that the observation of a particular type of pattern has been claimed. To claim that 'schizophrenia' refers to a syndrome is to claim that the cluster of phenomena which was originally and is now the source of the construct contains events which may be called signs and events which may be called symptoms, and that these fulfil the criteria set out earlier.

One of the problems of discussing the status of the necessary conditions for inferring schizophrenia is that various sets of regularities have been put forward as the source of the construct. But because it is generally accepted that Kraepelin's construct of dementia praecox marked the beginning of the modern construct of schizophrenia (for example, Kendell, 1975b; Wing, 1978a; Neale and Oltmanns, 1980; Gottesman and Shields, 1982) – indeed the terms dementia praecox and schizophrenia were often used interchangeably at least until the 1930s – the regularities in the behaviour of asylum inmates allegedly observed by Kraepelin will be taken here as the first set of necessary conditions for inferring schizophrenia. These, together with the clusters suggested by Bleuler and Schneider, will be examined in Chapter 3.

The sufficient conditions

It can hardly be overemphasised that if the necessary conditions for inferring a hypothetical construct have not been fulfilled, then the sufficient conditions cannot be either. It must be said, however, that if it were to be shown that the cluster from which schizophrenia was and is inferred did conform to the pattern denoted by 'syndrome', it would amount to the fulfilment of the necessary and just sufficient conditions for inferring it, because an originally postulated cluster would have been shown to be reliably associated with an independently and reliably measurable event, i.e. to have some predictive power.

But considerably more than this is claimed for 'schizophrenia'. A number of predictions have been derived from the construct but it is admitted that data relating to many of them (for example, that particular patterns of cognitive or psychophysiological or biochemical functioning will be observed) are in some disarray (for example, Neale and Oltmanns, 1980; Karson *et al.*, 1986; Wing, 1988). What users of 'schizophrenia' claim not to be in disarray are data relating to predictions about genetic inheritance. It is claimed, for example, that this hypothesis has been "proven" (APA, 1980) and that the evidence is "incontrovertible" (Kendell, 1975b). These claims will be examined in

Chapter 6. They will be examined in some detail first, because of their strength and near unanimity; second, because these data may be used to justify both the continuing search for supporting biochemical data and the retention of a particular theoretical model; and, third, because the presentation of this literature could offer examples of the ways in which the presentation of data in secondary sources might function to maintain the concept.

A second way by which it can be implied that the sufficient conditions for inferring a construct have been met is by changing the correspondence rules. It was noted earlier that the regularities from which a hypothetical construct is originally inferred form the first set of correspondence rules which tie the construct to observable events. It was also noted that these rules may change as the initial set of events is shown to be reliably associated with other, reliably and independently measurable phenomena, i.e. the construct is shown to predict new observations. The correspondence rules for inferring schizophrenia have been changed a number of times since the concept was introduced (these are usually called diagnostic criteria, but the term correspondence rules will be used here to help keep in mind the fact that the validity of 'schizophrenia' is to be evaluated by applying criteria used by the scientific community in general). These changes in correspondence rules will be examined in Chapters 4 and 5 in order to assess to what extent they reflect the processes described earlier. It is, of course, the case that the use of any set of correspondence rules implies that these refer to a pattern of phenomena. The rules set out in DSM-III and DSM-IIIR will therefore be examined, in Chapter 5, to assess the extent to which this can be said to be the case.

But before these criteria are applied to 'schizophrenia', it is important to set the introduction and use of the concept in their historical and social context. It is particularly important that this should have been done if the concept is found wanting, so as better to understand not only the problems it presents, but why these should have developed in the first place. The next chapter will therefore consider the historical background to the introduction of the concept.

Chapter two

The background: events leading up to the introduction of 'schizophrenia'

In Western Europe and the United States, the period between the middle of the eighteenth century and the beginning of the twentieth saw a number of important changes in theories and methods of dealing with the problem of deviant behaviour. Scull (1979) describes one of these changes as a shift in responsibility for social deviance from the family and local community to a formal and centralised authority. This transition, however, involved much more than the compulsory construction of state asylums. It was accompanied by the transformation of the term insanity from a "vague, culturally defined phenomena afflicting an unknown but probably small, proportion of the population into a condition which could only be authoritatively diagnosed, certified and dealt with by a group of legalised experts" (Scull, 1975: 218). Thus the segregation of those labelled insane from society in general and other deviants in particular was contemporaneous with the growth of medical influence over this population and with the emergence of the new specialty of psychiatry.

A third major change, which post-dated the others by several decades, was the importance attached to the activities of classification and differential diagnosis of what were claimed to be distinct varieties of insanity. There had certainly been attempts to bring order to the heterogeneity of strange behaviour (i.e. behaviour which observers could not understand) throughout the seventeenth, eighteenth and early nineteenth centuries, but these were armchair, academic exercises conducted by writers, philosophers and physicians with no consensus – and little discussion – of the principles on which such an endeavour might be based. The classification systems had little effect on practice, even that of their creators. This state of affairs contrasts with the role assigned to classification systems by Brill (1974) who states that he "know(s) of no psychiatry that can get along without one" (1121).

The most comprehensive account of the first two of these processes has been provided by Andrew Scull (1975; 1979). One of Scull's major contributions has been to demonstrate that the development of a state asylum system and the growth of medical influence over deviant behaviour cannot be seen as twin processes in a progression towards more humane and scientific treatment of the 'mentally ill'. A major part of the account which will be presented here draws heavily on Scull's work. The account will necessarily be briefer than the topic merits, but it is intended simply to set the scene for discussion of the introduction and later development of 'schizophrenia'. Although many of the details which will be given apply to England, there was a remarkable similarity in the nature of the changes in the remainder of Western Europe and in the United States (see, for example, Zilboorg, 1941; Bockoven, 1956a; 1956b). This was in part attributable to exchange of ideas and to similarities in economic structure. Where differences *are* apparent, they are in the timing rather than the nature of events and can in part be traced to the degree of reluctance to accept control from central government (Castel *et al.*, 1982).

The development of institutions

The building of state institutions for one category of deviant was a relatively late development from a trend towards an institutional response to deviance in general. Attempts to authorise institutions for vagrants who could not or would not support themselves began in England and the remainder of Western Europe around the time of the Reformation when the Catholic Church's tradition of almsgiving was destroyed. In England, these attempts collapsed with the outbreak of the Civil War but were more successful in the rest of Europe with its tradition of absolute monarchy and where the threat deviants presented to the social order was perhaps felt more acutely. The English, and, later, American, responses to deviant behaviour amongst the poor were therefore local and idiosyncratic, and included almshouses, houses of correction, charity hospitals and workhouses, each of which accepted a heterogeneous group of people. It was during this period that private madhouses first appeared. These developed out of the practice of some parishes of boarding out non-violent people who showed bizarre behaviour and the habit of relatives of giving over such people into the care of others, usually clergymen or physicians. The social and economic changes brought about by the first stages of the Agrarian and Industrial Revolutions transformed the problem of dealing with those who, for whatever reason, did not support themselves. From the middle of the eighteenth century, the numbers of receipt of Poor Relief escalated and it was easy to assume that the locally based and somewhat idiosyncratic systems of Poor Relief were laxly administered and encouraged rather than relieved poverty and idleness.

The idea that relief should go only to those who deserved it was not new; the distinction, however, had never been very carefully applied in practice, possibly because the numbers involved were relatively small and, in any case, work could easily be forced from those who did not conform. At the beginning of the nineteenth century the distinction was re-emphasised, partly because of the large increase in numbers in receipt of Poor Relief and the fact that the force used by absolute monarchs could no longer be applied. Scull has also suggested that the distinction was crucial to the operation of the modern wage system, whose beginnings can be traced to this period. Institutions, in the form of workhouses, came to be seen as the ideal solution. Their unattractiveness would deter the able bodied, while a disciplined regime within them would prepare those not so deterred for a life of industrial labour. If this were clearly out of the question, then the discipline would do no harm. The gathering together of indigents in one place would also make the administration of the Poor Law more efficient.

The construction of institutions at this time and the growing practice of segregating deviants lacked some important features which were later to typify western society's response to those who failed to conform to its norms. First, the segregation was on a relatively small scale in contrast with that achieved in the last quarter of the nineteenth century. Second, little attempt was made to distinguish different types of deviant, except in terms of deserving or non-deserving. Third, medical interest in institutional populations was insignificant. Scull has suggested that the great stress which was laid upon correctly distinguishing the able bodied from the non-able bodied unemployed prepared the ground for the later separation of what was called insanity "from the previous inchoate mass of deviant behaviours so that it was seen as a distinct problem requiring specialised treatment in an institution of its own" (1979: 36).

One result of failing to separate out different classes of deviant within the workhouse quickly became apparent. By definition, the label mad is applied to those whose behaviour is incomprehensible, who violate social norms in ways which inspire if not fear, then at least bewilderment. Some of these people would continue to break rules within the institution. But the government of the day could hardly be expected to be interested in the management problems of workhouse keepers to the extent of passing a law forcing the construction in every county of institutions for the particularly troublesome. The end of the eighteenth century and the beginning of the nineteenth therefore saw a marked increase in the number of private madhouses, some of which were a result of parishes contracting with individuals to provide care for some of those in receipt of Poor Relief. There was virtually no restriction on entry into the madhouse trade and these establishments were run for profit, or in the hope of profit, by interested laymen – and women – clergymen and physicians. This free trade in lunacy was to pave the way for the controversy over who should be given the status of expert in this area. The trade was, however, on a comparatively small scale. In 1816, for example, there were thirty-six madhouses in London, one-quarter of which were licensed for less than ten people. There was, of course, great disparity in conditions within these madhouses; as would be expected, conditions were worst in those which took in pauper lunatics. The inevitable abuses which occurred were to prove fertile ground for those active in the Reform Movement. To claim, however, that the reformers improved the lot of those labelled insane by showing that "cruelty and neglect play no part except a shameful one, in the care of the mentally ill" (Lewis, 1966: 581) is, at best, an oversimplification of events.

Lunacy and the reform movement

The early reformers' cause was made easier by the fact that the issue of the management and disposal of 'lunatics' had been brought to public attention by the now disputed madness of George III and by Hadfield's attempt on the King's life. In 1800, Hadfield was found not guilty by reason of insanity, thus raising the thorny problem of what was to be done with him, as no legal provision existed for detaining him. A retroactive piece of legislation was speedily put on the statute authorising detention of such people, for the duration of the King's pleasure, in the county gaol or other suitable receptacle. This legislation brought with it the paradox that a technically innocent man was to be locked up; it also raised the question of what constituted another suitable receptacle. There were no obviously acceptable answers to these questions, but they did ensure that government and the general public were disposed to view lunacy as a problem in its own right. At the same time, a number of English magistrates began to agitate for changes in the quality of care provided in madhouses. They did not base their suggestions on an ideology of madness, but they were charged with the inspection of madhouses and were unhappy about conditions there.

Scull has suggested that the Reform Movement was influenced by two competing philosophical systems – Benthamism and Evangelicalism. The latter emphasised humanitarianism and discipline; it also contained, although rarely made explicit, a large element of paternalism and moral control. Benthamism emphasised the virtues of expertise and efficiency and the need for a science of government. These ideas were to dictate the reformers' goals – a reduction in the cruelty and neglect which typified madhouses and a country-wide system of centrally controlled asylums, regularly and thoroughly inspected by government agents or county officials. These goals – humanitarianism and efficient, central control – were not, of course, confined to the problem of madhouses but were part of a much wider social and political movement.

In 1807, in England, a Commons Select Committee published the first national report on private madhouses. Although the Committee was mainly concerned with recording the number of inmates, it did consider the plight of criminal and pauper inmates and in 1808, an Act was passed recommending the building of asylums for pauper lunatics with public money. The vast majority of local magistrates simply ignored the recommendations and those few asylums which were built did not provide appreciably better living conditions than had their predecessors. Scull has suggested that before any real change could take place, either in support for a system of public asylums or in conditions within them, there had to exist a cultural view of madness which was radically different from that generally held in the early nineteenth century. Bynum (1964) has argued that the way in which those labelled mad were treated at this time cannot simply be interpreted as a result of cruelty and indifference. Rather, it must be seen as in part deriving from the popular view which linked loss of reason to loss of humanity. The Aristotelian and Elizabethan views of madness which linked it to genius and sensibility had been largely lost sight of by the end of the eighteenth century, to be replaced by the idea of the madman as a brute (Skultans, 1979). It was a short step to the idea that madmen must be tamed, if necessary by force.

The unhappy position of lunacy reformers at the beginning of the nineteenth century has been summarised by Scull:

> the desire to protect society, to simplify life for those charged with administering local poorhouses and gaols and an unfocused, unsystematic feeling that the insane deserved more 'humane' treatment, did not amount to a coherent alternative vision of what could or should be done.
>
> (1979: 64)

The reformers were therefore unable to provide strong justification for the vast expenditure and interference in local affairs which the realisation of their aims would involve.

The new view of madness which was to provide this alternative vision was embodied in the work of the moral managers, moral in this case being closer in meaning to 'psychological' than to its present-day connotations of virtue. The first attempt at systematic practice of these ideas can be traced to William Tuke, a layman who, in 1792, opened the York Retreat as an alternative to the York Asylum which had a reputation for gross mistreatment of inmates. The rationale of the Retreat represented a move away from the idea of the mad as animals to be tamed to the view that they were merely lacking in powers of self-restraint; the task of the asylum was to re-establish these, using ideas of behaviour–consequence relationships remarkably similar to those underlying the token economy system developed 150 years later by Ayllon and Azrin. This view of the mad as essentially human but as exhibiting a defect in self-control did not, of course, develop in a cultural vacuum. Grange (1962) sees its counterpart in the romantic movement in literature, which saw the cultivation and analysis of emotion as a necessary part of existence, rather than as something to be feared and avoided. In turn, as Skultans (1979) has pointed out, the moral managers emphasised the balance of passions rather than opposition to them. Asylum inmates were therefore to be taught the regulation of emotion.

Scull has suggested complementary reasons to account not only for changing cultural views of insanity in the nineteenth century but also for the fact that they were to become so influential in social policy. As he points out, supernatural accounts of events are favoured when people's control over important features of their environment is limited, as was the case in pre-industrial society. The Agrarian and Industrial Revolutions vastly increased the potential for control and brought with them new attitudes to human nature which emphasised change through training and internalisation of social norms, rather than control by external agents. Thus, the changing concept of insanity is seen as developing in parallel with changing ideas about people and their relationship with the environment. These ideas, however, not only reflected real events, they also served to justify the demands made on the new industrial working force to adapt to an alien environment. Equally, the idea that people could strive to improve themselves – whether in the asylum or out of it – was a basic tenet of the upwardly mobile middle classes and was in direct opposition to the medieval idea of a predestined social order.

The concept of rehabilitation was inherent in the new view of insanity. Moreover, the cure was to be effected not by esoteric medical means but by kindness and instruction through manipulation of the environment. While not denying the humanitarian motives of the reformers, Scull has pointed out that one of the major attractions of moral management was that it promised to transform into free, rational, self-determining and economically useful individuals, that part of the population which deviated most markedly from these ideals. American accounts (see, for example, Bockoven, 1956b) also emphasise the important roles played by manual labour and religious worship in the attainment of discipline.

But whatever their ideological base, Tuke's innovations at the Retreat quickly attracted attention. A French physician, de la Rive, imported the ideas to the Continent where they were to become, if anything, even more popular than in England. Phillipe Pinel, director of the Bicêtre hospital in Paris, was exploring a similar set of ideas, while in the United States moral management was popularised by the physicians Benjamin Rush and Eli Todd and was later used by Dorothea Dix as a justification for her energetic campaign for the building of state asylums.

The years between the setting up of the first Parliamentary Select Commission on Lunacy in 1805 and the second in 1815 therefore saw radical and well-publicised changes in ideas not only on the nature of insanity but also in methods of dealing with those labelled insane. The reformers had been active during this period gathering facts on conditions in asylums and madhouses. A particularly horrific (even by nineteenth-century standards) catalogue of abuses uncovered in the York and Bethlem Asylums resulted in private enquiries and in pressure to review the situation on a national scale. The result was the setting up of the 1815 Parliamentary Committee. The reformers came to this Committee with a very different and much stronger set of arguments with which to convince the government of the need for a network of humanely run county asylums than they had had at their disposal in 1805. It was not their intention that these asylums should be run by doctors; on the contrary, Wakefield, one of the Commission's witnesses, declared that he considered doctors to be "the most unfit of any class of persons" to control asylums (Bynum, 1964: 326). The reformers were able to argue that practices within existing asylums not only constituted a moral outrage but were also theoretically unsound. They further argued that because there now existed a remedy for insanity, then the segregation of the insane from other indigents, with less potential, was essential. The Commission was presented with a vast amount of evidence of cruelty and neglect within asylums and with details of the alternatives which were available at the York Retreat. These could be made available to all asylum inmates, it was argued, only through the construction of well-planned public asylums in every county and by the operation of a stringent system of inspection.

The evidence presented to the Commission, and its subsequent report, represented a humiliating critique of the medical profession's handling of the lunacy problem. As a result of the Commission's report, a Bill was introduced in 1816 directing the compulsory construction of county asylums with an extensive system of inspection. The Bill was passed by the Commons but rejected by the Lords. The rejection of this, and of two following Bills in 1818 and 1819, resulted partly (in the case of the 1816 Bill) from a clause authorising the stringent inspection of the conditions under which 'single lunatics' in private homes were kept, as well as (in the case of all three Bills) from fierce opposition on the part of proprietors of private madhouses and the medical profession. But one of the most important reasons for the defeat of the Bills, Scull suggests, was the localist basis of English politics. A similar Bill was to succeed only after parliamentary reform had seriously weakened the power of the rural aristocracy and the issue of central versus local Poor Law administration had been resolved.

In 1827, yet another parliamentary inquiry was set up into the condition of pauper lunatics, resulting in a Bill, in 1828, so wary of offending the Lords that its provisions made little difference to the existing state of affairs. But, as Scull has pointed out, the Commission which, by design, included the leading parliamentary reformers, was to become a most effective pressure group for the reformers' aims. In 1842, the chairman of the Commission introduced a Bill to extend its powers for three years so that it could produce a detailed report on all madhouses in the country. The report, which appeared in 1844, was the most comprehensive ever produced. It not only reiterated the merits of moral management but also provided an elaborate justification for its implementation via the provision of purpose-built public asylums. Asylums were necessary in the first place, the report suggested, because lunatics must be treated by experts, in buildings designed to optimise the effects of such treatment. But treatment must also be given by strangers, in an environment other than that which had induced the problem in the first place. More asylums were necessary because early admission was essential if a cure were to be effected, and existing asylums were already overfilled. This inconvenient fact, which suggested that a cure was not readily available, was easily dealt with by the assertion that the inmates had not been admitted early enough. The report served its purpose: in 1845 the Lunatics Act made compulsory the building of county asylums for pauper lunatics, and their regular inspection. A similar Act had been passed in France in 1838, with relatively little opposition. Castel *et al.* (1982) attribute this to the greater acceptance of centralised authority in Europe; in contrast, by 1890, only one US state – New York – had passed such an Act.

As Scull (1979) and Skultans (1979) have pointed out, the provision of public asylums in the nineteenth century cannot be separated from the general issue of the management of the poor and in particular from the issue of local versus central Poor Law administration and indoor versus outdoor Poor Relief. Similarly, the kind of regime to which the asylums aspired, and their goals for the inmates, cannot be separated from the view of human nature engendered in part by the Agrarian and Industrial Revolutions. To depict the provision of asylums and its underlying ideology as an enlightened, humanitarian move is to minimise this and the fact that the purely humanitarian motives of the reformers could have been satisfied simply by pressing for an end to cruelty and neglect. They might also have argued that because so many abuses took place in institutions, then the obvious answer was fewer of them. That they argued the opposite reflects the fact that their ideas were inextricably connected with prevailing economic and political concerns. The idea that those who are called mad should be treated with kindness may well be more in accord with twentieth-century ideals than is the idea that they should be chained and whipped. But this does not make the first idea, and the elaborate theoretical justification which surrounded it, any more rational or scientific than the second. Both were derived from prevailing lay theories of human nature which in turn had their roots in social, political and economic concerns.

The growth of medical influence

Medical interest in bizarre behaviour (i.e. that which cannot readily be understood by reference to social norms) has a long history. The Ancient Greeks, for example, incorporated such behaviour into their humoral pathology, which was to be influential in western thought until at least the seventeenth century. The physician's interest, however, was shared by philosophers, theologians and writers, each of whom felt competent to construct theories of the nature and causes of whatever was viewed as madness. Inevitably, writings on the subject reflect this diversity of views. Physicians and philosophers did not write from opposing stances; rather, both managed to combine, often incoherently, philosophical, psychological and medical ideas. The mingling of the physical and the psychological reflects, of course, a preoccupation with the relationship between mind and body; this, and the fact that medical, philosophical and literary writings on insanity were often indistinguishable, were later to prove important in facilitating public acceptance of insanity as a medical problem. On a practical level, medical interest in insanity was also shared by other groups. But the co-occurrence of disturbing behaviour and bodily disease (if only by chance) and the traditional designation of physicians as helpers, gave them something of an advantage, regardless of expertise. Scull has pointed out that until about the middle of the eighteenth century, physicians made little attempt to further their interest or to secure public recognition as experts in insanity, The first piece of English legislation to make separate mention of lunacy was the 1744 Vagrancy Act, which defined one category of vagrant as any persons "who by lunacy or otherwise are so far disordered in their Senses that they may be dangerous to be permitted to go Abroad" (Bynum, 1964: 321). The Act authorised any person to detain such a vagrant and two Justices of the Peace to decide whether confinement in some secure place was necessary. The wording of the Act emphasises the fact that lunacy, however defined, was not regarded as a medical problem, nor defined in law as an attribute of the person; it was defined in terms of behaviour which might prove harmful to others.

The years between 1744 and the next Act which dealt with lunacy – in 1774 – saw a marked increase in medical interest in the subject. A small number of institutions, called hospitals, were founded for the care of lunatics. Scull attributes medicine's growing interest in lunacy to the much larger number of private madhouses which appeared during this period and which provided a new source of potential status and profit for medical men, in competition with interested laypeople. The 1774 Act was, in fact, aimed at controlling these establishments. It confirmed that anyone who could obtain a licence could open a madhouse but put inspection in the hands of the Royal College of Physicians and ruled that a medical certificate had to be obtained before anyone could be confined. Bynum (1964) has suggested that these provisions amounted to a public recognition of medical jurisdiction in insanity. Whether this is the case is, however, debatable. As Scull points out, the final decision about confinement rested in legal hands and the power of the Royal College of Physicians to inspect madhouses did not extend beyond the metropolitan area; elsewhere, it remained the duty of magistrates. And although the Act required a medical certificate prior to confinement, it said nothing about the qualifications of those into whose care the lunatic was assigned. It hardly makes sense to recognise lunacy as a medical problem but to continue to allow anyone who can obtain a licence to be responsible for the care of lunatics. Nevertheless, in the latter part of the eighteenth and the beginning of the nineteenth centuries, the medical profession had begun to take a far greater *practical* interest in the management of those labelled insane. In addition, the medical teacher William Cullen had begun to include the topic of insanity in his curriculum, thus allowing his pupils to lay claim to some specialist knowledge, an essential prerequisite for public recognition as an expert.

Medicine and moral management

These first attempts to secure acceptance of the claim that lunacy was a medical problem were seriously threatened by the advent of moral management which, in both theory and practice, owed nothing to medicine. On the contrary, it explicitly denied the usefulness of medicine in managing the insane. In England, the threat was increased by the findings of the 1815 Select Committee, and by the Bills which followed, which explicitly sought to remove medical powers of inspection granted under the 1774 Act. Not surprisingly, physicians were amongst the most vociferous opponents. As Bynum has noted, the implications of moral management "for both medical theory and medical practice were not lost on the physicians of the early nineteenth century who attempted to assess its true significance ... their income, prestige and medical theories were all threatened" (1964: 324–5).

The threat which moral management presented must be seen in the context of the structure of the medical profession in the early nineteenth century. There was then no such body as the medical profession as the term is understood today; instead, medical treatment was offered by three distinct groups: physicians, the elite, drawn mainly from the upper and upper-middle classes; surgeons, regarded as craftsmen and who in England had severed their links with barbers as recently as 1745; and apothecaries, the lowest status group. In practice, it is unlikely that the quality of care offered by these groups matched their professional standing. Except in Scotland, where medical education was controlled by the universities, the training received by physicians was in many ways inferior to that of surgeons and apothecaries. The clientele treated by the three groups did, however, broadly match their social standing.

The Royal College of Physicians, formed in 1518, had been for some time engaged in a battle to keep surgeons and apothecaries, who were seeking to improve their status, in an inferior position. Medical proprietors of madhouses were drawn from all three groups but the most vociferous and articulate defenders of medicine's interest in this area were the physicians. Already much preoccupied with status, the physicians therefore found themselves in an invidious position in the first decades of the nineteenth century. If they supported the reformers' attempts to introduce legislation compelling the building of public asylums, they ran the risk that the new insitutions would be put in the hands of laypeople and that physicians would find themselves adopting a subordinate role. On the other hand, if they opposed the proposals, then the madhouse trade would presumably flourish and be open to all comers. Neither option augured well for physicians. Faced with this dilemma, the profession had a number of choices. First, they could present convincing evidence that those behaviours labelled insanity were caused by disease and could be cured by medical means. This they were unable to do. Second, they could agree to share the field with others and accept that moral management did not require any medical expertise. There is no evidence that this option was ever seriously considered. Third, they could attempt to persuade government and the public of their expertise by means of non-empirical argument, thus avoiding the awkward issue of their failure to provide empirical evidence in support of their claims.

In choosing the third option, physicians and their colleagues were committed to supporting the expansion of the public asylum system. As Scull has pointed out, however, government support for increasing the number of asylums had been won on the basis that moral management, not medical intervention, could restore sanity. The medical profession must therefore incorporate it into its scheme of things either by arguing convincingly that it was best suited to administer asylums and organise such care and/or that intervention by non-medical means did not invalidate the proposition that insanity was a disease and therefore a medical matter. It is not immediately obvious which set of arguments would lead, however illogically, to such conclusions. Possibly as a result, initial attempts by physicians to defend their interests consisted mainly of rhetorical repetitions of the superiority of a medical approach. Such claims continued to be made throughout the century but were gradually joined by a more subtle set of arguments. These were of two sorts: the first suggested that a *combination* of medical and moral management would be more efficacious than either alone. William Neale, for example, declared in 1836 that:

> To those acquainted with the workings of the malady and its peculiar characteristics, it will be easy to perceive the errors and partial views of such as profess to apply a medicinal agent only, as a specific, or those who advocate a course of moral treatment only as a cure. There is no doubt that a co-operation of medical and moral means is requisite to effect a thorough cure.
>
> (Scull, 1979: 161–2)

But as Scull has pointed out, this concession to moral management was a harmless one. It could, after all, be administered by anyone whereas medical treatment, it was claimed, required special training. Clearly, the medical profession could administer both but lay moral managers could not administer medical treatments. Thus, the medical position was not threatened.

The second set of arguments was derived from the long-standing debate on the nature of 'mind' and 'mental events'. Most western physicians of the nineteenth century adhered to the dualist position put forward by Descartes and Hartley in which the concepts of mind and soul were virtually identical. The idea of physical disease presented no problems; when disease was said to be mental, however, or curable by non-physical means, then taxing philosophical and theological problems were raised. The moral managers appeared to be putting forward just such a view. Pinel, for example, had stated explicitly that insanity was not an organic disease and that what was psychological (mental) was best dealt with by psychological means. Samuel Tuke adopted a more pragmatic position. If insanity were a disease of the mind, then therapy should be aimed at the mind. If, on the other hand, it were a disease of the brain, as yet undetected, moral management was indicated by the reciprocal action of mind on brain.

These arguments, however, failed to tackle the (apparently) central issue of what exactly happened to the mind in a case of insanity. Traditional theological and philosophical theory held that the mind (or soul) was an immaterial essence, incapable of destruction by mortal means and thus, unlike the brain, protected from disease and decay. To argue otherwise was to challenge Christian belief in an immortal soul. The mind was seen as operating through a material object, the brain. Taken separately or together these premisses seemed to lead to the conclusion that insanity must be seen as a disease of the brain, albeit one amenable in part to non-physical intervention. A corollary to these arguments was that the only alternative to viewing insanity as a brain disease was to see it as a spiritual matter, to be dealt with by the clergy. Forbes Wimslow, for example, stated that the contrary view to that which saw insanity as a medical problem was that it was: "a spiritual malady ... an affectation of the immaterial essence ... a disorder of the soul and not simply the result of the derangement of the material instrument of the mind interfering with the healthy action of its manifestations" (Scull, 1979: 167).

These arguments had particular force in an increasingly secular society where even the clergy were loath to view deviant behaviour as a spiritual malady; the reformers, too, had been anxious to distance themselves from the idea of insanity as divine retribution and of the insane as deserving of punishment. The arguments put forward by medical men appeared happily to solve the dilemma of admitting to the efficacy of moral management while protecting the status of the soul and, of course, justified a humane approach to the lunatic. The appeal of such arguments must be seen not only in the context of a strongly Christian society but also of one which lacked, first, the idea that it is possible systematically to study and modify *behaviour* (which is after all what was being discussed) without reference to the concepts of mind or brain and, second, the notion of certain behaviours as deviations from a particular set of cultural norms, rather than as phenomena which logically required the positing of some underlying disorder. But in spite of the appeal of these arguments, there remained the awkward fact that if insanity were a brain disease, it was one which frequently could not be detected. Two explanations were put forward to account for this. First, the instruments and methods available to physicians were said not to be sophisticated enough to detect what were probably subtle changes in the brain. Second, structural changes were said probably to occur only in the later stages of insanity and that, in effect, lunatics died too soon for these to be observed. Bynum (1964) has noted that the very absence of brain pathology was taken by a few physicians as evidence that even in insanity the mind is not subject to decay.

By the middle of the nineteenth century, the medical profession had assumed control of a large majority of public asylums in England, on the Continent and in the United States. Vacant posts which had been filled by lay superintendents were now almost invariably given to physicians. Although the arguments discussed above almost certainly contributed to this process, a number of other factors may have facilitated medical dominance. Scull has noted that many aspects of moral management worked against its being developed as a coherent *professional* ideology. The moral managers in general and the Tukes in particular had adopted an essentially pragmatic approach to intervention and had eschewed both premature theory building and the idea that moral treatment could only be carried out by a group of specially trained experts. This rendered the moral managers vulnerable to those less cautious in their theorising and in their claims. In addition, the language of moral managers was similar to that of medicine: they too spoke of afflictions, diseases and treatments. Like medicine, they saw bizarre behaviour in dispositional terms, as an attribute of the person. This is hardly surprising, given the pervasiveness, even now, of dispositional explanations of behaviour (Ross, 1977). The conceptual gulf which separated moral and medical management was therefore not as wide as it might at first glance have appeared.

Physicians were able to construct socially acceptable theories of insanity which incorporated moral management without compromising their professional status. Indeed, it could be argued that they enhanced it, by appearing to be broad minded and open to new ideas. Physicians also possessed the important advantage of having already formed a profession of sorts; they were thus able to argue that the best way of ensuring that asylum superintendents were conscientious, reliable and properly motivated was to choose them from an already existing profession, rather than encouraging a free-for-all which might allow disreputable elements to enter the business. In England, the originator of moral management was a layman; in the remainder of Europe and in the United States, its strongest advocates were physicians. This may have encouraged, or at least made less contentious, the idea that doctors should have charge of asylums. Each asylum must, in any case, employ a physician to deal with bodily ailments. Those responsible for the appointment of asylum superintendents increasingly came to see it as more efficient and economical to employ one person to do both jobs.

The decline of moral management and the rise of somatic theories

The large-scale construction of asylums was overtly justified by the assertion that lunacy could be cured by moral management. By the end of the nineteenth century, however, this approach had become little more than a hazy recollection in the minds of asylum superintendents and had been replaced by a wholly somatic view of lunacy, both in theory and in practice.

A number of reasons have been put forward for the demise of moral management. Bockoven (1956a) suggests that one of the most important was the failure of the innovators to train enough people to staff the growing number of asylums. To this was added an enormous increase in the numbers committed to asylums, a factor widely cited in accounts of the decline of moral management (for example, Bockoven, 1956a, 1956b; Leigh, 1961; Jones, 1972). It has been suggested that the ever-increasing number of asylum inmates made impossible the practice of moral management, with its emphasis on a detailed knowledge of the individual and its de-emphasis of regimented, custodial approaches. Bockoven (1956a) notes that the situation in the United States was further complicated by the fact that immigrants made the greatest contribution to the increase.

These two factors – lack of trained personnel and the vast increase in the number of inmates – might at first glance seem adequate as explanations of the decline of moral management, particularly as the pioneers of the approach had placed so much emphasis on asylums run as 'family' units. But closer examination shows the explanations to be unsatisfactory, or, at least, incomplete. First, one of the hallmarks of moral management was that it was essentially a pragmatic approach requiring, according to its proponents, no special training. It was this fact which, it was suggested earlier, partly contributed to the failure of lay moral managers to provide effective opposition to physicians in the competition for influence in asylums. In any case, the innovators had written extensively on the subject, giving details of what was thought to be the essence of the approach, so that any interested physician could easily acquaint himself with the few principles. Second, the citing of increased numbers of inmates as a cause of the decline of moral management can be shown to carry with it the assumption that the increase was relatively simple to explain and was one which the medical profession was powerless to prevent. Third, neither explanation can account for the vigour with which somatic theories were espoused in theory and practice.

It will be argued, instead, that the decline of moral theories and the growing influence of somatic theories cannot be understood separately from the increased numbers of asylum inmates, the problematic concept of insanity and the ambiguous professional position of mad doctors in the second half of the nineteenth century.

The rising population of asylum inmates

Throughout the nineteenth century, but particularly in the latter part, the number of people confined to asylums increased dramatically. In England and Wales, for example, the average number of inmates per asylum was 116 in 1827; by 1890, it was 802 (Scull, 1979). In addition, the estimated prevalence of insanity (a category made up of 'lunacy' and 'idiocy') in England and Wales increased from one in 802 in 1844 to one in 432 in 1868 and to one in 266 in 1914 (Hare, 1983). The increases were paralleled by a growing reluctance on the part of the state and local authorities to spend money on asylums, particularly as there seemed to be no limit to the numbers who needed to be contained within them. What had begun as purpose-built buildings for relatively small numbers gradually grew, in a haphazard fashion, into vast custodial receptacles where, not surprisingly, the emphasis on cure was replaced with concern with keeping the inmates under control. It is certainly true that moral management as practised by Tuke, Pinel and Rush would have been impossible under such circumstances; what is less clear is why the number of inmates should have increased at such a rate.

Both Scull (1979) and Hare (1983) have provided detailed evaluations of the nineteenth-century records of the numbers of the insane and of the sometimes fierce debate which surrounded their interpretation. The major question of concern was that of whether the increase in numbers was an administrative artefact or whether insanity really was, to use Hare's phrase, "on the increase". Both Hare and Scull are agreed that the rising population of the insane cannot be accounted for by more accurate registration in the second half of the nineteenth century, i.e. by the idea that a pool of hitherto unrecognised cases would now be included in official statistics. But thereafter, they reach opposing conclusions: Hare argues that the evidence supports the view that there was a real increase in what would now be called the functional psychosis, and in particular in schizophrenia, in the second half of the nineteenth century; Scull concludes that the increase was more apparent than real. There is some reason for supposing that Hare may, in a roundabout way, be partly correct in his suggestion of a real increase in schizophrenia at this time; the rather complicated issues surrounding this argument will be taken up at the end of the next chapter. Nevertheless, Scull's arguments remain relevant to the discussion of the demise of moral management. The first of these concerns nineteenth-century definitions of insanity and the second, the professional status of mad-doctors.

In the nineteenth century, there were almost as many definitions of insanity as there were medical men who cared to write on the subject. But the definitions were as vague as they were numerous, so that it was extremely difficult to see how such a phenomenon might be recognised in practice. The public was reassured that this was possible, however, via the now familiar appeals to 'clinical judgement'. Mayo, for example, claimed in 1817 that:

It must be borne in mind, that a great unanimity may exist among experienced observers as to the presence of certain mental states, characterised by certain generally accepted names, which states, at the same time, it would be very difficult to describe in any form of words, insomuch that the indefined name, in the use of which all experienced men are agreed respecting these states, will convey to all a more clear and distinct impression than any attempt at definition or even description.

(Scull, 1979: 237–8)

Vague definitions of insanity, based on subjective judgements, could, of course, be narrowly applied; their vagueness did not necessitate a rise in the number of asylum inmates. There are, however, good reasons for expecting a broad rather than a narrow application of the term in the nineteenth century. First, the perceived size and importance of a problem is likely to be directly related to the status of those who claim to be able to deal with it. The professional position of mad doctors in the late nineteenth century will be discussed in more detail in the next section; it should be noted, however, that it was not in medicine's professional interests to minimise the apparent size of the lunacy problem. The second factor which may have facilitated the use of a broad definition of insanity was the very existence of asylums designed to cure it. In assessing the importance of this factor, it should be borne in mind that the initial judgement of insanity was – and still is – made not by a doctor but by the lay public, on the basis of unwanted behaviour. Clearly, what is unwanted varies with time, place and the person making the judgement. It would be remarkable if such judgements were not influenced by the availability of a system for dealing with those labelled insane, on the apparently humanitarian grounds that they could be restored to health. Scull has therefore argued that the elastic concept of insanity was able to include a wider range of deviant behaviour than had hitherto been the case and that this could in part account for the rising population of the insane.

Hare has offered two arguments against this conclusion. First, the prognosis of asylum inmates apparently worsened during the last decades of the nineteenth century; contemporary observers attributed this to the admission of greater numbers of less favourable cases. Second, the 1909–13 statistics for England and Wales indicated that "the group of conditions which we would now include in the term 'functional psychoses' – mania, melancholia, delusional insanity and secondary dementia – formed at least 75 per cent of the total" (1983: 449). Hare, however, does not consider the possibility that the decline in prognosis could have been due not to less favourable cases, but to less favourable conditions, including overcrowding and an increasing reliance on physical methods, than had prevailed in the heyday of moral management. The major problem with his second argument is that we have no way of knowing whether, or in what ways, the referents of terms like melancholia or delusional insanity changed over the years. Both Scull and Hare are well aware that historical epidemiology of this sort is a very hazardous business. Nevertheless, the complete absence of any data on the reliability and accuracy of mad-doctors' diagnoses does mean that a widening of the vague concept of insanity remains a serious possible explanation for the apparent increase in the prevalence of insanity in the nineteenth century.

The professional status of mad-doctors and the development of somatic theories

It may have been the case that, by the middle of the nineteenth century, the superintendents of almost all public asylums in England were medical men;

this administrative superiority, however, did not amount to an ideal of professional autonomy and recognition as experts. The final decision as to whether or not an individual should be confined remained in legal hands, although a medical certificate was needed. There remained also the theoretical and practical difficulties faced by medicine in relation to deviant behaviour. It was recognised by the public and medical men alike that, rhetoric notwithstanding, the behaviour of asylum inmates could not, in many cases, be shown to be accompanied by brain or any other lesions nor to be responsive to the plethora of medical interventions available. Asylum doctors were uneasily aware of the fact that the existence of asylums had been justified by the claim that the inmates could be cured by purely non-medical means which they, trained in medicine, were supposed to administer. Worse, they did not appear to be making a very good job of it, as witness the rising number of admissions and the falling number in the category of discharged cured.

In the second half of the nineteenth century the medical profession therefore sought, in a number of ways, to enhance its status *vis-à-vis* deviant behaviour. As Zilboorg (1941) has pointed out, one of the more obvious ways of doing so is by forming professional organisations and by publishing specialist literature not easily available to, nor comprehensible by, lay people. In 1844, the newly formed Association for Medical Superintendents of American Institutions for the Insane began publication of the *American Journal of Insanity*. A similar organisation had been founded in Britain in 1841, called the Association of Medical Officers of Asylums and Hospitals for the Insane. Its journal, *The Asylum Journal*, appeared in 1853 but the title was soon altered to the more prestigious-sounding *Journal of Mental Science*. The editorial of the second volume declared that "Insanity is purely a disease of the brain. The physician is now the responsible guardian of the lunatic and must ever remain so." In 1855 John Gray, one of the most vociferous proponents of a somatic theory of bizarre behaviour, became editor of the *American Journal of Insanity*. Not surprisingly, the number of papers on moral management declined, and the number on pathology increased during his thirty years of editorship (Dunton, 1944).

There was, in addition, a considerable literature aimed at both the specialist and the general reader, attempting to prove that the treatment of insanity, whatever it might entail, must remain in medical hands. John Millar, for example, argued in 1856 that:

> The shower bath is used as a corrective discipline. The matron uses the shower bath for swearing, bad language and filthy habits ... the whole question of its use I consider to be entirely within the province of the Superintendent as much as any other medical treatment he may think it necessary to employ.
>
> (Scull, 1979: 202–3)

As Scull points out, this kind of argument neatly illustrates one paradox faced by the medical superintendents: if asylum inmates were suffering from brain disease, they could not be held responsible for their behaviour and therefore punishment was pointless. Somehow or other, however, their behaviour had to be controlled and, of course, the time-honoured methods of reward and punishment were used. But this implied that the inmates *were* responsible for their behaviour. The only solution to this paradox was to incorporate everything that was done to the inmates into 'medical treatment'.

The mind(soul)–body question continued to preoccupy mad-doctors. The strength of feeling on this matter is illustrated by Pliny Earle's remark that:

> Were the arguments for the hypothesis that in insanity the mind itself is diseased ten-fold more numerous than they are, and more weighty, I could not accept them. My ideas of the human mind are such that I cannot hold for a moment that it can be diseased, as we understand disease. This implies death as a final consequence, but Mind is eternal. In its very essence and structure (to use the term we apply to matter), in its elemental composition and its organisation, it was created for immortality, beyond the scope of the wear and tear and disorganisation and final destruction of the mortal part of our being.
>
> (Bockoven, 1956a: 193; parentheses in original)

Given this context, both professional and theoretical, it would perhaps be naive to expect mad-doctors to give their whole-hearted support to moral management, regardless of the ease or difficulty with which it could be applied. Rather, it is to be expected that they would do everything they could to advance the notion that the behaviour of asylum inmates was a manifestation of brain disease and was amenable only, or mainly, to purely medical remedies. The ambiguous position of medical superintendents is well illustrated by their response to the increase in the number of asylum inmates. The 1845 Act, requiring the building of county asylums, had specifically recommended that these be for curable cases only and that, wherever possible, separate receptacles be constructed for the incurables. The distinction between the two was made simply by assuming, in general, that an inmate of more than two years standing was incurable. Retaining asylums for curable cases would, it was supposed, allow the concentration of skills on those most likely to derive benefit. It might be expected that asylum superintendents would be only too pleased to see the implementation of these recommendations which would, among other things, allow them to practise moral management and concentrate on perfecting the cure in whose name the asylums had been built. But, as Scull illustrates, the medical profession strongly resisted the idea of moving 'incurables' to a separate place. The apparently plausible justifications were that such a system would foster the very abuses reform was supposed to halt and that there was always the hope of a cure, regardless of the length of the inmates' confinement.

The seemingly humanitarian basis of these arguments should not obscure the fact that any attempt to provide separate refuges for the 'incurables' could be seen as presenting a threat to asylum doctors. It was not envisaged that these places, which would be cheaper to run than asylums, would be under the control of doctors; the decreasing discharged-cured figures suggested that the vast majority of lunatics would soon pass out of the profession's hands. This prospect was obviously unwelcome to an embryonic profession whose status was already precarious. Instead, asylum doctors were able to continue to justify their failure to cure by citing the huge number of inmates, which made the task impossible. A few individual doctors protested about the situation and demanded action, but the profession as a whole took no concerted action, in marked contrast with their vigorous attempts to secure the construction of asylums. Scull (1979), reviewing the Reports of the Lunacy Commissioners (which included a large number of doctors), has noted that the distinction between praise and blameworthy asylums gradually came to be seen in terms of cleanliness, order and comfort, rather than in terms of numbers discharged 'cured'. Local magistrates had suggested another solution to the problems faced by asylum doctors, which would have freed them to concentrate on curing the inmates. This was the appointment of a lay administrator who would relieve the physician of the burden of paperwork and allow him to spend more time with the inmates. But asylum doctors vigorously opposed such suggestions to the point in two cases, at Hanwell hospital, of the medical superintendents' resigning in protest. Thus the relationship between the decline in moral management and the rising number of asylum inmates was not quite as straightforward as it might appear.

During the second half of the nineteenth century, asylum doctors increasingly behaved as if the inmates were literally sick. Microscopes became a standard part of asylum equipment; post-mortems were regularly performed to find the hypothesised brain lesions which were the cause of the inmates' strange behaviour; it became commonplace for asylums to have their own laboratories and to emphasise the importance of histopathological investigations; drugs were increasingly used to sedate the inmates. Bockoven (1956a) has linked this behaviour on the part of asylum doctors to the fact that the vast size of asylums made it impossible for the superintendents to become acquainted with the inmates and their problems. But while it is true that superintendents could not easily get to know all the inmates, this hardly necessitated their acting as if the inmates were sick to the point of examining their brains under a microscope. It is reasonable to suggest that what did necessitate such behaviour was the ambiguous professional status of mad-doctors. In order to convince the public and government that insanity was a medical matter, mad-doctors had to behave in the same fashion as their more secure colleagues who enjoyed the luxury of never, at least in recent history, having had to convince people that bodily ailments were a medical matter. And it was not only the public who must be convinced. Asylum doctors occupied the lowest rung of the professional ladder and were, as their title 'alienist' might suggest, as separate from the rest of medicine as were their charges from the rest of society. Thus, every innovation in medicine was faithfully reproduced in the asylum, at the expense of the non-medical moral management.

For the most part, these imitations of medical practice were conspicuously unsuccessful either in discovering the causes of the inmates' behaviour or in altering it. It might therefore seem that it was only a matter of time until the professional pretensions of mad-doctors collapsed. The perceived, and actual, relationships between medicine and deviant behaviour were, however, radically altered by two processes. The first was the increasing interest in deviance shown by the new (and prestigious) medical specialty of neurology; the second the mounting evidence of a link between syphilis and the well-known cluster of features called, among other things, dementia paralytica.

Neurology and insanity

By the seventh decade of the nineteenth century, public asylums, and particularly those in the United States, had become huge, custodial receptacles with low standards of care. The necessary emphasis on the inmates' supposed sickness, plus the obviously unsuccessful attempts of the asylum doctors to discover either cause or cure, had induced a profound pessimism amongst them. They dealt mainly with lower class-groups, had few funds or facilities for research and lacked professional status. The situation did not, of course, go unnoticed and in 1879, the American Neurological Association launched a series of attacks on mad-doctors and their asylums. The Association, representing the new and growing specialism which dealt with disorders of the brain and nervous system, had been formed in 1875, although their *Journal of Nervous and Mental Disease* had first been published in 1874. The Association specifically excluded asylum doctors from its membership. They sought, via various speeches and publications, to gain acceptance for the view that asylums were damaging to the insane.

There are some interesting similarities and differences between the attitudes of American neurologists at the end of the nineteenth century and those of the lunacy reformers at the beginning. Both groups were intent on exposing abuses in asylums; both were intent on showing that asylum inmates and anyone labelled mad should be dealt with in a manner quite dissimilar from the traditional way. But there the similarities end. For the lunacy reformers, the answer was *more* asylums, an increase in custodial care; for the neurologists the answer was *fewer* asylums, a decrease in custodial care. The two opposing solutions probably reflect the mixed motives of the two groups. The lunacy reformers' efforts to increase institutional provision were inseparable from their desire to establish an efficient system of centrally controlled indoor Poor Relief; the neurologists' efforts to discredit asylums were almost certainly linked to their desire for professional advancement. It appeared that neurologists wanted the insane to be their customers and not those of asylum doctors. As neurologists came, in general, from fairly high status backgrounds and worked mostly in prestigious urban teaching hospitals, they were naturally disinclined to go where the insane were; instead they sought to bring the insane to them. To this end, Hammond, in 1879, declared that "the medical profession (outside the hospital) is, as a body, fully as capable of treating cases of insanity as cases of any other disease ... in many instances, sequestration is not only unnecessary, but positively injurious" (Bockoven, 1956a: 182). Obviously, neurologists must uphold the idea that those labelled insane were suffering from brain disease and they did this as vociferously as had mad-doctors.

Around the turn of the century, there appeared in the cities of the United States a new type of medical institution called a psychopathic hospital, which combined treatment with teaching and research and where out-patient clinics were first opened in 1912. A number of 'psychiatric institutes' were opened, as were 'psychiatric' wards in general hospitals. The ease and speed with which these developments took place is a reflection partly of the professional aspirations of neurologists but also of the American distaste for a unified, centrally controlled response to the lunacy problem. One important consequence of these developments was that people brought to the attention of neurologists those relatives who displayed behaviours which were less deviant and which disturbed fewer people, than did those of asylum inmates. The opening of out-patient clinics encouraged this trend, because neurologists declared themselves happy to see what they called milder cases. The already elastic criteria for applying the label insane or mentally disordered were thus widened still further.

It is notable that the relationship between mad-doctors and neurologists in Germany – from where Kraepelin's concept of dementia praecox was to emerge – was quite different from that in the United States or Britain. An institutional response to the problem of deviant behaviour and a system of non-restraint had been established there far more quickly and without the bureaucratic wrangling which had characterised the process in England and the United States. In Germany, the main proponents of asylums and of non-restraint had been doctors and the number of them who specialised in insanity increased rapidly in the first decades of the nineteenth century. Zilboorg (1941) has commented that:

> The whole system of life in Germany reflected the tempo of rapid industrialisation and the ever increasing sense of communal relationship and these were in turn reflected in the psychiatric profession. The individual worker, no matter how gifted, became part of a whole; the total accomplishment began to count more than the performance of any individual. As a result, a certain uniformity spread itself across German psychiatry. There was little strife. The rift between somatologists and the psychologists was well-nigh forgotten. German psychiatrists were almost without

exception good neurologists and good neuroanatomists who in fact if not in spirit followed Griesinger's postulate and equated mental and nervous disease.

(446–7)

This may have meant that German neurologists and mad-doctors, who were in any case often the same people, did not waste time attacking each other; it also meant that the idea that the behaviour of most asylum inmates was caused by brain disease had been a virtually unchallenged article of faith in Germany for longer than in England and the United States. Moral management as an ideology had never had much impact in Germany but was quickly transformed to an ideal of strict order and discipline.

Thus, by the end of the nineteenth century, the links between medicine and disturbing behaviour were firmly forged. The links were to be strengthened further by the results of research into the infectious diseases.

Psychiatry and syphilis

It had been noted as early as 1814, by the French physician Esquirol, that some asylum inmates showed a consistent pattern of behaviour and physical features: the expression of beliefs which were clearly false, incoherent and inarticulate talk, tremors and loss of muscle power followed by almost complete loss of the use of limbs and death. By the third decade of the nineteenth century, this pattern had been described frequently by French physicians and, later, by physicians in other parts of Europe and the United States. It was also observed that the brains of these people showed various pathological changes at post-mortem, but the relationship between earlier syphyilitic infection and these changes was not to be unambiguously demonstrated until the beginning of the twentieth century.

The fact that the link between the bizarre behaviour of these people, the physical changes observed before death and the brain pathology found afterwards *and* the link between all of these and syphilis was not fully appreciated during the nineteenth century was partly a result of the then current ideas about insanity. Hare (1959) has pointed out that the nineteenth century physician was unhappily aware of the fact that, while some of the inmates who expressed strange beliefs or spoke incoherently showed pathological brain changes at post-mortem, an equal (or greater) number did not. Similarly, a great many inmates (who might now be diagnosed as having, say, Parkinson's disease or Huntington's chorea) showed marked changes in motor behaviour. To add to the confusion, the term paralysis and its related term paresis had a number of different referents. The physicians of the early nineteenth century therefore did not fully appreciate the significance of the co-occurrence of features called dementia paralytica, nor did they regard those displaying them as a distinct and homogeneous group for research purposes. Nor was the nature of the relationship between bizarre behaviour, the motor changes and the brain pathology easily grasped. A paralytic disorder might be seen as both a cause and an effect of strange behaviour, rather than both being seen as products of pathological brain changes. The cerebral changes noted in asylum inmates were so varied, or completely absent, that some physicians, including Pinel, despaired of relating them in any systematic way to the inmates' behaviour. A number of physicians did grasp the possible implications of the co-occurrence of features called dementia paralytica but, lacking conceptual and methodological sophistication and technical expertise, were unable to provide more than indirect – and often ignored – evidence for their theories. It was not until 1912, following significant technical innovations and conceptual advances which were both antecedent and result of work on the infectious diseases, that the debate was closed by the finding of syphilitic spirochetes in the brains of those who had displayed the dementia paralytica cluster. The diagnosis of dementia paralytica had become objective in the 1890s when specific reactions of cerebro-spinal fluid were demonstrated and the indirect evidence linking dementia paralytica and syphilis had been mounting for some time before Noguchi's convincing direct evidence emerged in 1912. It is interesting to note that Kraepelin was one of those convinced by the indirect evidence.

Szasz (1976) has placed strong emphasis on the role of the dementia paralytica–syphilis link in fostering somatic theories of bizarre behaviour. Skultans (1979) disagrees and suggests that:

> the consequences which Szasz draws do not necessarily follow: the elaboration and proliferation of nomenclature did not take place. Early diagnosis and careful classification as preconditions for successful treatment were emphasised by the moral managers in the first half of the nineteenth century....With the increase in the size of asylums and the asylum population, the general standard of care deteriorated. Since cure was no longer a goal, classification was neglected.

(7)

Skultans' argument, however, is based on a misunderstanding not only of developments in classification around the turn of the century but also of the crucial differences between these and the earlier classificatory attempts of the moral managers.

Syphilis and the classification of deviant behaviour

Medical men had always striven to accommodate strange behaviour into whatever theoretical framework was then being employed to study physical ailments. They did this partly because they knew of no other way to think about the matter; later, of course, it was to become a practical necessity to maintain their *professional* claim that deviant behaviour was a medical matter.

Theories of physical suffering, however, were so firmly rooted in general theories of man and nature that to include behaviour seemed a perfectly reasonable way to proceed. Thus, as was pointed out earlier, philosophical, medical and literary writings on madness were often indistinguishable. Medical ideas about the nature of diseases and how or whether they should be classified were therefore faithfully reflected in writings about deviant behaviour. Ontological theories, with their emphasis on careful classification, were more popular in medicine than was the idea of disease as a quantitative deviation from some norm. Transferred to behaviour they resulted, during the eighteenth and nineteenth centuries, in a plethora of classification systems, no two of which appeared to agree on either the number or nature of what were claimed to be types of insanity. One problem was the lack of consensus as to the principles on which the endeavour should be based. Some insisted that classification should be by the most prominent symptom (it was apparently assumed that it would be obvious to an observer which behaviour merited this label); others claimed that groups of symptoms should be the basis of a classificatory system. Henry Maudsley insisted that the only good classificatory system was one based on etiology. To add to the confusion, words and deeds did not always match. As Zilboorg (1941) has pointed out, Skae and de Sauvages, who insisted on a classification based on symptoms, slipped, apparently unnoticed by themselves, into classifying on the basis of assumed cause.

There was also the problem of the uses to which these various systems might be put. It is difficult to avoid the conclusion that one of the systems' major functions was to convince medical men and the public of the complexity of insanity and of the detailed and expert knowledge needed to deal with it. Certainly, when it came to intervention, the niceties of classification seemed to be forgotten. Until relatively recently, medicine possessed a small number of cure-alls, and when these were discussed in the context of behaviour, the writers reverted to general terms such as cerebral irritation or, more usually, insanity. They had, of course, little option because the precise connections between the behaviour of those labelled insane, the various interventions and the abstract groups named in the classification systems were, to say the least, tenuous.

The moral managers. by contrast, adopted their usual pragmatic approach to the business of classification. For them, it must serve practice. Tuke (1813) suggested that "the general comfort of the patients ought to be considered; and those who are violent require to be separated from the more tranquil, and to be prevented, by some means, from offensive conduct towards their fellow sufferers". Thus, inmates should be "arranged into classes, as much as may be, according to the degree to which they approach to rational and orderly conduct" (141). This separation was also designed to teach inmates that 'good' behaviour earned different consequences than did 'bad'.

In the more abstract world of the physicians the chaos of classification systems for insanity was such that more than one recommended abandoning the whole business. Neumann, for example, suggested in 1859 that: "We shall never be able to believe that psychiatry will make a step forward until we decide to throw overboard the whole business of classification....There is but one type of mental disturbance and we call it insanity" (Zilboorg, 1941: 438). The problem for psychiatrists was that as long as their medical colleagues continued to emphasise the importance of grouping phenomena in particular ways, they must follow suit or risk creating professionally damaging gaps in theory and practice. In any case, as psychiatrists were trained as doctors, it is hardly surprising that the majority should bend what they observed to fit prevailing medical theories, rather than the other way round. As the nineteenth century progressed and medical research slowly began to show signs of being productive, it became increasingly unlikely – if, indeed, it ever had been likely – that medical theories would change in any way to accommodate the awkward behaviour of asylum inmates. Another reason why psychiatry must follow medicine was that the last decades of the nineteenth century, like the first, lacked anything resembling a scientific theory of behaviour. This is not to suggest that had such theories been available psychiatrists would have gladly used them; professional considerations must still be taken into account. Those psychiatrists who wished to be scientific, however, could see no way of doing so that did not involve imitating medicine. The alternative, as they saw it, was to return to abstract philosophy or, worse, to theology or mysticism.

This insistence on scientific practice and the conviction that it involved studying the brains of those who behaved strangely were particularly strong in Germany where neurology and psychiatry were virtually indistinguishable. There were, however, limits to the extent to which medicine could be imitated. Virchow's theory that classification and diagnosis consisted in naming pathological organ changes obviously could not be taken up as so many asylum inmates did not show them and any changes which could be found could not be systematically related to behaviour. Nevertheless, the search for disease entities must proceed. There were some attempts to characterise these in terms of 'psychological structures' but no agreement could be reached on what these might be and the theories were short lived. In the absence of well-demonstrated physical lesions, it became increasingly necessary to emphasise the importance of phenomena which presented themselves to the clinician. Fortunately, this emphasis had a long and respectable history in medicine, even if it was now being replaced by an emphasis on laboratory analysis. In the last decades of the nineteenth century, Kahlbaum reiterated Sydenham's view that progress would only be made by observing the onset, course and outcome of various groups of symptoms. It is interesting to note, although it was not stated explicitly, that it seems to have been taken for granted that these groups of symptoms would somehow present themselves to the physician in a readily recognisable form; his main task was to chart their course, to discover whether or not they constituted specific disease entities.

There can be little doubt that the growing body of evidence about the nature of infectious diseases, including syphilis, must have helped to convince psychiatrists that they were on the right track as far as methodology was concerned. For probably the first time in medical history, there were strong indications that adopting a particular theoretical framework would lead to a successful outcome. Moreover, medicine's successes had begun with – indeed, would never have been attainable without – careful observation of phenomena as they presented themselves to the clinician, *not* by speculation about unknown causes. Dementia paralytica appears to have been particularly common in northern Germany and Kraepelin – who was greatly influenced by Kahlbaum – wrote extensively on the subject. The role of the discovery of the dementia paralytica–syphilis link may therefore have been to confirm and extend the belief in a particular way of working, rather than in a somatic theory of deviant behaviour, which was in any case already well-established. And the length of time it had taken to discover the link may have given psychiatrists hope in the face of their poor empirical results.

But it is notable that those who emphasised the importance of the clinical observation of symptoms, which included bizarre behaviour, did so in apparent ignorance of the considerable methodological problems of observing and recording behaviour; indeed, from their emphasis on brain pathology, it was easy to lose sight of the fact that, in many cases, their subject-matter *was* behaviour. They also ignored the problem of knowing which behaviours should be thought of as symptoms, given that no pathology could be demonstrated in many inmates and, in those in which it could, there were no clear links between it and behaviour. Instead, it was implicitly reasoned that people were confined to asylums because they suffered from mental disorders. Therefore, what the clinician observed in the asylum, and considered abnormal, must be the symptoms of mental disorder. But the concepts of insanity and mental disorder were lay and not scientific concepts and their referents were idiosyncratic, many and varied. It is also possible, as was mentioned earlier, that the number of referents increased in the latter part of the nineteenth century; it is certainly beyond dispute that the apparent number of cases of insanity increased considerably. Indeed, Zilboorg (1941) has suggested that detailed clinical observation had to be stressed to bring order to "the welter of clinical material which accumulated with such suddenness" (447). It is not being suggested here that theoretical order could not be brought to the apparent chaos of the inmates' behaviour. What is suggested is that mad-doctors had failed to confront the consequences of their history, the implications of their ignorance and the conceptual and methodological difficulties of the task they had taken on. Nevertheless, it is against this background that Kraepelin is credited with having "delineated syndromes from the midst of chaos" (Kendell, 1975b: 62). Given the enormity of the task and the fact that Kendell's statement – together with the continued use of 'schizophrenia' – amounts to a claim that the necessary conditions for inferring it have been fulfilled, it is important that Kraepelin's putative achievements be examined in detail.

Chapter three

The necessary conditions for inferring schizophrenia: the work of Kraepelin, Bleuler and Schneider

This chapter will examine in detail the writings of Emil Kraepelin, Eugen Bleuler and Kurt Schneider to assess the extent to which they provide evidence that the necessary conditions for inferring dementia praecox or schizophrenia – i.e. the observation of a set of regularities – have been fulfilled. These writers have been chosen because Kraepelin's ideas are said to mark the beginnings of the modern construct of schizophrenia; because Bleuler and Schneider were influenced by him, though in different ways and because all three profoundly influenced future generations of psychiatrists. Bleuler's influence has been stronger in the United States, while Schneider and Kraepelin have proved more influential in Europe (Cooper *et al.*, 1972; Neale and Oltmanns, 1980). The three also represent a chronological sequence which illustrates not only the development of the concept of schizophrenia but also many of the problems associated with it. Others, notably Adolf Meyer, were involved in the development of the construct but their work will not be examined here because their ideas post-dated Kraepelin and Bleuler, their influence has been less and the criticisms which could be made of them are similar to those which will be made of Kraepelin *et al.*.

It must be emphasised that the issue being addressed here is not whether Kraepelin and his successors observed bizarre behaviours in asylum inmates; it is beyond doubt that the inmates behaved in ways which were both uncommon and incomprehensible to observers. Neither is it questioned that many of the inmates were distressed by their experiences. What is being examined is whether Kraepelin *et al.* were justified in claiming to have observed regularities amongst this mass of deviant behaviours which would justify inferring the constructs dementia praecox and schizophrenia.

The writings of Kraepelin, Bleuler and Schneider will be assessed in terms of the extent to which they support the observation of a pattern of phenomena which would justify the label syndrome. This criterion has been chosen for two reasons. First, as was noted in Chapter 1, modern writers are apparently unanimous in claiming that schizophrenia is inferred from such a pattern (what is actually and misleadingly claimed is that schizophrenia is a syndrome).

Second, this pattern is the minimum which allows the conclusion that a postulated cluster is not either the chance co-occurrence of unrelated phenomena or illusory (see, for example, Chapman and Chapman's 1967 demonstration of the perception of co-occurrences in random data). It is not possible to apply a less stringent criterion to the work of those said to have 'discovered schizophrenia' and maintain any semblance of support for its claims to scientific status.

The work of Emil Kraepelin

The term dementia praecox, which Kraepelin was to bring to such prominence, had been introduced (as démence précoce) by Morel in 1852 but with referents different from those suggested by Kraepelin in 1896. Kraepelin himself had used the term in 1893 with referents somewhat similar to Morel's but different from those he was later to employ. Kraepelin's 1896 writings are the starting-point of this evaluation because it is these which are most frequently said to mark the beginnings of the modern construct of schizophrenia. Kraepelin developed his ideas in a series of texts published between 1896 (5th edition) and 1913 (8th edition). Material from the latter was published separately in 1919. Writings from the 1896, 1899 and 1913/19 texts will be discussed in order to describe both the introduction and development of Kraepelin's 'modern' concept of dementia praecox. Two aspects of his work will be examined in detail: first, the evidence he presented in support of his claim that a particular cluster of phenomena could be the source of the construct of dementia praecox; and second, the way in which his population and the setting in which he worked might have influenced his theorising.

Some general considerations

One problem which is immediately encountered in any attempt to describe the evidence Kraepelin presented in support of his construct is that he more than once changed his mind about the putative regularities which allowed dementia praecox to be inferred. In 1896, for example, he described what he claimed was a meaningful cluster of behaviour from which he inferred dementia praecox. He also described a second cluster from which he inferred catatonia and a third from which he inferred dementia paranoides. Kraepelin suggested that the second cluster probably had the same antecedents as the first, although he offered no direct evidence for this; he therefore suggested that both clusters should be the source of dementia praecox. The cluster from which dementia paranoides was inferred was thought to have different antecedents, although again no direct evidence was offered; Kraepelin therefore suggested that this cluster should continue to be the source of a construct different from dementia praecox (Kraepelin of course did not use this language but talked misleadingly of separate illnesses). By 1899, in the 6th edition of his text, Kraepelin had apparently reversed this decision. He now postulated a new set of putative regularities said to justify inferring dementia praecox and which included some of the behaviours from which he had previously inferred dementia paranoides.

Between the 6th and 8th editions of his text, Kraepelin further increased the number of behaviours said to be symptoms of dementia praecox. The scale of the increase can be gauged from the fact that in 1896 a discussion of the constructs of dementia praecox and catatonia took up about thirty-seven pages. In the 6th edition, 'dementia praecox' occupied seventy-seven pages; by the 8th edition, the discussion had grown to 356 pages. This increase was almost wholly accounted for by the proliferation of behaviours said to be symptoms of dementia praecox. As the number of behaviours said to fall within the scope of the construct increased, so too did the number of sub-groups, i.e. regularities within the larger pattern, which Kraepelin claimed to have observed. In the 6th edition, he suggested three major sub-groups – putative regularities from which he inferred dementia praecox, hebephrenic type; dementia praecox, catatonic type; and dementia praecox, paranoid type. Within each of these, Kraepelin made further sub-divisions but without inferring new constructs. In his 1913 text, he claimed to have observed eleven major sub-groups within the larger cluster said to justify inferring dementia praecox.

These changes in what Kraepelin claimed to have observed parallel apparent changes in the criteria he used to attribute meaningfulness to any postulated cluster. Both changes reflect the conceptual and methodological problems he encountered, but did not always recognise, in trying to make sense of the multitude of bizarre behaviours displayed by asylum inmates. Because of these apparent changes in criteria, Kraepelin's earlier and later writings will be discussed separately.

Kraepelin's early writings: 1896 and 1899

In 1896, Kraepelin adopted the criterion of similarities in onset, course and outcome to assign meaningfulness to any postulated cluster of bizarre behaviour whose antecedents were unknown. He was thus claiming that if he could identify a group whose behaviour changed in a similar way at one point (onset), showed further similarity in development over a period of time (course) and reached a similar end-point (outcome), he would be entitled to postulate a common, as yet unobserved, event or process to account for this supposed pattern, i.e. a hypothetical construct with its surrounding assumptions.

Some of the problems of this argument have already been mentioned but are sufficiently important to be repeated here. First, although the terms onset, course and outcome are often used as if they referred to simple, discrete events, in practice they are usually summary terms for a set of extremely complex and continuous processes, particularly when they are applied to behaviour. Thus, what is actually recorded under these headings may be quite arbitrary and will differ across researchers. Second, the complexities of describing onset, course and outcome are compounded by the difficulties in specifying *important* similarities among the range of phenomena observed. An investigator using this criterion to assign meaningfulness and faced with a heterogeneous population showing a wide range of similarities and differences in behaviour (as was the case with Kraepelin's population) has no easy way of knowing which groupings are likely to result in the observation of 'new' phenomena. If this criterion is applied to a heterogeneous population, the likely result is unstable and ever-changing groupings as different investigators, or the same investigator at different times, apply varying criteria for assessing importance. Thus, the mere description of a set of similarities within a population and of differences between it and other populations, is not enough to attribute meaningfulness to the 'pattern' of similarities described. It is for this reason that evidence is demanded that these are a function of another independently and reliably measurable event – in medical parlance, a sign.

A third problem of this criterion is that the inclusion of 'outcome' requires that no statement can be made about the population of interest until all members have reached a point where no further change is possible. Even if this were achieved – say the population was studied until every member was dead – it would still not be possible to identify any new exemplars of a postulated pattern until they too had reached an agreed end-point. Thus, diagnosis would be delayed and research progress minimal. Taken together, these problems account for the unpopularity of this criterion in medicine.

It is unlikely that Kraepelin was wholly unaware of these problems; it is more likely that he employed the criterion as a last resort, having been unable to establish order from the apparent chaos of the inmates' behaviour using more useful and conventional criteria. He certainly did not adopt similarities in onset, course and outcome as a general criterion for classification. It might be argued, however, that Kraepelin's employment of a problematic criterion does not invalidate his work; that if he did describe similarities in onset, course and outcome, it would at least be a starting-point for a search for an independently measurable event associated with this supposed cluster. As this analysis will show, however, there is no evidence from Kraepelin's early writings that he even reached this starting-point.

Similarities in onset, course and outcome?

At first glance, it might appear that Kraepelin did indeed make use of his stated criterion to identify a pattern of behaviour from which he inferred dementia praecox. He suggested, for example, that the phenomena from which he inferred catatonia probably shared an antecedent with those from which he inferred dementia praecox because "both in their development and in their origins and prognosis we find an extensive correspondence between the two forms of illness" (1896: 461). He also suggested that the events from which he inferred dementia paranoides were different from these because "Not only does [dementia paranoides] develop on average at a rather higher age, it has a course and an outcome which is considerably different" (1896: 469). Indeed, the name Kraepelin chose for his construct reflects his belief that he was using this particular criterion: dementia refers to the alleged outcome and praecox to the time of onset. A closer examination of Kraepelin's work, however, gives a much less orderly impression of his methods and conclusions.

If medical researchers are engaged in a search for regularities in a heterogeneous population, it is assumed that they should present data showing that some members of this population share features which are either not present in other groups or, if present, appear to have different antecedents (for example, congenital vs. acquired immune deficiency). Data should also be presented in support of any claim that the first group is homogeneous in some important respect, that the features they share do not co-occur by chance. Having presented these data, the researchers would *conclude* by inferring a new hypothetical construct. Although Kraepelin saw himself as a scientific medical researcher, his presentation of the construct of dementia praecox in 1896 was quite different from that outlined here. Instead of *concluding* by inferring his construct, having presented evidence in support, Kraepelin *began* with the construct and proceeded to describe what he called cases of dementia praecox. He did not report the number of these who conformed to the descriptions he presented. These data, however, are crucial to claims that important shared features have been identified. Rather, Kraepelin's descriptions are in the form, 'one often notices'; 'it is occasionally observed'; 'in some cases', and so on. Thus, Kraepelin wrote as if by some independent and valid criteria, established by past research, dementia praecox had already been inferred in this sample and he was merely engaged in recording his impressions of the group. He wrote, that is, as if data supporting the introduction of his concept had already been presented when in fact they had not.

If Kraepelin failed to follow the required first step to inferring new constructs in medicine, the question remains as to the evidence he did present in support of his contention that he had identified a group of asylum inmates who had in common that their behaviour developed and changed in similar ways and reached a similar end-point. The only source of evidence is Kraepelin's subjective and unquantified accounts of alleged cases of dementia praecox. In this analysis, these will be examined under the headings of onset, course and outcome, although Kraepelin did not use these headings himself in spite of the importance he is supposed to have placed on them. Readers of his work can only extract information which appears to be relevant from the global accounts he provided.

Initial changes in behaviour (onset)

Kraepelin appears to have paid scant attention to two fundamental problems of discussing 'onset' in this context. There is, first, that of knowing which behaviour changes were important within his framework, i.e. indicative of some unobserved but assumed biological change, and second, that of the reliability of information collected retrospectively. The problems of retrospective data collection are well known – events may be distorted in memory by the passing of time, by attempts to understand the present, by leading questions from an interviewer and so on. Kraepelin, however, does not say from what source or how he obtained his accounts of alleged behaviour changes, how long after the event or what efforts were made to verify the information. These problems are highlighted by Kraepelin's claims that:

> The whole upheaval can take place so imperceptibly and with such indefinite indications that those around imagine that they are confronted simply with the outcome of an unhappy development, perhaps even of some character fault.
>
> (1896: 426)

> In more than half the cases, the upheaval occurs so imperceptibly and with such indefinite indications that its actual beginning cannot be determined in retrospect.
>
> (1899: 149)

It is difficult to understand how Kraepelin could have made use of his stated criterion of similarities in onset, course and outcome when he believed that onset could not be observed in more than half of those to whom he applied the term dementia praecox.

The issue remains of the extent of within-group similarity and between-group differences in what were claimed to be important initial changes. It is an issue which is impossible to resolve from the information provided by Kraepelin. Not only are his accounts of the postulated changes so vague that the observations which led to them are obscured, there is no indication of the number of people to whom each applied. Clearly, they did not apply to everyone labelled as suffering from dementia praecox, otherwise it would have been unnecessary for Kraepelin to have qualified his accounts thus:

> Somewhat less often the beginning of the illness is signalled by a markedly unhappy mood.
>
> (1899: 150)

> One often notices, particularly at the beginning, hypochondriacal complaints, self-recriminations, fears for the future.
>
> (1896: 427)

> One is often struck at this stage by a bluntness of feeling and indifference.
>
> (1896: 431)

It appears that quite different, indeed sometimes opposite, behaviour could signal the onset of dementia praecox:

> In the patient's behaviour, either a marked inertia and lassitude or typically childish characteristics make themselves apparent.
>
> (1896: 428)

> The psychosis begins as a rule with indications of a light or severe psychological depression (1896: 442). In a second group of cases one sees the illness set in with the sudden onset of a state of excitation with little prior warning.
>
> (1896: 443)

But Kraepelin also appeared to use the age at which some change was said to have occurred, rather than any specific changes, as one criterion for inferring dementia praecox. He suggested, for example, that "I think it is useful to divide dementia paranoides from the first named illnesses. Not only does it develop on average at a rather higher age ..." (1896: 469). The use of age of onset, of course, begs the question of how Kraepelin could possibly know that some alleged change was a function of whatever processes were said to underlie the illness of dementia praecox – in other words, of how he could claim that it marked the onset of dementia praecox as well as the question of why age was considered to be a useful criterion. It is difficult to avoid the conclusion that the population from whose behaviour Kraepelin inferred dementia praecox had in common only that their behaviour had changed in some disturbing way and to an extent sufficient for their relatives or the authorities to report them to the profession which claimed expertise in dealing with incomprehensible behaviour. Even those said to have "collapsed imperceptibly" must have changed perceptibly at some point in order to be brought to Kraepelin's notice. But Kraepelin's account of the changes is so vague and the changes themselves apparently so varied that little else can be said about the extent of similarity within the group, far less about the extent of difference between it and groups to which the term dementia praecox was not applied.

It might be objected that for any diagnostic category in medicine, similar variability would be observed: that for a group given label X, some would report initial changes A, B and C and others D, E and F. To argue like this, however, is to confuse the initial identification of regularities which justify inferring a new hypothetical construct, and which would not, in this case, include 'initial changes', with later observations about new exemplars of this pattern. It is to miss also the crucial point that Kraepelin was – or should have been – engaged in the former activity, not the latter.

Changes in behaviour over time (course)

Kraepelin introduced his 1896 concept because he claimed to have observed a group of people whose behaviour initially changed, developed and 'ended' in similar ways. It is therefore somewhat surprising to find reference to large amounts of within-group variability in the way in which the behaviour of the group was said to change over time:

> The course of this process of illness can take the most varied forms.
>
> (1896: 426)

> The further course of the illness in these cases is a varied one insofar as the imbecility sometimes develops more rapidly, sometimes more slowly and can in fact stop progressing at very different stages.
>
> (1896: 429)

Kraepelin thus appears to be claiming that the course of the illness in different people was simultaneously very similar and very different.

It was mentioned earlier that in 1896 Kraepelin suggested that the constructs of dementia praecox and catatonia were probably synonymous and gave as one of the reasons that the behaviour of those to whom the two constructs were applied changed in similar ways over time. It is therefore, again, surprising to find him describing the putative courses in quite different ways:

> The course of dementia praecox is in general one of regular progression. Only very seldom does one see an extensive remission of the signs of illness.
>
> (1896: 436)

> An unusually important phenomenon of the course of catatonia is the remissions which occur.
>
> (1896: 455)

Just as Kraepelin had attempted to 'join' the constructs of dementia praecox and catatonia in 1896, he wished to keep separate the construct of dementia paranoides, arguing that "it has a course and an outcome which is considerably different" (1896: 469). It is not unreasonable, then, to expect that the later 'joining' of 'dementia praecox' to some of the behaviours which had been the source of dementia paranoides, should, within Kraepelin's framework, have been accompanied by an explanation of why what had been, in 1896, "a considerably different course" was now, in 1899, apparently a similar one. Not only was such an explanation not forthcoming, but Kraepelin appeared to be unaware that it was called for. In 1896, he apparently used extensive and persistent visual and auditory hallucinations and delusions as one source of dementia paranoides; less extensive and transient displays of these phenomena were one source of dementia praecox. In 1899, Kraepelin did not offer evidence that the extent and persistence of these phenomena were actually the same in both groups; nor did he indicate that a common antecedent had been found, to justify disregarding differences in behaviour. Rather, he apparently abandoned 'extent and persistence of hallucinations and delusions' just as arbitrarily as he had chosen it, as a criterion for differences in course. Alternatively (and it is difficult to know from Kraepelin's writings which was the case), he may have abandoned 'course' altogether as part of the criterion for assigning meaningfulness, and merged the constructs on the basis of alleged similarities in outcome. This still, however, leaves the problem of how a "considerably different outcome" had now become a similar one.

Kraepelin's own admission of a large amount of within-group variability and his apparently arbitrary choice of criteria for similarity cast serious doubt on his claim to have identified a group who showed important similarities in behaviour change over time. The group to whom the term dementia praecox was applied presumably did show some similarities in their behaviour; as with Kraepelin's discussion of 'onset', however, it is impossible to know from Kraepelin's account either their extent or their significance.

'End-point' behaviour (outcome)

In attempting to identify regularities in the behaviour of asylum inmates, Kraepelin appeared to place more emphasis on 'outcome' than on 'onset' and 'course', although there is no obvious justification within his framework for doing so; certainly, Kraepelin never offered one. An early attempt to clarify the concept of dementia praecox illustrates this emphasis on an alleged end-point: "Dementia praecox is the name we give to the development of a simple more or less severe state of psychological weakness with manifestations of an acute or sub-acute disturbance of mind" (1896: 426). This statement also, however, illustrates one of the major problems in Kraepelin's discussion of 'outcome', as indeed of 'onset' and 'course' – his failure to specify the referents of the term, although he did provide descriptions of some of the behaviour from which he inferred 'simple more or less high grade state of psychological weakness'. The descriptions, however, are highly varied and no indication is given of the number of inmates to whom they applied. For the most part, however, the reader is left not with descriptions but with only vague statements about psychological weakness with no indication of the observations which were the source of this term or its (apparent) synonyms:

> although patients are more placid, it is only to reveal ever more clearly the indications of a fairly high grade psychological weakness.
>
> (1896: 433)

> The common outcome of all severer forms of dementia praecox is idiocy.
>
> (1896: 436)

The end state [of one type of paranoid form of dementia praecox] is feeble minded confusion.

(1899: 188)

Most frequently, however, the illness seems to lead to an insane confusion.

(1899: 200)

Kraepelin's failure to specify behaviours which were the source of the concepts of feeblemindedness, idiocy, and so on, or of the gradations of which he wrote, makes it impossible to know the extent of similarity amongst those to whom 'dementia praecox' was applied or of difference between them and other inmates. This problem is compounded by Kraepelin's indirect admission that the same behaviour might lead him to infer feeblemindedness in one inmate and not in another depending on past behaviour: "so that often enough we must remain in doubt as to the meaning of a particular final condition, should we be without the preceding history" (1905: 205). Not only did Kraepelin apparently use past behaviour to decide whether feeblemindedness should be inferred from present behaviour, he also used present behaviour to reconstruct the past when no information was available:

Still, even now, in a considerable number of cases, the careful observation of clinical symptoms makes it possible for us to trace out at least a rough outline of what has gone before from the final stages of the malady.

(1905: 205)

But Kraepelin's claim that this was possible is difficult to understand in the light of his statement that: "Unfortunately, I have not yet been able to discover particular indicators for drawing conclusions about the likely outcome of the illness in individual cases" (1899: 180). Kraepelin confirmed his pessimism in 1920 when he again claimed that it was impossible to predict prognosis in spite of careful observation (Astrup and Noreik, 1966).

This tendency to indulge in the dubious practices of interpreting present observation to fit constructions of the past, and, perhaps, a tentative diagnosis, and of re-construing an unknown past to fit present observations and diagnosis is, of course, yet another reason for the disfavour with which 'similarities in onset, course and outcome' is viewed as a criterion for assigning meaningfulness to a postulated cluster.

It was pointed out earlier that Kraepelin's first task was not to 'diagnose dementia praecox' but to search for regularities amongst the behaviour of inmates which might justify inferring new constructs. Kraepelin was clearly aware of the importance of the latter task, but was apparently either ignorant or dismissive of its primacy, i.e. of the dependence of the diagnostic task on the previous observation of regularities. Thus, his question-begging approach complicates still further his account of alleged outcome. In the 5th and 6th editions of his text, Kraepelin does not even discuss diagnosis, so that no information is available on the criteria he used. If Kraepelin had been following his own rules, then no judgements should have been made about inmates whose behaviour did not conform to any previously observed set of regularities, until they had reached a point where no further change was possible, if, indeed, such a point could be identified before death. But Kraepelin provided no information about the point(s) at which he made decisions about 'outcome', although photographs suggest that the label dementia praecox was applied to some inmates while they were relatively young. The important point, however, is that there is no reason to believe that the alleged end-point behavour from which Kraepelin inferred idiocy, feeblemindedness, and so on did not change at some future point. Kraepelin in fact failed to provide any evidence that he had identified a group of people who displayed similar 'end-point' behaviours.

It was suggested earlier that the mere description of a set of putative similarities in behaviour change at one point, in changes over time and in end-point behaviour, does not in itself justify inferring a hypothetical construct but that it might serve as a starting-point in a search for a meaningful cluster. It appears, however, that Kraepelin came nowhere near even this starting-point; rather, he fell victim to the problems known to attend the use of this criterion for grouping a heterogeneous population.

Kraepelin's later writings: 1913/1919

A recurring problem in Kraepelin's early writings is that of knowing what he actually *did* – what data he collected and how. The problem is in part a result of his question-begging approach and use of popular lay terms of the day (for example, weak-minded; degeneration), whose referents were never specified. But in these early writings, Kraepelin appeared to remind himself, at least intermittently, that he was required to demonstrate that certain phenomena 'went together' – that they co-occurred above chance level – in order to justify his construct of dementia praecox. Although he chose a highly problematic criterion and failed to provide evidence that a group of people conformed to it, at least his goal (to demonstrate co- occurrence) was appropriate. In his later writings, Kraepelin's goals are obscure. Wender (1963) claims that Kraepelin had now adopted a new criterion – that of identifying 'common characteristics of the disorder' – for assigning meaningfulness to a postulated cluster. It is, however, very difficult to know from Kraepelin's writings if this was his intention; he appears largely to have lost sight of the importance of demonstrating that certain phenomena 'went together', possibly because he erroneously thought that the demonstration had already been made.

What *is* clear is that in 1913, Kraepelin placed much less emphasis on putative similarities in type and timing of initial behaviour changes, in changes over time and in end-point behaviours, and instead introduced the new topic of "disorders which characterise the malady". This change of emphasis is signalled by his introductory statement: "Dementia praecox consists of a series of states the common characteristic of which is a peculiar destruction of the internal connections of the psychic personality" (1919: 3). The new emphasis on a 'common characteristic' was probably at least in part the result of criticism of his earlier emphasis on 'similarities in onset, course and outcome'. Criticism was not, as might be thought, based mainly on the deficiencies of this criterion; rather, it was based on the claim that it was possible to find cases of dementia praecox whose behaviour had changed in some disturbing way relatively late in life and whose end-point behaviour, or, more accurately, behaviour at the last point at which observations were made, apparently differed little from what the medical profession designated as normal (see, for example, Bleuler, 1911/1950). Kraepelin appeared partly to accept these criticisms:

It has since been found that the assumptions upon which the name chosen rested are at least doubtful ... the possibility cannot in the present state of our knowledge be disputed that a certain number of cases of dementia praecox attain to complete and permanent recovery and also the relations to the period of youth do not appear to be without exception.

(1919: 4)

Highlighting the apparent inappropriateness of the term dementia praecox, Serbski (cited in Zilboorg, 1941) commented on Kraepelin's statement that about 13 per cent of his cases apparently recovered, and enquired whether these were to be thought of as deterioration without deterioration, as dementia without dementia. Rowe (1906) pointed to the lack of reliability in the measurement of 'outcome', to the fact that the term deterioration was used very loosely and to its questionable use as a diagnostic criterion.

Kraepelin's critics are interesting, however, not so much for the problems they saw as for those they missed: the fallacy of their arguments was apparently overlooked. If Kraepelin's justification for originally inferring dementia praecox was the claim that he had identified a group who showed similarities in type and timing of initial behaviour changes, change over time and end-point behaviour, then it was logically impossible to have 'some cases of dementia praecox' whose behaviour changed relatively late in life and then reverted to 'normal'. Such a claim was incompatible with the use of Kraepelin's concept *unless* evidence was presented that a new and different set of regularities had been observed which would justify inferring it without recourse to 'onset, course and outcome'. This evidence was never presented. Rather, by the early 1900s, 'dementia praecox' seemed to have taken on a life of its own, quite detached from any examination of its origins. Critics spoke as if a new 'disease' had been 'discovered' which had, perhaps, been inappropriately named, about whose symptoms there might be disagreement, but which could easily be recognised in 'unequivocal cases':

A clinical picture is necessary to a concept of disease, and the predominant symptoms are what in the majority of cases will give us the classification. I would throw out the weak, meaningless, ill-defined symptoms which serve only to confuse and lessen the wealth of more reliable data; and the stilted verbosity and generalisation should be replaced by constant and well-cut symptoms true to the disease. These not being present, I should hesitate before stamping it dementia praecox.

(Rowe, 1906: 393; see also Bleuler, 1950)

It was against this background of ill-informed discussion, characterised by reification and question-begging, that Kraepelin published what was to be his last major set of writings on the construct of dementia praecox. Before these are examined, it is important to note the methods by which Kraepelin reached the conclusion that "there are apparently two principal groups of disorders which characterise the malady". He appears in doing so to have committed the same fallacy as his critics: in claiming that "the possibility cannot in the present state of our knowledge be disputed that a certain number of cases attain to complete and permanent recovery" and that "the relations to the period of youth do not appear to be without exception", Kraepelin was admitting that the group of people from whose behaviour he had originally inferred dementia praecox did *not* show the kind of similarities in 'onset, course and outcome' he had first claimed. Given that he had used this criterion to assign meaningfulness to a putative cluster and, therefore, to justify the introduction of his 1896 construct, it follows that, within his framework, he was no longer justified in using it; nor could he arbitrarily alter its correspondence rules. Instead, he must re-start his search for regularities amongst the heterogeneous group of asylum inmates whose behaviour did not conform to any known pattern. Not only is there no evidence that Kraepelin did re-start his search; he appeared, like his critics, to have been unaware of the problem. His writings, however, are in a form from which it is extremely difficult to deduce what he actually did; not only did he fail to describe how he sought "disorders which characterise the malady" (he claimed only to have found them), he failed also to describe what he meant by "characterise the malady". It is possible that he meant 'criteria I use to infer dementia praecox', but, if so, these should have been derived only after abandoning the construct, and should have been accompanied by evidence that they were a set of regularities such as would justify re-introducing the concept. Alternatively, Kraepelin may have meant 'disorders shared by every inmate called a case of dementia praecox'. The problem here, of course, is that in order to seek such 'disorders', 'dementia praecox' must first, by some independent and valid criteria, be identified. Kraepelin was no doubt helped in this task by his belief that he too could recognise unequivocal cases when he saw them:

In the first rank of course the delimitation of dementia praecox comes into consideration. We shall see later that on this point, in spite of the ease with which the great majority of cases can be recognised, there is still great uncertainty.

(1919: 186)

Unfortunately, Kraepelin did not even describe the criteria by which he recognised this great majority, far less provide evidence of their validity. Instead, he continued to beg the question of the validity of 'dementia praecox'. His failure to deal with these fundamental problems makes it extremely unlikely that his later writings will allow the conclusion that he was justified in introducing and later using the construct. Nevertheless, they will be examined here in order to emphasise the weakness of the foundations on which his considerable influence rests and because the analysis is relevant to the work of Bleuler, which will be discussed in the next section.

" ... two principal groups of disorders ..."

On the one hand we observe a *weakening of those emotional activities which form the mainsprings of volition*....The second group of disorders, which gives dementia praecox its peculiar stamp ... consists in the *loss of the inner unity* of the activities of the intellect, emotion and volition in themselves and among one another.

(1919: 74–5; emphasis in original)

Unfortunately, Kraepelin did not describe the observations on which these inferences were based. What he did instead was to list literally hundreds of what were claimed to be "psychic symptoms of dementia praecox", grouped according to unstated but apparently multiple criteria. The headings included: Influence on thought; Hallucinations of sight, smell and taste; Morbid tactile sensations and common sensations; Sexual sensations; Orientation; Consciousness; Retention; Association experiments and Evasion, with some headings claimed to be disorders of others. It is difficult to understand the rules by which Kraepelin generated these headings and listed behaviour under them, particularly as apparently identical phenomena appear to be listed under several different symptom headings.

Under many of the headings, Kraepelin discusses behaviour or 'states' which he claims are connected in some way with disorders of volition, to which he apparently attached much importance. It is, however, impossible to deduce which behaviour Kraepelin used to infer the putative disorders or the nature of the connection between the behaviours and the 'disorders of volition'. Some behaviours and 'states' are presented as alleged *results* of a disorder of volition; others are apparently cited as *causes* of disorders of volition while still others are used to infer this concept. There is no indication of how these choices of behaviour were made; for the most part, Kraepelin writes of the putative association between various behaviours and 'disorders of volition' in such a way that it is extremely difficult to know what he is trying to convey.

" ... which characterise the malady"

It was pointed out earlier that it is difficult to interpret what meaning Kraepelin attached to "characterise the malady". His writings not only fail to clarify this problem, they obscure it. One interpretation of the phrase is that Kraepelin was claiming to have identified behaviour shared by all those to whom he had already applied the label dementia praecox, but not by other inmates. On Kraepelin's own admission, however, this does not appear to have been the case:

> We may well suppose that also the development of such stereotypes, which give such a peculiar appearance to the terminal states of the disease *and likewise to many forms of idiocy*, is specially favoured by the failure of healthy volitional impulses.
>
> (1919: 45; emphasis added)

More specifically, a group of inmates from whose behaviour Kraepelin inferred paraphrenia appeared also to display behaviour which Kraepelin had previously connected with 'disorders of volition': "At the same time there are also abnormalities in the disposition, but till the latest stages [of paraphrenia] not that dullness and indifference which so frequently form the first symptoms of dementia praecox" (1919: 283).

It may be, then, that Kraepelin was suggesting that those he called dementia praecox had in common that they displayed whatever behaviours were the source of disorders of volition with greater intensity or frequency than did other inmates. As Kraepelin failed to identify the behaviour in question, far less the intensity and frequency in all inmates, it is impossible to know whether this was the case. The details are hardly relevant, however, unless accompanied by evidence that grouping inmates according to such variations is useful, i.e. leads to the prediction of previously unobserved events. An alternative interpretation of "characterise the malady" is that Kraepelin was proposing that the two "principal disorders" could be used as diagnostic criteria. Setting aside for the moment the necessity for a prior demonstration that the principal disorders referred to a pattern of behaviour, it is clear from Kraepelin's discussion of 'diagnosis' that, whatever his intentions, he did not consistently use these criteria to diagnose dementia praecox.

The meaning which Kraepelin attached to "characterise the malady" remains obscure. What is clear, however, is that in his later writings as much as in his earlier work, he failed to provide evidence that he was justified in inferring and using the construct of dementia praecox. His failure is well illustrated by his discussion of diagnosis. If Kraepelin had identified a pattern which justified inferring a new hypothetical construct, the chapter entitled 'Diagnosis' would have contained a clear description of this pattern, accompanied, perhaps, by discussion of how to avoid confusing it with other overlapping patterns (for example, the pattern from which lung cancer is inferred may be confused with the pattern from which tuberculosis of the lungs is inferred unless certain discriminating observations are made). Kraepelin did indeed include a discussion of possible confusion between the alleged symptoms of dementia praecox and alleged symptoms of other 'disorders'. Quite apart from the fundamental problem of justifying any choice of behaviour as symptomatic of dementia praecox or any other 'condition', Kraepelin gave the asylum doctors the futile and indeed impossible task of distinguishing the unstated referents of various popular lay terms:

> From genuine impulsive negativism there must be distinguished the
> surly, stubborn self-will of the paralytic and the senile dement, the playful reserve of the hysteric, the pertly repellent conduct of the manic and
> from the senseless perversities in action and behaviour, as they occur in
> dementia praecox, the conceited affectation of the hysteric, as also the
> wantonly funny solemnity of the manic patient.
>
> (1919: 258)

Kraepelin in fact appeared to use different criteria for diagnosing dementia praecox in different inmates, while claiming that he was actually using the 'whole clinical picture'. This claim might have been quite reasonable if the 'clinical picture' corresponded to a previously observed pattern, but it clearly did not. On the contrary, it is interesting to note that when he talked of the 'whole clinical picture', Kraepelin appeared to fall back on his old, problematic criterion of similarities in onset, course and outcome:

> But what hardly ever is produced in quite the same way by morbid processes of different kinds is ... *the total clinical picture*, including development, course and issue.
>
> (1919: 261; emphasis in original)

> The states in dementia praecox which are accompanied by confused excitement and numerous hallucinations, have often been called amentia and traced to exhausting causes. Experience has shown me that cases of that kind cannot be separated from the remaining forms of dementia praecox according to the origin, course and issue.
>
> (1919: 275)

That the judgement of 'issue' still lay in the eye of the beholder, however, is illustrated by Kraepelin's justification for separating out a group of inmates to whom he applied the term paraphrenia systematica, but whom other doctors called dementia praecox because, they claimed, the outcome of the two groups was indistinguishable. While agreeing that the outcome of 'dementia praecox, paranoid form' and of 'paraphrenia systematica' might *look* the same, Kraepelin nevertheless claimed that:

> it is obvious that in the terminal states [of those I call dementia praecox, paranoid form], we have to do with morbid processs which have run their course and ended in recovery with defect, and just on that account these cases have not progressed to the more severe forms of dementia such as form the issue of other paranoid cases of dementia praecox. *We may well imagine*, and may occasionally even really experience it, that a fresh outbreak of the disease may yet transform the hallucinatory or paranoid weak-mindedness into a drivelling, silly, negativistic or dull dementia.
>
> (1919: 299; emphasis added)

It is not, then, surprising to find Kraepelin noting that agreement amongst observers about putative outcome, and many other aspects of the inmates' behaviour, was virtually non-existent. Indeed, he goes even further to note the obvious fact, applicable to himself, that:

> In this uncertainty about the delimitation the statements of different observers can in the first place not be compared at all, not even the diagnoses of the same investigator at different periods of time separated by a number of years.
>
> (1919: 186)

It is unfortunate that Kraepelin, having noted this lack of reliability, proceeded as if he had noted exactly the opposite. Kraepelin did, of course, have the option of searching for regularities which would justify inferring a new construct by the accepted medical method of identifying a pattern of signs and symptoms. He certainly tried to find biological events, including changes in brain structure, which reliably co-occurred with whatever behaviours he thought of as symptoms of dementia praecox. By his own admission, however, the attempt failed and it is interesting to note, in spite of his claim to be a medical scientist, Kraepelin's repeated appeals to his own authority, rather than to empirical evidence, in support of his claim to have identified a pattern which justified his concept:

> we shall no longer need to refute in any detail the objection formerly brought from different sides against the establishment of [dementia praecox] that it was a case of unjustified grouping of uncured psychosis of very different kinds....Clinical experience has demonstrated innumerable times that it is possible from the conception of the pathology of dementia praecox to tell with great probability the further course and issue of a case belonging to the group.
>
> (1919: 252)

We have therefore even yet to rely purely on the valuation of clinical experience....

(1919: 255)

Although I must doubt that all of the disease pictures of Kahlbaum actually belong together, I nevertheless feel that my extensive experience justifies the recognition of the great majority of these cases as examples of a single characteristic illness form.

(1899: 160)

The context of Kraepelin's work

Kraepelin arrived at the study of deviant behaviour after most of the events described in Chapter 2 had taken place. He was therefore the product of an environment which accepted unquestioningly the appropriateness of the methods and theories of medicine to the study of disturbing behaviour, but which had never seriously considered the problems this might present. While Kraepelin has been mildly criticised by modern writers for his insistence on a disease-entity model, it may be argued that this aspect of his belief system, by acting as an obvious target for attack, has tended to obscure the problems of the wider framework within which he worked, as well as the fact that he failed to provide any evidence in support of his concept (see, for example, Wing, 1988). Kraepelin in fact appears to have been unaware of, or to have chosen to ignore, even the most basic principles of empirical enquiry – the need to present systematically gathered data, rather than to rely on personal experience and beliefs; the importance of clear description so that others can try to replicate the observations; the importance of reliability of observations and the dangers of question-begging. He appears also to have been unaware of the problem of how he could possibly know, in the absence of independent evidence, which of the many disturbing behaviours shown by asylum inmates were products of an unspecified brain disease. Given that the social context in which Kraepelin worked was one of relative naivety in conceptual and methodological matters, perhaps these deficiencies are not surprising. What is surprising is that Kraepelin's work is given serious consideration by his successors – Strauss and Carpenter (1981) even consider it to be the cornerstone of scientific psychiatry – and is subjected only to mild criticism by modern writers.

One further aspect of Kraepelin's working environment and population deserves detailed comment but as the discussion applies equally to the work of Bleuler, it will be postponed till the end of the next section.

The work of Eugen Bleuler

Bleuler's major text – *Dementia Praecox or the Group of Schizophrenias* – was published in 1911. Gottesman and Shields (1982) stated that "Bleuler had no major disagreements from Kraepelin's views on schizophrenia" (39). This was unfortunate, for it meant that Bleuler took for granted that Kraepelin had described a pattern which justified introducing the new concept of dementia praecox. Bleuler compounded the error by adopting his own set of criteria for inferring the construct as well as suggesting the new word schizophrenia, although he contined to use the term dementia praecox. Wing (1978a) claims that Bleuler's "schizophrenia covered all Kraepelin's sub-classes with the addition of paraphrenia" (2). But the lack of specificity of Kraepelin's descriptions, the confusion of his account of diagnosis and the lack of specificity in Bleuler's account make it impossible to know whether the two were using the construct(s) as Wing claims. Because Bleuler, like Kraepelin, took for granted the validity of 'dementia praecox', his work was at best misconceived and at worst futile. In addition, most of the criticisms which were made of Kraepelin's writings apply also to Bleuler's. His work will therefore be reviewed less extensively than was Kraepelin's.

The word 'schizophrenia'

Bleuler put forward three reasons for introducing the term schizophrenia. He claimed, first, that the words dementia praecox (which he called the name of the disease) "only designates the disease, not the diseased" (1950: 7). Why it should be thought appropriate to coin a term denoting the person is not clear, and Bleuler offered no explanation. Wing (1978b) claims that the availability of an adjectival form of the word made it more convenient, but for what or whom he does not explain. Bleuler's second reason reflected his belief that certain behaviours were "characteristic of the illness": "in every case we are confronted with a more or less clear-cut splitting of the psychic functions" (1950: 11). The problems of the first part of this belief will be discussed below; it is worth noting, however, that Bleuler used the term 'splitting of the psychic functions' so loosely that it is impossible to know what range of behaviour was its source. Bleuler's third and, he suggested, most important, reason for "coining a new name" was that although he believed that the *construct* of dementia praecox was properly applied to people whose behaviour changed (in some unspecified way) relatively late in life and who did not merit the term demented, the *words* were inappropriate. The problems of holding this belief and retaining the construct, albeit re-titled, were discussed in the previous section.

Bleuler created two dichotomies, in writing at least, within whatever behaviours were the source of his concept of schizophrenia. He called these fundamental and accessory symptoms and primary and secondary symptoms. Although the two are sometimes, apparently, taken as synonymous (see, for example, Gottesman and Shields, 1982), Bleuler's writings give no indication that he meant this to be the case; on the contrary, he appears to have attached quite different meanings to primary and fundamental and to secondary and accessory. In addition, some behaviours called fundamental symptoms appear later as secondary, while behaviours called accessory symptoms were later labelled primary. The number of dichotomies Bleuler created and the names he attached to them, however, are of much less importance than are the justifications he advanced for creating them. Because Bleuler did apparently create two dichotomies, they will be discussed separately.

The fundamental/accessory dichotomy

Bleuler claimed that:

> Certain symptoms of schizophrenia are present in every case and at every period....Besides these specific, permanent or fundamental symptoms, we can find a host of other, more accessory manifestations....As far as we know, the fundamental symptoms are characteristic of schizophrenia.
>
> (1950: 13)

Bleuler's claim to have identified behaviour "permanently displayed in every case of schizophrenia" raises problems similar to those discussed in relation to Kraepelin's discussion of "disorders which characterise the malady": Bleuler's claim demands that an independent and valid criterion be used to infer schizophrenia in the first place, before any statements can be made about 'behaviour displayed in every case'. Alternatively, if Bleuler was claiming to have observed a group, all of whom displayed behaviour not observed in other inmates, and that he introduced *his* schizophrenia on the basis of these, he was not justified in doing so unless he also provided evidence that the behaviour formed a meaningful cluster. A third interpretation, that these behaviours were Bleuler's diagnostic criteria, makes the statement self-evident, as every 'case' would have to display these to qualify as a 'case'.

Bleuler failed to meet either of the requirements demanded by the first two interpretations; indeed, he seemed to be unaware of the problem. He also made no attempt to provide evidence to support his assertion that all those whom he called schizophrenic, by whatever criteria, showed the same behaviour permanently. Bleuler dealt with this detail simply by claiming that "it was proven that there exist certain constant symptoms..." (1950: 284). Bleuler appeared to contradict even his own use of "fundamental symptoms" by claiming that "at ... times [the accessory symptoms] alone may permanently determine the clinical picture" (1950: 13). This claim is apparently incompatible with his earlier claim that whatever behaviours he called fundamental symptoms were permanent and were present "at every period of the illness", although it must be admitted that Bleuler's meaning here is obscure.

Bleuler claimed that certain behaviours were displayed only at some times by some of those he called schizophrenic; these were also, he claimed, shown by other inmates. The scope of the term accessory symptoms, which he applied to these behaviours, was sufficiently wide for Bleuler to group them into twenty-eight categories. The question arises as to why Bleuler believed he was entitled to call the hundreds of behaviours in these categories symptoms of schizophrenia. This is not to suggest that his designation of some forms of behaviour as fundamental symptoms raises no problems – far from it; but Bleuler at least advanced criteria, however inadequate and unfulfilled, which he believed himself to be using. No criteria were put forward for the choice of behaviour as accessory symptoms. Nor did Bleuler describe any consistent relationship between fundamental and accessory symptoms. It is difficult to avoid the conclusion that the choice was arbitrary.

Although Bleuler did not spell out any clear relationship between fundamental and accessory symptoms, he appeared at times to imply that the latter were a result of the former. If Bleuler had observed a syndrome pattern, then such a claim might have been reasonable if 'fundamental symptoms' merited the term signs and if plausible theoretical links existed between his signs and symptoms. Not only did Bleuler fail to describe any of this, he apparently suggested a variety of directional links between fundamental and accessory symptoms. For example, fundamental symptoms were said to cause other fundamental symptoms and accessory symptoms were said to cause fundamental symptoms.

Primary and secondary symptoms

Bleuler's second dichotomy was, he claimed, one which separated "the symptoms stemming directly from the disease process itself" from "those ... which only begin to operate when the sick psyche reacts to some internal or external processes" (1950: 348). Bleuler also claimed that "The primary symptoms are the necessary partial phenomena of the disease" (349), thus seeming to imply that whenever events designated as the disease process occurred, then primary symptoms must follow. Yet Bleuler also stated that "To start with [the disease] remains latent until an acute pathological thrust produces prominent symptoms, or until a psychic shock intensifies the secondary symptoms" (1950: 463). He therefore implied that primary symptoms could not always be observed, which raises the interesting question of how Bleuler could infer them. He did not deal with this important problem, but it appears that his reasoning could be tautological. The secondary symptoms of hallucinations and delusions, for example, indicated to Bleuler the presence of a primary symptom, the predisposition to hallucinations, which was, in turn, claimed to be a necessary condition for the development of hallucinations (1950: 349).

The choice of primary and secondary symptoms

Bleuler stated that *"We do not know what the schizophrenic disease process ac-*

tually is" (1950: 466; emphasis in original). Yet he still felt able to provide a list of "symptoms stemming directly from the disease process". It is difficult to understand how Bleuler was able to recognise the consequences of a totally unknown antecedent; inevitably, then, his criteria for applying the term primary symptom varied from symptom to symptom.

The 'disturbance of association', for example, was regarded as primary "insofar as it involves a diminution or levelling of the number of affinities", and because some "confusional states usually occur without psychic occasion" and are "sometimes ... accompanied by a syndrome which we ordinarily associate with signs of infection or autointoxication" (1950: 350). Certain pupillary disturbances were regarded as primary symptoms for no stated reason but the conclusion was said to be "assisted" by the claim that when such disturbances were observed, the "cases ... show a poorer termination than those with other kinds of pupillary disturbances" (1950: 352). Bleuler at least made some attempt to justify these choices; with other types of behaviour said to be primary symptoms, no justification was given. Bleuler claimed, for example, that:

> most of the manic episodes appear to belong to the disease process itself.
>
> (1950:351)

> We can assume that the tendency towards stereotypy originates directly from the disease process.
>
> (1950: 351)

> A part of these edemas appear to be directly conditioned by the disease process.
>
> (1950: 352)

Bleuler's choice of behaviour as secondary symptoms appears to be based on the belief that they were "subject to psychic influences". Quite apart from the problem of how this decision was made and of the justification for regarding some of the many inmate behaviours which must have varied with the environment as symptoms of schizophrenia, there are some interesting inconsistencies in Bleuler's writing. He claimed, for example, that the disturbances of affect were secondary because "real destruction of affectivity cannot be proved, even in the most severe cases; ... some affects may be present and others not" (1950: 353). But Bleuler also claimed that "Even in the most severe cases the majority of the associations take the usual pathways" (1950: 355), which can reasonably be interpreted, using Bleuler's language, to mean that 'real destruction of associational activity cannot be proven, even in the most severe cases'. Whatever Bleuler thought of as the association disturbances, however, were "conceived of as being primary" (1950: 355).

As with 'primary symptoms', Bleuler designated various unspecified behaviours as secondary symptoms on the basis only of his authority:

negativism is certainly a complex secondary phenomenon.

(1950: 354)

it should need no proof that the disturbance of the complex functions of intelligence ... the impaired synthesis of the total personality, the disordered strivings and efforts of the patients ... the altered relations to reality ... are comprehensible only in connection with the already mentioned secondary symptoms; therefore they themselves are secondary manifestations for the most part.

(1950: 354)

These problems highlight yet again the important general issue of how the 'symptoms of schizophrenia' were chosen. It must be borne in mind that Bleuler, like Kraepelin, assumed that the brains of those called schizophrenic had changed in some uniform way in structure or function. Whatever behaviour was said to be symptomatic of schizophrenia was assumed to be a direct or indirect consequence of these changes. Bleuler, however, never demonstrated that either of these assumptions was justified; indeed, he did not even systematically investigate them. Nevertheless, he believed that he could diagnose schizophrenia and correctly designate some forms of behaviour as symptoms of schizophrenia. Bleuler's account of diagnosis shows that, like Kraepelin, he used many different criteria. These included unspecified styles of writing or playing the piano; a 'will o' the wisp' gait; pupillary disturbances; the overall impression (unspecified) received from an inmate and the inmate's remaining "quantitatively and qualitatively rigid with regard to the same feelings, even though he responds to ideas of varying values" (1950: 300). If Bleuler's criteria appear non-specific, this may be because "just how prominent the various symptoms have to be in order to permit a diagnosis of schizophrenia can hardly be described" (1950: 298). In addition to these diagnostic criteria, Bleuler designated many other behaviours as symptoms of schizophrenia. *Which* behaviours were rarely specified, perhaps because, according to Bleuler, speaking of his criteria for inferring affective disturbance "it is easier to sense these phenomena than to describe them" (1950: 42).

One criterion which Bleuler did appear to use in designating behaviours as symptoms was his *beliefs* about how normal people reacted to events:

Even when the affects change, they usually do so more slowly than in the healthy....During an interview, a female patient was repeatedly shown the picture of a child. It took one-quarter of an hour for the corresponding sorrowful affect to appear.

(1950: 45)

All the nuances of sexual pleasure, embarrassment, pain or jealousy may emerge in all their vividness which we never find in the healthy when it is a question of recollecting the past.

(1950: 46)

During celebrations one can observe how much longer it takes the schizophrenic to get into the party mood than it does the healthy person.
(1950: 45)

With this criterion in mind, it is interesting to note Bleuler's general account of some of the phenomena from which he inferred schizophrenia simplex:

On the higher levels of society, the most common type is the wife (in a very unhappy role, we can say), who is unbearable, constantly scolding, nagging, always making demands but never recognising duties. Her family never considers the possibility of illness, suffers for many years a veritable hell of annoyances, difficulties, unpleasantnesses from the 'mean' woman ... the possibility of keeping the anomaly secret is facilitated by the fact that many of these patients still manage to conduct themselves in an entirely unobtrusive way. Frequently, one is veritably forced to keep the situation secret from the world at large because there are many people who readily step in and defend these women who themselves know how to play the role of injured and persecuted innocence.
(1950: 236; parentheses in original)

Kraepelin's and Bleuler's population

Strauss and Carpenter (1981), Cutting (1985) and Hare (1986) have remarked on the fact that the kind of 'severe and long-standing cases' described by Kraepelin and Bleuler are no longer seen, while Seeman *et al.* (1982) claim that certain symptoms of schizophrenia are now rare. These comments suggest that there is some difference between Kraepelin's and Bleuler's population and that called schizophrenic today. There are indeed striking differences between the two populations. It is possible to say this because, although both Kraepelin and Bleuler consistently failed to specify the range of phenomena which was the source of their symptom concepts, they did provide many specific descriptions of inmates said to be cases of dementia praecox or schizophrenia. Seeman *et al.* consider that the reasons for the changes are unknown while Strauss and Carpenter imply that the difference might have arisen because 'schizophrenia' has inexplicably become less severe or is halted by modern drugs, but they provide no evidence that this is the case. A more plausible explanation of the difference is that Kraepelin and Bleuler were dealing with a quite different population from that called schizophrenic today, and one to which the term would not now be applied. It was mentioned earlier that in Europe close links existed at this time between neurology and psychiatry and that, in Germany at least, the two professions were virtually one, in contrast with the modern position of two quite separate groups. The close links between psychiatry and neurology were in part the result of ignorance about both brain and behaviour; the separation of the groups increased as *neurologists'* knowledge increased.

65

Inevitably, then, Kraepelin and Bleuler would have seen people who would now fall within the orbit of neurology and not psychiatry. There is, in fact, a remarkable similarity between their descriptions of 'cases of dementia praecox/schizophrenia' and later descriptions of people said to be showing Parkinsonian sequelae to the (assumed) viral infection called encephalitis lethargica. It is important to note that the *pattern* from which this concept was inferred was not described, by von Economo, until 1917, after Kraepelin and Bleuler had completed their major writings. Sacks (1971), however, has pointed out that various singular phenomenon which were part of this pattern had been described often in the past, but that each generation apparently 'forgot' the observations of the previous one. Von Economo himself acknowledges that he was helped in 'seeing' the pattern by the devastating European epidemic of 1916–27 and by his mother's recollection of the Italian epidemic (the great *nona*) of the 1890s. Just how similar are the descriptions of Kraepelin, Bleuler and von Economo, and how different from modern descriptions of 'schizophrenia', can be seen from Table 3.1. In addition to the phenomena listed there, Kraepelin, Bleuler and von Economo also described marked peculiarities of gait (Bleuler considered that he could identify schizophrenics simply by watching inmates walking); excess production of saliva and urine; dramatic weight fluctuations; tremor; cyanosis of hands and feet and the inability, in spite of effort, to complete 'willed' acts. All three also described delusions and hallucinations of many sensory modalities while both Kraepelin and von Economo provided details of the severe structural brain damage which was revealed microscopically at post-mortem. Both stressed the great damage to nerve tissue and the proliferation and 'infiltration' of abnormal glia cells. Given that Kraepelin and Bleuler are credited with having first described schizophrenia "so thoroughly and sensitively" (Gottesman and Shields, 1982) it is remarkable that, with the exception of delusions and hallucinations, not one of the phenomena described above, and in Table 3.1, appears in the index of a comprehensive academic text on 'schizophrenia' (Neale and Oltmanns, 1980).

Contemporary neurologists, of course, noticed that von Economo's descriptions of 'encephalitis lethargica' and the sequalae were very similar to what they had been used to calling dementia praecox or schizophrenia. Von Economo claimed that some people said to be suffering from schizophrenia were in fact cases of encephalitis lethargica while Hendrick (1928) pointed to cases of "acute psychosis", where the diagnosis of encephalitis lethargica was confirmed at post-mortem. The problem was, however, that the validity of 'dementia praecox/schizophrenia' was taken for granted, so that it was assumed that Kraepelin and Bleuler had described a different disorder from von Economo but that it could be very difficult indeed to tell the difference between them. The criteria suggested for making this differentiation were, inevitably, vague and subjective:

the [encephalitis lethargica] patient ... can be shown much more easily than the schizophrenic to be highly sensitive and his withdrawal from contact with others is a motivated defence rather than a product of preoccupation and dulling of external interests.

(Hendrick, 1928: 1007)

Stransky in 1903 established the fundamental thesis that in the schizophrenic diseases an intra-psychic ataxia (that is a dissociation of the 'noö- and thymo-psyche') exists as a basic symptom. In this division he meant 'noö-psyche' to be the representative of the purely intellectual functions, while the 'thymo-psyche' embraced the urges, emotions and volition....In encephalitis lethargica, though no genuine dissociation as in dementia praecox occurs, an isolated disturbance of the thymo-psyche takes place, leaving the noö-psyche intact ....

(von Economo, 1931: 163; parentheses in original)

Hauptman (cited in Jelliffe, 1927) considered that schizophrenics were unable to relate their psychomotor disorders to the soul life. The problem was compounded by the fact that the diagnosis of encephalitis lethargica was not straightforward. As von Economo pointed out, the initial infection was sometimes mild and sometimes severe and the sequelae could appear immediately or after many trouble-free years. In addition, what von Economo described as 'a remarkably constant' picture of brain damage was obviously not visible until post-mortem, while many other physiological functions were apparently within normal limits. It is possible, then, that, in trying to tell the difference between 'schizophrenia' and 'encephalitis lethargica' the psychiatrists and neurologists were actually distinguishing amongst exemplars of 'encephalitis lethargica'. We must be very careful indeed, however, of concluding that this was the case. There is no reliable way in which the diagnostic status of Kraepelin's and Bleuler's populations can be checked and, certainly, it might be objected that before the great epidemic, the prevalence of encephalitis lethargica/post-encephalitic Parkinsonism in Europe would be insufficient to account for the large numbers said to be suffering from dementia praecox or schizophrenia. Sacks (1971), however, has claimed that the prevalence of Parkinsonian sequelae of encephalitic infection prior to the great epidemic may have been underestimated; he argues that variously named European epidemics from the sixteenth to the nineteenth centuries may well have been forms of post-encephalitic Parkinsonism. It is interesting to note here also William Perfect's suspicion, recorded in 1787, that one contributor to the increasing prevalence of insanity was "the epidemic catarrh, more generally known by the name of the *Influenza* which raged with such violence ... in the year 1782" (Hare, 1983: 449; emphasis in original). It could be speculated that, if these epidemics increased in extent or frequency in the nineteenth century, or if more people survived the initial infection only to experience the sequelae, then this – and not an increase in schizophrenia, as Hare claims – might in part account for the rising numbers of cases of insanity. But to return to Kraepelin and Bleuler: there are at least good circumstantial grounds for supposing that they were for the most part dealing with the consequences of some forms of encephalitic infection and that at least a sizeable minority of their patients would later have been diagnosed as cases of post-encephalitic Parkinsonism.

Table 3.1 Descriptions of dementia praecox, schizophrenia and encephalitis lethargica/post-encephalitic Parkinsonism

The spasmodic phenomena in the musculature of the face and speech which often appear, are extremely peculiar.

(Kraepelin, 1913/1919: 83)

Fibrillary contractions are particularly noticeable in the facial muscles and "sheet lightning" has long been known as a sign of a chronically developing [schizophrenic] illness.

(Bleuler, 1911/1950: 170)

As a rule, other spontaneous movements are associated with the choreic movements of Encephalitis Lethargica, the myclonic and fasciscular twitches of the disease: an important point with regard to differential diagnosis .... These myclonic movements are more or less rhythmical and symmetrical flash-like short twitches of separate muscles or groups of muscles.

(von Economo, 1931: 39)

Dufour has described disorders of equilibrium, adiadochokinesia and tremor which he regards as the expression of a "cerebellar" form of dementia praecox.

(Kraepelin, 1913/1919: 79)

Constraint is also noticeable in the *gait* of the patients. Often indeed it is quite impossible to succeed in experiments with walking. The patients simply let themselves fall down stiffly, as soon as one tries to place them on their feet.

(Kraepelin, 1913/1919: 148; emphasis in original)

In some cases the ataxia attains such a degree that the instability of gait, the deviation towards one side, the tendency to fall backwards on standing, the tremor, the giddiness and the nystagmus can only be ascribed to an involvement of the cerebellum in the inflammatory process.

(von Economo, 1931: 32)

[Ermes] found that a fall of the leg held horizontally only began after 205 seconds [in cases of dementia praecox], while in healthy persons it made its appearance on an average after 38 seconds, at latest after 80 seconds. There followed then [in dementia praecox] either a repeated jerky falling off with tremor or a gradual sinking.

(Kraepelin, 1913/1919: 79)

if ... one lifts up the forearm of a patient [suffering from the amyostatic-akinetic form of encephalitis lethargica] the arm remains raised for quite a time after having been released, and is only gradually brought back in jerks and with tremors.

(von Economo, 1931: 44)

It is notable, too, that papers which appeared at the time on 'organic aspects of schizophrenia' (for example, Hoskins, 1933; Hoskins and Sleeper, 1933) described phenomena – pupillary disorders, polyuria, cyanosis – certainly not claimed today to be part of 'schizophrenia' (see APA, 1980, 1987). And it was exactly these symptoms, amongst others such as chronic constipation and

Table 3.1 *Continued*

During acute thrusts [of schizophrenia], though rarely in the chronic conditions, we often encounter somnolence. Patients are asleep all night and most of the day. Indeed, they often fall asleep at their work. Frequently, this somnolence is the only sign of a new thrust of the malady.

(Bleuler, 1911/1950: 169)

In the now increasing somnolence [of the acute phase of the somnolent ophthalmoplegic form of encephalitis lethargica] one often observes that the patients, left to themselves, fall asleep in the act of sitting or standing or even while walking ... [somnolence] is repeatedly found in quite slight cases as the only well marked symptom.

(von Economo, 1931: 27)

Hoche also mentions the markedly increased secretion of the *sebaceous glands* [in schizophrenic patients].

(Bleuler, 1911/1950: 167; emphasis in original)

A hypersecretion of the sebaceous glands (probably centrally caused) causes the peculiar shining of the faces of these patients.

(von Economo, 1931: 46; parentheses in original)

The tendency to edema (*sic*) is usually ascribed to poor circulation, but it may have other causes....In a physically strong female patient with a beginning mild schizophrenia, edemas were noted in the thigh area....At times more severe edemas may make movement painful.

(Bleuler, 1911/1950: 166)

oedema of hands and feet ... are ... more frequent in the amyostatic than in the other forms of encephalitis lethargica.

(von Economo, 1931: 46)

In the most varied [schizophrenic] conditions, [the pupils] are often found to be unequal without having lost their ability to react ... this pupillary inequality is rarely persistent; it often varies within a few hours, becoming equal or reversed.

(Bleuler, 1911/1950: 173)

[The] behaviour of the pupils is of great significance. They are frequently in the earlier stages [of dementia praecox] and in conditions of excitement conspicuously wide ... here and there one observes a distinct difference in the pupils. The light reaction of the pupils often appears sluggish or slight.

(Kraepelin, 1913/1919: 77)

pupillary disturbances are very common. In patients [with the hyperkinetic form of encephalitis lethargica] one generally finds unequal and myopic pupils with a diminished and sluggish reaction but sometimes also one-sided or double or complete absence of reaction or an absence of light reaction only. These pupillary disturbances often vary considerably [in the same patient].

(von Economo, 1931: 38)

A differential diagnosis between [encephalitis lethargica and chorea] must necessarily be very difficult except where there exist for our guidance pupillary disturbances or other objective signs of encephalitis lethargica.

(von Economo, 1931: 39)

greasy skin, which were said to be shared by patients with schizophrenia and encephalitis lethargica (Farran-Ridge, 1926).

What appears to have happened since is that, as post-encephalitic Parkinsonism and other severe infectious diseases became rarer, and as neurology and psychiatry separated into two distinct specialisms, the referents of 'schizophrenia' gradually changed until the diagnosis came to be applied to a population who bore only a slight, and possibly superficial, resemblance to Kraepelin's and Bleuler's. This transformation of the concept, while at the same time retaining the idea that Kraepelin and Bleuler discovered or first described schizophrenia, has probably proceeded without critical comment for several reasons. First, the taking for granted of the validity of 'schizophrenia' has now, as much as in the 1920s, encouraged the idea that the concept, although problematic, could eventually be sorted out and discouraged any fundamental re-assessment; thus, its gradual transformation might have been mistaken for progress because the nature of the transformation – from a neurological, physical and behavioural concept to an entirely behavioural/experiental one – and its implications were never made explicit. The transformation may have been aided, second, by the fact that changes in the social and 'moral' behaviour of those said to be suffering from encephalitis lethargica were emphasised by some writers. A gradual shift in emphasis to disturbing *behaviour* as diagnostic criteria for schizophrenia might not, therefore, have been very obvious, particularly as the same profession claimed jurisdiction over both disturbing behaviour and disturbing neurology. Thus, the events described in the previous chapter, and particularly those at the end of the nineteenth century, were especially important in allowing the transformation to a behavioural concept, and in allowing the retention of somatic explanations. The idea that Kraepelin, Bleuler and modern psychiatrists are studying the same phenomena may, finally, have been encouraged by an emphasis on the similarities in Kraepelin's, Bleuler's and modern descriptions of 'schizophrenia', and by a lack of discussion of the differences.

Those who use the modern construct of schizophrenia might object that any similarity between Kraepelin's and Bleuler's populations and that of von Economo is irrelevant, for two reasons. First, Kraepelin's and Bleuler's inclusion of these people might be seen as a simple case of misdiagnosis. Second, it might be suggested that the validity of the modern construct of schizophrenia does not depend on Kraepelin and Bleuler and that the modern construct is justified by later research. Both of these arguments are questionable. The first again confuses the tasks of construct formation and of diagnosis, and thus begs the question of the validity of 'dementia praecox' and 'schizophrenia'. If Kraepelin and Bleuler did use phenomena from which we would now infer, say, post-encephalitic Parkinsonism, as part of a putative pattern said to justify the introduction of dementia praecox, then, if these are removed, it must be demonstrated that the remaining phenomena form a pattern which justifies inferring a new construct. This rule is central to the construction of scientific theories (Cronbach and Meehl, 1955). It is clear from Kraepelin's and Bleuler's writings that neither the separation nor the demonstration was even attempted, far less achieved. The second objection is, of course, one of the major issues being addressed in this book, but it is worth noting here that it is difficult to reconcile with the attention paid by modern writers to the work of Kraepelin and Bleuler and with the kind of claims made about it.

It may be reasonably argued, of course, that the question of Kraepelin's and Bleuler's populations is irrelevant because their writings provide no evidence that they were justified in inferring any hypothetical construct. The issue is raised here, and will be discussed again in later chapters, because it may help explain some of the undoubted differences between Kraepelin's and Bleuler's population and that called schizophrenic today, as well as some of the problems encountered by the construct.

Before the work of Kurt Schneider is reviewed, it would be useful to bring the discussion up to date for a moment, because the suggestions made here about the origins of 'schizophrenia' might encourage the conclusion that recent suggestions of 'schizophrenia's' being an infectious disease have some validity (see, for example, Crow, 1984; Hare, 1983, 1986). There are, however, good reasons for assuming that this is not so. The first is that the suggestions take no account of the lack of evidence to justify the introduction of 'dementia praecox' and 'schizophrenia': they are based, as were the writings of neurologists at the time, on the assumption that Kraepelin's and Bleuler's concepts were valid. The same confusion is evident in Tyrrell *et al.*'s (1979) and Crow's (1984) suggestion that schizophrenic symptoms are found in a variety of disorders, including infectious encephalitis. It might as well be claimed that humoral disorders are infectious diseases, or that symptoms of humoral disorders are found in a vartiety of other disorders. The second reason for doubting the validity of these claims is that the results of research relating to them are both inconsistent and extremely difficult to interpret (Crow, 1984; King and Cooper, 1989). What could, with reason, be suggested, however, is that some instances of bizarre behaviour which are at present construed as symptomatic of schizophrenia may have a viral or other infection as one antecedent. This is quite different from arguing that some types of schizophrenia may be viral in origin. Again, to use the previous analogy, that is like arguing that some types of humoral disorder may have been viral in origin. Looked at in one way, of course, they probably were, but we no longer consider it a useful kind of statement to make.

The work of Kurt Schneider

Schneider's ideas have exerted a considerable influence on modern psychiatry. Clare (1976), for example, points out that they appear to inform the diagnostic activities of psychiatrists not only in Britain but world-wide (WHO, 1973).

Schneider's 1959 writings will be examined here as they are a comprehensive and representative expression of his views (see also 1974).

Three aspects of Schneider's writings are noteworthy. First, he too begged the question of the validity of 'schizophrenia'. He took for granted that there existed a disease called schizophrenia but failed to provide any evidence in support of this notion. This lack is unfortunate not only because none of his predecessors had provided the necessary evidence but also because Schneider added to the confusion by adopting yet another set of correspondence rules for inferring schizophrenia; more correctly, he adopted several sets because, like Kraepelin and Bleuler, he used different criteria to diagnose schizophrenia in different people. Second, Schneider was closer to Kraepelin than to Bleuler in his orientation in that he tended to eschew theory and claimed to prefer pragmatic description. It is perhaps not surprising that many of his conclusions conflict with Bleuler's. Third, Schneider made virtually no mention of inmates' neurological or physical state but concentrated on behaviour; he was, however, unable to ignore the fact that no reliable organic antecedents of whatever behaviour was the source of his schizophrenia had been identified.

Schneider saw his major task as that of setting out criteria whereby schizophrenia might be recognised. He was, therefore particularly interested in diagnosis or, more accurately, the identification of new exemplars of a previously observed pattern. Given that neither Schneider nor any of his predecessors presented evidence that such an observation had been made, it was inevitable that any attempt to pursue the task of diagnosis and to justify it would end in confusion.

Schneider's concept of illness

Schneider stated that:

> Illness is always a bodily matter ... if [some organic disease process] is absent, description of psychic or indeed social peculiarities as if they were illnesses involves the use of unscientific metaphor ... our criterion for psychiatric illness becomes reduced to the simple establishment of morbid organic change ... our concept of psychiatric illness is based entirely on morbid bodily change.
>
> (1959: 7)

> In medicine, we take [symptom] to mean the sign of an illness, an understandable indication of an illness.
>
> (1959: 130)

Setting aside Schneider's confusion of the two very different terms sign and symptom, he was apparently claiming that phenomena designated as symptoms are those which indicate that some morbid bodily change has occurred.

Schneider also admitted, however, that morbid bodily change could not reliably be demonstrated in those whom he wished to call schizophrenic. The logical conclusion to have drawn, therefore, was that the terms illness and symptom were inappropriately being applied to 'social peculiarities'. But Schneider could hardly abandon these terms and still claim expertise over these behaviours. He therefore retained them by *assuming* an as yet unobserved morbid bodily change and by altering the meaning he had previously applied to symptom:

> It would be wiser ... [in the case of psychosis with no demonstrable somatic base] to understand by "symptom" some generally characteristic, constant feature of a purely psychopathological nature that can be structured into an existing state with a subsequent course. In this case, the medical connotation of "symptom" is abandoned....Thought withdrawal is at bottom not a symptom of the purely psychopathologically conceived state of schizophrenia, but is frequently found and therefore a prominent feature of it.
>
> (1959: 131)

Schneider offered no justification for this circular argument nor for having altered what he claimed was the medical meaning of symptom other than that "It seems well worth preserving this particular meaning of 'symptom' " (1959: 131–2).

Schneider thus appeared to designate as symptoms of schizophrenia any phenomena claimed to be frequently found and therefore prominent features of schizophrenia. This reasoning is, of course, similar to that of Kraepelin and Bleuler when they spoke of 'characteristic' or 'fundamental' symptoms and the same problems attend it: Schneider's statement demands the use of a valid criterion for inferring schizophrenia in the first place and one which is independent of whatever behaviours are said to be found in association with 'it'. Because no such criterion was available, and Schneider certainly did not suggest one, his criteria for calling certain behaviours symptoms of schizophrenia must have been other than he claimed. It is, however, extremely difficult to deduce from his writings what these might have been.

First- and second-rank symptoms

Schneider divided whatever phenomena he had chosen as symptoms of schizophrenia into first-rank and second-rank. The former included audible thoughts, the experience of influences playing on the body and delusional perceptions; the latter consisted of "All the other modes of experience that attend schizophrenia" (1959: 134). Schneider's criteria for calling some phenomena first-rank symptoms are unclear. At one point, he seemed to suggest that they are behaviours which appear only in schizophrenia and not in cyclothymia (1959: 135) and that some of them are highly specific for schizophrenia

(1959: 120). Such arguments, however, can be criticised on the same grounds as was Schneider's definition of symptoms of schizophrenia. Alternatively, these statements may be interpreted to mean that 'first-rank symptoms' form a pattern which would justify inferring a hypothetical construct. Schneider, however, did not even attempt to present evidence that this was the case. He did, however, appear to make use of another criterion for choosing first-rank symptoms, which was the reliability with which, it was claimed, they could be observed. But no data were actually provided on reliability and in any case it would have been irrelevant without evidence that the behaviours formed a pattern.

Schneider claimed that his first-rank symptoms had "special value in diagnosis" (1959: 133) and were (for various individual 'symptoms') "of extreme importance in the diagnosis of schizophrenia" (1959: 97); "a particularly important sign for the diagnosis of schizophrenia" (1959: 99); "of exceptional diagnostic importance" (1959: 104). It might be supposed that Schneider would infer schizophrenia only if these behaviours were observed, although such an inference would not, of course, be justified. But this was not the case. Clinicians were, apparently, "often forced to base their diagnosis on the symptoms of second rank importance, occasionally and exceptionally on mere disorders of expression alone, provided these are relatively florid and numerous" (1959: 135). Why these clinicians should be forced to make a diagnosis, rather than admit ignorance, is not explained. It is rather like claiming that a clinician was forced to make a diagnosis of diabetes mellitus in the absence of an abnormal response to glucose intake or of sugar in the urine, or forced to make a diagnosis of cancer in the absence of cells of a certain type, simply because someone reported tiredness or nausea. The analogy is not exact, however, because Schneider had never identifed events of the status of glucose tolerance, and so on, so that even in the presence of 'first-rank symptoms' he would still not be entitled to make a diagnosis.

The problem is compounded by Schneider's apparent confusion over the status of his first-rank symptoms. He claimed, for example: "Delusional perception ... is always a schizophrenic symptom, if not always an indication of what we clinically are used to calling a schizophrenia" (1959: 104–5); and "Where there is delusional perception we are always dealing with schizophrenic psychosis" (1959: 106).

That Schneider's understanding of the activities of construct formation and diagnosis was limited is further emphasised by his claim that: "[The value of first-rank symptoms] is ... only related to diagnosis; they have no particular contribution to make to the theory of schizophrenia" (1959: 133). It is difficult to understand how such a claim can reasonably be made by a member of a discipline where the activities of theory construction and diagnosis are so closely related.

An overview of the work of Kraepelin, Bleuler and Schneider

It was suggested earlier that Kraepelin and Bleuler described a population quite different from that to which the term schizophrenia would be applied today. There are indications that Schneider was already working with a population somewhat different from that of his predecessors, although the paucity of his descriptions makes it difficult to know if this was the case. Schneider, for example, placed much less emphasis on problems of voluntary movement and on various physical features (indeed, he scarcely mentioned them). He claimed also that insight into the illness was rare, where Bleuler had claimed it to be typical. (By 'insight' they apparently meant simply that the person agreed that their behaviour was strange or alien to them; von Economo and Kraepelin also provided many very similar descriptions of patients' attempts to account for their, to them, bewildering behaviour.) Schneider also mentioned a group of what he called elderly cranks who showed unspecified eccentric movement and speech; he claimed that these people were quite dissimilar to those to whom the term catatonic was now applied but unfortunately he did not say in what ways.

But the nature of the population studied by Kraepelin, Bleuler and Schneider is less important than the fact that none of them presented evidence of having observed a set of regularities which would justify inferring a new hypothetical construct, even without attendant assumptions about brain disease. Certainly, none of them identifed a syndrome, although their frequent misuse of the term 'sign' might convey the erroneous impression that they, or someone, had done so. But what is perhaps most remarkable about their work is that, in spite of aligning themselves to a scientific framework, not one of them presented a single piece of data relevant to their assumption that they were justifed in introducing and using the concepts of dementia praecox and schizophrenia. They presented instead their own beliefs, backed up by authority.

Nevertheless, in spite of the lack of evidence that the necessary conditions for inferring schizophrenia had been fulfilled, the construct continued – and continues – to be used. This raises the important questions of what correspondence rules are now used to infer the concept and where they have come from. As correspondence rules can be seen, at their most basic level, as a statement of 'necessary conditions which have been fulfilled', the question is obviously an interesting and extremely important one. The next two chapters will therefore examine what are conventionally known as diagnostic criteria for schizophrenia but which will also be called here official correspondence rules for inferring schizophrenia.

Chapter four

The official correspondence rules for inferring schizophrenia –
1: The development of diagnostic criteria

Official guidelines as to what should be observed for schizophrenia to be inferred are set out in a series of publications by the World Health Organisation (WHO), the Registrar General's Office (based on those of the WHO) and the American Psychiatric Association (APA). WHO guidelines for inferring schizophrenia are included in the medical manual, *The International Statistical Classification of Diseases, Injuries and Causes of Death*. Their inclusion there implies that the construct is similar to that of constructs used in medicine and that the activity of psychiatric diagnosis is similar to that of medical diagnosis. The guidelines for inferring schizophrenia are therefore best examined, and the problems surrounding them best understood, in the context of a general discussion of medical diagnosis. The first part of this chapter will therefore be concerned with describing the activity of medical diagnosis and its theoretical background as well as with some of the most frequently occurring misconceptions to be found in the literature on psychiatric diagnosis. The second part will describe and evaluate the early development of 'official' diagnostic criteria for inferring schizophrenia.

The nature of diagnosis

The word diagnosis is derived from Greek and means to distinguish, to discern through perception. It is unfortunate that the term has come to be closely associated in the public mind with 'finding out what is wrong with someone' and, indeed, it is even used in this way by some professionals (for example, Silberman, 1971; Clare, 1976). Just as misleadingly, Kendell (1975b) describes diagnosis, in its active sense, as "the process by which a particular disease is attributed to a particular patient" and, as a noun, as "the decision reached, the actual illness attributed to that individual" (23). These definitions are unfortunate not only because Kendell's reifies constructs inferred from various biological and behavioural phenomena, but also because they obscure the complexity and variety of activity subsumed under the term diagnosis. They obscure also its relationship to the activities of non-medical scientists. Given that users of the concept of schizophrenia claim scientific status for it, i.e. claim that their activities in relation to it are similar to the activities of other scientists in relation to their concepts, it is particularly important that these two aspects of diagnosis are not obscured.

Put at its simplest, diagnosis is a matching task. Medical practitioners, faced with people displaying various physical phenomena ask themselves to which, if any, pattern or set of regularities *already observed by researchers* these phenomena correspond. Obviously, in order to answer that question, the clinican must collect a considerable amount of information about the phenomena displayed by the patient, few of which may be visible at first examination. Clinicians will, however, look only at those aspects of the person's functioning that they think likely to yield useful information. They will, in other words, ask themselves which already-observed patterns include the immediately available information, for example, headache, blurred vision, nausea, and so on. As was pointed out in Chapter 1, the same 'symptoms' form part of a number of different patterns which may only be differentiated by the presence or absence of events not immediately observable by the clinician, for example, a malignant brain tumour. But the clinican may not be sufficiently knowledgeable about what researchers have observed and/or be unskilled at eliciting information about symptoms and so make investigations which lead nowhere. Those who earn a reputation as good diagnosticians tend to be distinguished by their extensive knowledge of regularities suggested by researchers, by their skill in eliciting information about symptoms and by their unwillingness to reach hasty conclusions as to which set of regularities is matched by the phenomena displayed by their patients. It may happen, of course, that an experienced clinician does not know of any already observed pattern to which a patient's signs and symptoms correspond. This may mean that the phenomena are unrelated or that they represent a 'new' pattern – one which has not previously been observed.

Clinicians, however, do not communicate their conclusions in this kind of language. They do not say that Mr X displays a set of physical phenomena which match those observed by Dr Y in a group of subjects. Instead, they use one or two words, usually with the verb 'to have' – Mr X has multiple sclerosis/throat cancer/osteoarthritis, and so on. There are two main reasons for this. The first is that when researchers, both medical and non-medical, observe what is considered to be a set of regularities, their habit is to infer constructs from them in the way described in Chapter 1 and it is the construct name which often becomes the diagnostic label. The second reason for adopting this style of communication is quite different. It seems to stem from our persistent and problematic habit of talking about constructs derived from biological or behavioural phenomena as if the constructs were located somewhere within the person. To be accurate in communication, diagnosticians would have to report that "The phenomena observed in Mr X seem to match those already observed by Dr Y on research subjects and from which Dr Y inferred the construct Z. I am therefore inferring the construct Z from the phenomena I have observed in Mr X." Not surprisingly, such cumbersome, if accurate, speeches are rarely made.

Part of the complexity of medical diagnosis arises from the fact that the various sets of regularities suggested by researchers, and which form the basis of the matching task, are of very different type. Engle and Davis (1963) have outlined five different forms of regularity which vary in terms of their specificity, the amount of variability shown from person to person and the extent to which the antecedents are known. Those clusters known as syndromes, and which were described in detail in Chapter 1, have been placed at the bottom of the list. This is because their antecedents are generally unknown and there is considerable variability amongst those who share some of the features which make up the clusters. Engle and Davis describe diagnoses based on these different patterns, i.e. claims to have observed a new exemplar of the pattern, as being of "decreasing orders of certainty" from the first to the fifth type of pattern. By this is meant simply that as the patterns suggested by researchers become less distinct and the variability amongst those who share some of the features increases, then the less 'certain' can a diagnostician be that the phenomena displayed by a particular patient correspond to one of them. The patterns from which, for example, frost-bite and, to a lesser extent, cholera are inferred are more specific, and show less variability from person to person, than do the patterns from which multiple sclerosis or rheumatoid arthritis are inferred. It follows that constructs derived from these different types of pattern will have more or less well-developed theoretical networks. Some are hypothetical constructs with well-developed networks; others, such as essential hypertension or dermatitis, are little more than summary descriptions with no theoretical network to speak of. It is the richness of constructs' theoretical networks which determines the amount of information clinicians can give patients about 'their illnesses'. If constructs inferred at diagnosis have previously enabled predictions to antecedent events or processes, then patients will be told about 'causes'; if the progress of the pattern over time and the variables which influence it are known, then information about 'prognosis' can be offered. And, if it is known which factors can be applied systematically to alter the pattern in a desired direction, then 'effective treatment' may be given.

Kendell (1975b) rightly describes the constructs inferred from these patterns (and which he misleadingly calls diseases) as having variable conceptual bases. For example, the correspondence rules for some of the constructs are based on morbid anatomy, for some on histopathology and for others on the presence of a particular antecedent, for example, a bacterial or viral agent. Kendell has therefore suggested that "our present [medical] classification is rather like an old mansion which has been refurnished many times but always without clearing out the old furniture first, so that amongst the new inflatable plastic settees and glass coffee tables are still scattered a few old Tudor stools,

Jacobean dressers and Regency commodes and a great deal of Victoriana"
(20). Kendell appears, however, to be unnecessarily disparaging of medicine
here. The range of patterns on which diagnosis is based will *always* be a mixture because they represent all that is hypothesised in medicine at any time.
Because knowledge is always imperfect and some areas are always better described than others, the result will inevitably be this kind of hierarchy. As
research proceeds, some constructs, for example Down's syndrome, move 'up'
as their theoretical networks expand; others, for example wasting diseases,
general paralysis, are abandoned as it is realised that they referred to several
different patterns. Still others, for example tuberculosis, 'expand' as a common antecedent for what were thought to be different patterns is found. And
new constructs will be added as new patterns are described. There is no reason
to suppose that this process of grouping and re-grouping phenomena, of en-
richening, abandoning and adding constructs, will not continue indefinitely.
The result will only be a hierarchy whose contents change, so that two centuries from now it may look, to use Kendell's analogy, like a mixture of Art
Deco, High Tech and whatever style is in vogue at the time. The twenty-second
century's medical constructs will no doubt have as varied conceptual bases as
have ours.

International classification systems in medicine

When clinicians officially record the results of their assessments of patients,
including their diagnoses, they do so in accordance with the *International
Classification of Diseases, Injuries and Causes of Death* (ICD; 9th ed., WHO,
1978). The starting-point of attempts to devise international classifications is
usually taken to be 1853, when the International Statistical Congress asked
William Farr and Mark d'Espine to draw up a nomenclature of the causes of
death, which could be used in all countries. It was hoped that this would bring
some order to the then rather chaotic system of recording medical statistics.
Some clinicians, for example, were in the habit of recording a proximal cause
of death, for example renal failure, but not the events leading up to it, for
example carcinoma of the liver. Others might record a major antecedent but
not its sequelae. Similarly, only some might record that the patient had just
given birth or was known to be a heavy drinker. To add to the confusion, different names might be given to one construct, so that it looked as if two
patterns were being referred to instead of only one.

The term nomenclature refers to a list of approved terms for recording observations. In this context, nomenclature is, in fact, mainly a list of constructs
and summary descriptive labels, derived from patterns of varying complexity
suggested by researchers. The lists devised by Farr and d'Espine were regularly
revised. Such revisions are essential, to incorporate new constructs suggested
by researchers as well as modifications of existing constructs. In 1899, the International Statistical Congress approved a resolution recommending that

revisions be made every ten years. The modern International Classifications are not simply of causes of death. Their title – the International Classification of Diseases, Injuries and Causes of Death – reflects the fact that a much wider range of phenomena is incorporated, an expansion which began in 1949, with the 6th revision. But nor is the International Classification just a nomenclature or list of constructs. It attempts to group together patterns from which the constructs are derived and which are thought to have important features in common, like an admittedly primitive Periodic Table. What might be called higher order constructs, whose names usually reflect the supposedly important shared features, are then inferred from these larger groupings, for example 'congenital abnormalities'. It is this attempt at grouping which earns the title classification system.

It was pointed out earlier that the constructs included in medical classification systems are derived from different types of patterns. Some include events thought to be antecedents of other phenomena in the cluster; in other patterns, the antecedents are unknown. In the first type, the antecedents are varied – genetic, traumatic, viral, bacterial, and so on. Some patterns are defined in terms of a type of bodily reaction or by site of visible damage. Because some patterns may meet more than one criterion and because our ignorance of bodily dis-ease is so great, any attempt to group patterns according to what are thought to be important shared features will inevitably be both a compromise and temporary. The groupings and headings, or 'higher order constructs' adopted by the 9th revision conference, include Diseases of the Respiratory System; Diseases of the Nervous System and Some Organs; Endocrine, Nutritional and Metabolic Disorders and Symptoms, Signs and Ill-Defined Conditions. Each heading is allocated a range of digits, for example 240–279; the number of 3-digit categories represents the number of constructs or terms which have been included under the main heading, i.e. the number of clusters which have been grouped together to form the larger group. This number represents a best guess as to how many, given the present state of medical knowledge, are necessary and may be the subject of heated debate within the revision committees. The clusters may be subdivided again according to various criteria, by the use of a fourth digit, for example by body site or age of onset. The International Classification was thus envisaged by Farr, and remains today, a best estimate of the state of medical knowledge, with implications beyond the mere listing of approved medical terms. Researchers, of course, are not bound by this classification; indeed, as the system reflects a mixture of well-agreed empirical data, best guesses and ignorance, it is their task to provide data which will alter it. It is to this system that diagnosticians refer when they record their asessments of new patients or complete death certificates or other official forms. The system, however, tells them only in what terms and in what order to record their observations; it does not tell them how to make a diagnosis. It does not, in other words, set out the correspondence rules for the constructs it lists. It does not do this because its devisers are presumably aware that these are set out in numerous specialist texts; it is to these that clinicians can refer to familiarise themselves with patterns suggested by researchers, with constructs derived from them, with their theoretical networks and with the empirical data offered in support.

The ICD and deviant behaviour

The ICD has, since 1949, included a section (Section V) whose subject-matter is not unwanted physical phenomena but unwanted or disturbing behaviour. Some of the events which led to medical men's claiming expertise in deviant behaviour were described in Chapter 2. It was emphasised there that, in order to claim equality with their colleagues in physical medicine, alienists had to behave, as far a possible, in similar ways. It is therefore not surprising that, as well as calling the odd behaviour of asylum inmates 'symptoms of illness', and searching for a particular type of pattern amongst these 'symptoms', alienists also sought to develop international classification systems of their subject-matter. Having done so, they tried, like their physician colleagues, to use them as a basis for diagnosis. Before their development is described, however, some common misconceptions about diagnosis in psychiatry and, in some cases, about diagnosis in general, will be discussed.

Diagnosis – some misunderstandings

The subject-matter of diagnostic systems

Many of those who apply the diagnostic terms of psychiatry and medicine seem to believe that their subject-matter is 'diseases', 'illnesses' or 'disorders' (for example, Stengel, 1959; Engle and Davis, 1963; Silberman, 1971; WHO, 1974; Kendell, 1975b; Klein, 1978; Spitzer and Endicott, 1978; APA, 1980, 1987). These claims are suspect because they smuggle into existence the problematic terms disease and illness and give the false impression that there exist 'out there' readily recognisable phenomena called diseases which naturally form the subject-matter of psychiatry. In doing so, they obscure the fact that the terms disease and illness are popular or lay constructions whose referents change in idiosyncratic ways with time and place. This leads to reification and to the erroneous belief that researchers and diagnosticians 'name diseases' which are somehow possessed by people. WHO (1974), for example, claims that "the classification of diseases cannot begin without a list of agreed names of diseases in which each name stands for only one disease" (11), while DSM-111 states that "A common misconception is that a classification of mental disorders classified individuals, when what are being classified are disorders that individuals have" (6).

But it is no more possible accurately to define the subject-matter of medicine or psychiatry than that of, say, chemistry or geography. All that can be said is that people who call themselves psychiatrists or geographers or whatever tend, by convention or even by public demand, to study certain phenomena. For medicine, these are usually physical events or processes which are distressing to, and unwanted by, the sufferer or others. For psychiatry, the phenomena of interest are experiences and behaviours which are unwanted by the person themselves or by others, and which are often assumed to be outside the person's control. The fact that some of these phenomena have, in our culture, been popularly construed as 'illnesses' or 'diseases', and have had various popular assumptions made about them, is no more relevant to their scientific study than is the fact that some of the phenomena now studied by astronomers or physicists were once popularly construed as 'magical' or 'miraculous'. What psychiatrists and medical researchers therefore try to classsify are putative patterns of unwanted physical and behavioural phenomena. The arbitrariness with which particular phenomena are deemed to be part of, or not part of, the subject-matter of psychiatry and therefore deemed to form illnesses or disorders can be seen in the way in which 'homosexuality' was removed, by committee vote, from the subject-matter. This behaviour pattern therefore ceased, from one moment to the next, 'to be a disease'.

Because what are seen as unwanted and uncontrollable behaviours and experiences vary with time and place, so too does psychiatry's subject-matter. The variation is more noticeable in psychiatry because what are construed as unwanted behaviours are generally more variable than are unwanted physical phenomena, although there is considerable variation even in these. It follows that any attempt to define the subject-matter of medicine or psychiatry (which usually appears as attempts to define disease) can amount to nothing more than a description of how the term disease is currently used. This point is emphasised by the views of Spitzer and Endicott (1978) in their discussion of the 3rd edition of the APA *Diagnostic and Statistical Manual of Mental Disorders*:

> We believed that without some definition of mental disorder, there would be no guiding principles that would help determine which conditions should be included in the nomenclature, which excluded and how conditions should be defined. As we considered the many conditions traditionally included in the nomenclature, we realized that although the definition of mental disorder proposed at the time of the controversy regarding homosexuality was suitable for almost all of them, a broader definition seemed necessary.

(18)

Unfortunately, Spitzer and Endicott do not say for what a broader definition seemed necessary, but it is clear from their statement that all they can – and do – do is to describe the way in which the APA used the term mental disorder in 1978. They can, that is – and do – attempt to find common features amongst behaviours said *by tradition* to form the subject-matter of psychiatry and call this a definition of mental disorder. Such an exercise would be of interest mainly to etymologists were it not for the fact that definitions constructed in this way are then illogically used to 'prove' that certain behaviours 'are manifestations of mental illness' and that they should therefore fall under the jurisdiction of psychiatrists (see, for example, Kendell, 1975a; Clare, 1976).

The ideas that the subject-matter of medicine and psychiatry is disease or illness and that practitioners find diseases in people are extremely tenacious. This is perhaps best illustrated by the fact that even those writers who are clearly well aware of the popular roots of terms like disease and of the dangers of reification persist in talking as if they had never made these points. Klein (1978), for example, after thoughtfully discussing the social conventions surrounding the terms disease and illness, proceeded to put forward his own definition, as if it were somehow independent of these, as if it enabled him properly to call some behaviours manifestations of mental disorder or mental illness. Kendell (1975b), although clearly aware of the problem of reification, talks of "diseases as concepts". The confusion here is that it is not diseases that are concepts, but that Kendell and others talk of *concepts* which claim scientific status as if their referents and theoretical networks were synonymous with those of the popular term disease. In other words, they call concepts 'diseases'.

Syndrome as a cluster of symptoms

It was pointed out in Chapter 1 that the term syndrome refers to a type of pattern made up of events known as signs and symptoms and whose antecedents are unknown. It is the presence of the signs in the cluster which suggests that it is not the chance co-occurrence of unrelated phenomena. Because signs, by definition, can be more reliably observed than symptoms, it is they also which enable clinicians, however tentatively, to claim to have observed a new exemplar of a cluster, albeit at a 'low order of certainty'. It follows that the term, 'cluster of symptoms' refers to a cluster which is quite different from that of a cluster of signs and symptoms. There are, however, many examples in the psychiatric literature of the term syndrome being used to mean a cluster of symptoms, as if this usage were synonymous with a cluster of signs and symptoms. Kendell (1975b), for example, appears to use the word 'syndrome' to mean both a constellation of symptoms and a constellation of symptoms and signs. Spitzer and Endicott (1978) claim that "A syndrome is a collection of symptoms (or signs) that co-vary" (29) while Silberman (1971) takes syndrome to mean "a cluster of symptoms ... which occur in combination relatively often" (12).

To use syndrome to mean a cluster of symptoms is not an incorrect usage; there is, of course, no correct meaning of the term. The problem lies in the fact that before a hypothetical construct can be inferred from a putative cluster, there must exist some evidence that the cluster is meaningful, that it is not the chance co-occurrence of unrelated events or even illusory. It has already been pointed out that we may 'find' clusters in random data or mistake chance co-occurrence for meaningful co-variation. Frequent co-occurrence, as in Silberman's definition, is not sufficient to impute meaningfulness. It is for these reasons that the inclusion of an event which may be reliably observed and is thought to be an antecedent of the symptoms is so important in any cluster from which a new construct is inferred. The use of the word 'syndrome' to refer to suggested clusters both with and without signs may therefore create the spurious impression that one is as likely to be meaningful as is the other.

The validation of psychiatric diagnoses

There are a number of references in the psychiatric literature to the idea that diagnoses should be valid or can be validated (for example, Robins and Guze, 1970; Kendell, 1975b; Neale and Oltmanns, 1980). But because diagnosis is a matching task, the result can only be described as more or less accurate, in the sense that what is claimed to be a new exemplar of a previously observed pattern is more or less similar to it. The term validity is, of course, applicable to the construct originally inferred when the pattern was first described; obviously, if the construct was not derived from a meaningful cluster, there can be no matching and no diagnosis. Thus, to make a diagnosis is to claim, implicitly, that the validity of the construct inferred has already been established.

The confusion evident in the literature appears to arise from a failure to make the crucial distinction between the original research which seeks to identify new patterns and infer new constructs, and the later activity of identifying new exemplars of these patterns. This confusion is apparent in Kendell's claim (1975b) that "diagnostic validity is a neglected issue" and that one of the most important reasons for the neglect of the "predictive validity" of psychiatric diagnoses is that "much of the basic evidence for the validity of our Kraepelinian diagnostic categories accumulated long before people began to ask questions about reliability and validity" (41). But if the basic evidence for the validity of diagnostic categories has been accumulated, then the issue of 'diagnostic validity' cannot have been neglected. If it has been, as Kendell claims, then the basic evidence cannot have accumulated. Unfortunately, Kendell gives no indication of where this evidence is to be found; as was shown in Chapter 3, it was certainly not presented by Kraepelin or his immediate successors. It would appear from Kendell's examples that the neglected research to which he refers is of a type designed to extend the theoretical network of an existing construct. Such research is obviously futile if the construct was originally inferred on insufficient evidence. The failure to distinguish between research which results in a new construct and the identification of new exemplars of the pattern from which it was derived, is widespread in the psychiatric and psychological literature. Because the implications are important, the issue will be discussed in more detail in relation to 'schizophrenia' in the next chapter.

The confusion of reliability and validity

It is axiomatic that constructs which claim scientific status should be derived from observations about which there is a high level of agreement. It is readily admitted, however, that agreement amongst psychiatrists as to whether a particular construct should be inferred from someone's behaviour may be unsatisfactorily low (for example, A.T. Beck et al., 1962; Ward et al., 1962; Spitzer and Fleiss, 1974; Kendell, 1975b). Perhaps because of this, when high levels of agreement have been achieved, they have often been over-valued. The sources of most examples of this practice are two large-scale studies – the US–UK Diagnostic Project (Cooper et al., 1972) and The International Pilot Study of Schizophrenia (WHO, 1973). Two different types of agreement are discussed in these studies. The first is that obtained by training, by instructing interviewers to use a particular set of correspondence rules for inferring schizophrenia and other constructs. It is hardly surprising that higher levels of agreement are found after training, but they provide no information about the constructs' validity. It is not on this type of agreement, however, that most of the exaggerated claims have been based, but on a second type found in surveys of diagnostic practice in different countries. These revealed, via various statistical techniques, that if someone displayed certain behaviours, they were likely to be diagnosed as schizophrenic. This is not to say that there was strong agreement about schizophrenia's correspondence rules; some people were called schizophrenic without displaying these behaviours while others who displayed them received different diagnostic labels. Nevertheless, there were behaviours which, either singly or in combination, were more likely to lead to an inference to schizophrenia. Prominent amongst these were those behaviours called first-rank symptoms by Schneider, and which were discussed in Chapter 3.

When members of a particular discipline agree on some aspect of their belief system, one explanation is that they have, for whatever reasons, been convinced by the same authorities. Without independent evidence that the agreement is based on more than shared idiosyncratic beliefs, then nothing else may be assumed. It is this requirement of additional evidence, of replicated observations, of the predictive power of constructs, which separates those disciplines which confidently claim scientific status from those, for example theology or literary criticism, which do not. A survey of Catholic theologians would no doubt reveal a consensus that certain 'core' behaviours should lead to the inference, sin; about other behaviour there would be less agreement. But it is unlikely that we should see this as a contribution to a scientific literature or as other than a reflection of shared beliefs. Yet Clare (1976), for example, noting that 72 per cent of those who had a diagnosis of schizophrenia in the US–UK diagnostic project showed one or more 'first-rank symptoms', claimed that this suggests that "schizophrenic first rank symptoms may delineate a *nuclear or core group* of schizophrenics" (124; emphasis in original). Similarly, Neale and Oltmanns (1980), discussing the International Pilot Study of Schizophrenia, claimed that they "are now in a position to offer a specification of what seem to be the most salient features of schizophrenia" (50) and spoke of "clear cases of schizophrenia" (38). Hawk *et al.* (1975) discussed "discriminating symptoms" – meaning those about which there was a consensus – as being "empirically derived for their value in establishing a schizophrenic diagnosis" (344). Neale and Oltmanns have also misleadingly used the terms 'accurate diagnosis' and 'correct diagnosis' to refer to nothing more than diagnosis based on the behaviour revealed by these surveys to be the most popular source of schizophrenia. This process of developing diagnostic criteria is obviously quite different from that described in Chapter 1. Consensus about correspondence rules is essential for any construct which claims scientific status, but consensus of opinion is not enough. Hawk *et al.* and Kendell *et al.* (1979) use the term 'empirically derived' to refer to what are, in fact, the results of complex opinion surveys. This may give the false impression that agreement about schizophrenia's correspondence rules is based on the kind of careful empirical work which produced constructs like electricity or malaria. Obviously, the correspondence rules for these constructs and claims for their validity do not rest on opinion surveys but on repeatedly observed patterns and repeated demonstrations of the constructs' predictive power.

Categories versus dimensions

As Hempel (1961) has pointed out, the development of classification systems may be thought of as a special case of scientific construct formation. Unfortunately, these systems are often described in a language which obscures this important similarity: the defining characteristics of a human, a case of AIDS, and so on. The impression is often given and, indeed, the claim may be made explicitly (for example, Blashfield and Draguns, 1976) that classification systems consist of a set of entities which 'possess' certain definite characteristics. (The idea that medical classification systems name single diseases is another example of this fallacy.) As was pointed out earlier, classification systems are in fact attempts to group what are assumed to be meaningful patterns, on the assumption that some patterns are similar in important ways. But the patterns which form these groupings are often not discrete in that it may be difficult to observe a clear division between their presence and absence. The question then arises as to whether the same construct should be inferred from the 'semi-pattern' as from the 'full pattern'. An answer can only be derived empirically by asking in what way it would alter the construct's predictive power. It is this problem which is sometimes, rather misleadingly, referred to as that of borderline cases versus clear cases or typical cases. It is more usefully described by asking whether the correspondence rules should be stated in a dimensional (quantitative, quasi-linear) fashion and if so at what point it apparently ceases to be useful to infer the construct. Even when there is general agreement about this, there may still be gradations within the patterns. In medicine, these are usually called more or less severe cases. Some of the patterns which form the basis of medical classifications are thought to represent the co-occurrence of dimensional attributes, others categorical. In fact it is rarely possible to claim that a pattern either 'exists' or 'does not exist'. A pattern which appears to be either present or absent may only seem so because measurement is unsophisticated and subtle gradations in the attribute in question cannot yet be detected. The claim can perhaps most confidently be made for those few patterns whose antecedents include a known single dominant gene or a specific traumatic event, such as a snake bite or a gunshot wound.

Although it appears regularly in the literature of 'schizophrenia', and has apparently been used in an attempt to defend the construct (see Wing, 1988), the issue of categories versus dimensions is not especially relevant to the construct, for two reasons. First, to ask whether a postulated pattern represents the co-occurrence of graded characteristics or is qualitatively distinct, is to assume that a pattern has been observed in the first place. Thus, discussion as to whether schizophrenia should be a categorical or a dimensional concept begs the more important question of whether the concept is justified at all. Second, it might be argued that the discussion is of limited relevance in the more general sense that constructs are inferred to aid the observation of 'new' events. This can be achieved by grouping either graded or either/or characteristics, although the theoretical networks derived from the former may be more complex. Perhaps the best reason to be aware of the issue is that ordinary language so encourages us to believe that we are dealing with distinct and specific 'things'.

The development of international and American classification systems for deviant behaviour

Some of the many attempts by medical men to describe patterns of disturbing behaviour were briefly described in Chapter 2. These were distinguished mainly by their vagueness and multiplicity; by the last decades of the nineteenth century it was obvious, even to the most uncritical observer, that the result was chaos. In 1885, the Congress of Mental Medicine appointed a Commission to consider existing classifications and to derive one system "which the various associations of alienists could unite in adopting" (Kendell, 1975b: 87). It is unfortunate that the Commission's brief was not more modest and realistic: that they should consider why classification systems were so numerous, why no two of them were in agreement, why the constructs were not tied to specified phenomena and whether it was possible at that time to derive *any* system based on more than the opinion of authority. Unfortunately, these issues were never given serious consideration; the Commission duly devised a system which can at best be described as arbitrary but which was officially adopted by the now renamed International Congress of Mental Science in 1889. The system consisted of eleven construct names and included those "upon which the majority [of the Commission's members] were unanimous" while omitting those "upon which opinion was divided". The Commission claimed to have attempted, in spite of these disagreements, to include "the principal forms of madness" (Kendell, 1975b: 88). The list included Moral and Impulsive Insanity, Insane Neurosis and Progressive Systematic Insanity.

There is no indication that the validity of these constructs was based on other than the opinions of the Commissioners; no reference was made to where the empirical evidence which would have justified inferring them was to be found. Not surprisingly, the system was not much used. Indeed, in the absence of clear statements in the psychiatric literature of the constructs' correspondence rules and evidence of their validity, most of it *could not* be used for any constructive purpose, apart from to discover which terms were fashionable amongst some medical men of the day. This official attempt to classify disturbing behaviour was paralleled and followed by numerous others, equally devoid of an empirical base and none of which enjoyed extensive usage.

Kendell (1975b) has suggested some reasons why these systems were not accepted by asylum doctors. The Commissioners were, he suggests:

> forced to choose between several existing classifications, each acceptable only to its own authors; they were handicapped by ignorance of the aetiology of the conditions they were trying to classify; they were unable to agree amongst themselves whether classifications should be on the basis of symptomatology, psychology, aetiology or outcome or a combination of all four; and they were dealing with professional colleagues who were often as disinclined to have a uniform nomenclature imposed on them as they would have been to have uniform methods of treatment imposed on them.

(89)

These supposed reasons for the system's failure deserve comment, if only because they illustrate some of the ways in which psychiatric classification and diagnosis are misrepresented.

In the first place, neither the Commissioners nor the organisations they represented were *forced* – except by their own dictates – to choose between existing rival systems. They could have admitted the truth: that they were not in possession of the empirical data which would allow them to infer most of the constructs in their classification systems. Second, by claiming that the Commissioners were "handicapped by their ignorance of the aetiology of the conditions they were trying to classify", Kendell implies that patterns of deviant behaviour which would justify inferring hypothetical constructs had already been observed and that the problem lay in ignorance of the antecedents of these patterns. This was not so. It is worth remembering that these constructs were suggested before Kraepelin's dementia praecox. Unfortunately, his habit of introducing constructs – of claiming to have observed patterns in the behaviour of asylum inmates – but without providing evidence in support, had a long history amongst asylum doctors, and the devisers of the early classification systems did not depart from this tradition. They were, in fact, hampered by nothing more – or less – than their ignorance of what might be the regularities in asylum inmates' behaviour *and* by their disregard of their ignorance. Kendell's accurate comment that the Commissioners' colleagues were "disinclined to have a uniform nomenclature imposed on them" reflects a remarkable state of affairs on which Kendell does not comment. Asylum doctors, or, at least, those desirous of professional advancement, repeatedly claimed to be scientific. They should, then, have recognised that this claim was incompatible with 'to each his own nomenclature' and have declared themselves powerless *without* agreement on constructs and their correspondence rules. This is not to suggest that they should have accepted the Commissioners' opinions but that they should at least have recognised the implications of their disagreements.

The next few decades saw no important developments in attempts to produce international classifications of deviant behaviour. Although Kraepelin's dementia praecox and Bleuler's schizophrenia were used by asylum doctors, their lack of an empirical base rendered them useless, except in so far as they gave an impression of progress where none existed.

The beginnings of the modern international classifications

In 1948, a major administrative change took place, with the setting up of the World Health Organisation. The old medical International List of Causes of Death was revised and renamed The International Statistical Classification of Diseases, Injuries and Causes of Death. This 6th edition contained, for the first time, a section listing constructs mainly derived from behaviour, so-called mental, psychoneurotic and personality disorders. The construct of schizophrenia appeared in this section as "Schizophrenic disorders (dementia praecox)". This was followed by a number of constructs, such as paranoid, paraphrenic and primary schizophrenia, said to represent subdivisions of the major construct (the term construct was never actually used). WHO obviously assumed that reliable correspondence rules were available for these and the many other constructs listed in Section V, although in fact they were not, and took their validity for granted. The classification was therefore of very limited usefulness and, inevitably, was widely ignored. Those who did use the terms it contained presumably used their personal criteria for inferring them. This WHO attempt at the classification of deviant behaviour was ignored by

United States psychiatrists (who had nevertheless co-operated in drafting it) to the extent that they devised their own system: the first edition of the *Diagnostic and Statistical Manual of Mental Disorders* was published by the APA in 1952. The construct of schizophrenic reactions was used in place of schizophrenic disorders and again the main construct was subdivided.

Kendell (1975b) has claimed that the American classification was "in many ways superior to its contemporaries elsewhere" (92). Given the purpose of the classification, the only relevant way in which it could have been superior would have been in listing constructs derived from reliably observed regularities and grouped according to shared features of demonstrated importance. There is no indication that this was the case. Rather, the 'superiority' apparently lay in the fact that the classification was "widely available in a carefully prepared booklet" and that "adequate publicity was given to its existence and to the need for all American psychiatrists to bring their own diagnostic predilections into line with its requirements" (92). Kendell has claimed that the new classification was also superior in that it provided "working definitions or thumbnail descriptions of the syndromes concerned" (92). As with his comments on the earlier classifications, Kendell is again taking it for granted that the constructs listed in DSM-I had been derived from observed patterns. For the construct of schizophrenic reaction, the 'working definition' was:

> This term is synonymous with the previously used term dementia praecox. It represents a group of psychotic reactions characterised by fundamental disturbance in reality relationships and concept formations, with affective, behavioural and intellectual disturbance in varying degrees and mixtures. The disorders are marked by a strong tendency to retreat from reality, by emotional disharmony, unpredictable disturbances in stream of thought, regressive behaviour, and in some, by a tendency to "deterioration". The predominant symptomatology will be the determining factor in classifying such patients into types.
>
> (26)

Each 'sub-construct' was followed by a similar type of description, emphasising some aspect of the main description.

This kind of thumbnail sketch (though usually much less vague) is often used in medicine in answer to the question, for example, 'What is AIDS?' The answers, which vary from writer to writer, are usually a mixture of imprecisely stated correpondence rules and parts of the construct's theoretical network. The accounts are not intended for diagnosticians but are often used to reduce a complex theoretical network to manageable proportions. They are often found in, for example, medical dictionaries or in books or magazines for the general public. But this kind of imprecise and incomplete account can be given only because a more complex set of correspondence rules and empirical data is available for the construct – the thumbnail description is merely a distillation of them. But neither reliable correspondence rules nor, therefore, theoretical network existed for 'schizophrenic reaction'; the impression of superiority produced by the working definitions was entirely spurious. The inevitable state of affairs prevailed after the introduction of DSM-I: many ignored it and those who tried to use it had to employ their own correspondence rules.

Attempts at solutions

In 1959, Erwin Stengel published a lengthy and influential report under the auspices of the WHO. In this he detailed the extent of rejection of Section V of the 6th (and similar 7th) editions of the International Classification. More importantly, he suggested possible reasons and remedies. Stengel described only some of the large number of classifications recommended for use by Psychiatric Associations in different countries and discussed some of those devised by particular individuals. He noted two features of these systems. First, they were based on what Stengel called symptomatology or syndromal classification; some classifications were based on assumed aetiology of putative clusters (usually simply organic or non-organic) and some on assumed psychological features. Second, Stengel noted that the concepts contained in these systems had not been defined, i.e. there were no clearly stated rules for inferring them. Stengel's proposed solution to this problem was remarkable, as too was the fact that it had taken the best part of a century for the problem to be officially noted. In reaching his solution, Stengel was strongly influenced by a conference paper delivered by the philosopher of science, Hempel. Hempel had pointed out that the development of nomenclature and of classification systems was a special case of scientific construct formation and that these activities should therefore follow similar rules. He emphasised one of the fundamental tenets of scientific practice, that constructs must be tied to observable events. Where these consisted of a series of well-described operations, they might be called the operational definition of the construct. Hempel suggested, however, that "mere observations" could and should count as operations. Hempel may have created some semantic confusion by suggesting this usage of operational definition, but the important point remains that he was simply emphasising that constructs must be tied to, inferred from, an agreed set of observable events. Hempel then pointed out that psychiatric concepts were not tied to observables in this way, i.e. there were no clear rules for inferring them.

Unfortunately, Stengel drew from this the conclusion that the answer lay in developing operational definitions for existing psychiatric concepts. It must be emphasised that Hempel did not suggest this solution but merely described the problem. The conclusion is false because, in scientific activity, the observations or 'operations' come *first* and the constructs *second as a consequence of them*. Constructs developed in this way come, as it were, ready equipped with correspondence rules; to suggest that it is reasonable to try to find these for existing concepts is nonsensical. It is, of course, not so outside of scientific practice. In, for example, politics, law and religion, authorities frequently suggest or impose new criteria for inferring what are acknowledged as non-scientific concepts, such as fair wage, criminal act, sin, basic necessities, and so on. These rules are developed according to a quite different set of procedures from those used by scientists. The rules vary, for example, with political or religious creed, with cultural beliefs or with economic factors. Concepts derived in this way are often then used for administrative purposes; they are certainly not expected to have predictive power.

In proposing that psychiatrists work in a direction opposite to that of scientists and try to find correspondence rules for their constructs, Stengel overlooked the resulting problem of how it could possibly be known which constructs justified the search – what criteria were to be used in choosing them? Constructs are included in classification systems because they are assumed to be valid. But validity cannot be demonstrated without correspondence rules. Thus, to choose to include a construct in a classification system which claims scientific status is to imply that it is already tied to an agreed set of observables. Not surprisingly, Stengel's suggestions did not immediately result in the publication of a classification system complete with operational definitions. The Manual of the 8th edition of the International Classification was published without them. In 1968, a glossary of thumbnail sketches for each of the constructs in ICD-8 was published by the British General Register Office; in 1974, WHO published its own glossary. It has already been pointed out that these sketches presuppose that a construct is both tied to observables and has a theoretical network, and are neither intended for, nor usable as, diagnostic criteria. The compilers of the sketches were apparently unaware of this; Wing (1970) pointed out that the glossaries were produced in response to Stengel's call for operational definitions. The APA agreed, albeit reluctantly, to tailor the 2nd edition of their Diagnostic and Statistical manual to the nomenclature of ICD-8 (APA, 1968). Like the HMSO (Her Majesty's Stationery Office) and WHO glossaries, DSM-II presented thumbnail sketches for its constructs. 'Schizophrenia' (the DSM-I term schizophrenic reactions had been abandoned) now had three different sketches.

Unfortunately, it was still thought that the resulting confusion and rejection of the International and United States Classifications could be overcome by printing 'proper' operational definitions of schizophrenia and other constructs. Kendell (1972), for example, declared this the "remedy for diagnostic confusion". He reiterated Stengel's arguments and claimed that "there is no alternative to defining schizophrenia in terms of its clinical features" (386). Kendell did not specify what he meant by clinical features, although he appears to be using the term to mean certain types of abnormal behaviour. These must, therefore, be the behaviours from which schizophrenia is inferred. Kendell thus appears to be arguing that there is no alternative to defining schizophrenia than in terms of the behaviours from which schizophrenia is inferred. His argument in fact reduces to the circular statement that the devisers of the International Classifications must develop an operational definition for schizophrenia in terms of its operational definition. In other words, Kendell, like Stengel, was instructing them to begin their task by assuming that they had already successfully completed it. This kind of tautological and question-begging argument is a predictable result of the suggestion that psychiatrists work backwards from construct to correspondence rules and of a failure to appreciate the problems which will result.

Neither Stengel nor Kendell were able to suggest how the devisers of the International Classification might find this operational definition of schizophrenia, and the 9th edition (WHO, 1978) did not contain one. The manual, however, did depart from tradition by including the thumbnail sketches which had previously been published separately. As before, the glossary was prepared for Section V only. Kramer *et al.* (1979) called this integral glossary a major innovation. It was certainly an innovation; it also highlighted the potentially embarrassing fact that the subject-matter of Section V and the constructs based on it were claimed to be both the same as and different from those in the other, medical, sections. The devisers of Section V sought to explain this paradox:

> This section of the classification differs from the others in that it includes a glossary, prepared after consultation with experts from different countries, defining the contents of the rubrics. The difference is considered to be justified because of the special problems posed for psychiatrists by the relative lack of independent laboratory information on which to base their diagnoses. The diagnosis of many important mental disorders still relies largely upon descriptions of abnormal experience and behaviour and, without some guidance in the form of a glossary that can serve as a common frame of reference, psychiatric communications easily become unsatisfactory at clinical and statistical levels. Many well-known terms have different meaning in current use, and it is important for the user to use the glossary descriptions and not merely category titles when searching for the best fit for the condition he is trying to code.
> (cited in Kramer *et al.*, 1979: 247)

At first glance, these arguments may have an air of reasonableness, but it is one which is fallacious. The 'special problems' referred to are not, as is claimed, a lack of laboratory information (criteria) on which to base diagnoses, but a lack of any independent, agreed criteria. It was precisely this lack which led to the inappropriate call for operational definitions. It is not a necessary condition of medical classification systems that the patterns included in them include events observed in a laboratory. It happens, however, that 'laboratory information' often refers to phenomena which can be reliably observed and which reliably co-occur with symptoms. Without information of this type, whether observed in or out of a laboratory, there can be no claim to have observed a pattern and therefore no construct and no diagnosis. The devisers of ICD-9 thus overlooked the same problem as had their predecessors: how could a construct such as schizophrenia, lacking an agreed and valid set of correspondence rules and, thus, a theoretical network, come to have a thumbnail sketch based on these? The development of ICD-9 was, in fact, preceded by a series of international seminars, attended by "experts" (Kramer *et al.*, 1979); the results of the seminar concerned with 'schizophrenia' were published in 1965 (WHO, 1965). Participants took part in 'diagnostic exercises' in which they inferred constructs from written descriptions of people and from video recordings of interviews. The results were then scrutinised for areas of agreement in the use of the constructs. This kind of exercise is similar to the opinion surveys described earlier. The method could equally be used to discover how people use popular terms like 'moral' or 'ambitious' and so on, but it implies nothing about validity. In an exercise such as this, the opinion of one person carries as much weight as that of another: there are no experts in the social construction of behaviour. How the results of this seminar were translated into the sketch of 'schizophrenic psychosis' is unclear. It is difficult to avoid the conclusion that this sketch, and those which preceded it, represent simply an amalgam of the personal beliefs of prominent users of the concept of schizophrenia – that is, it is a social stereotype.

The development of DSM-III

ICD-9 was criticised for failing, yet again, to provide clear operational definitions of the constructs it contained; the sketches were rightly seen as unusable as diagnostic criteria. They were seen as such, however, not because of the way in which they had been developed, but because they were not specific enough. The 3rd edition of the Diagnostic and Statistical Manual of Mental Disorders (APA, 1980) is the first serious attempt to provide clear operational definitions for its major constructs. It is claimed that one of the goals of DSM-III was to achieve "consistency with the data from research studies bearing on the validity of diagnostic categories" (2). This carefully worded statement does not claim that the definitions in DSM-III *are* based on research evidence; that most are not is evidenced by the later statement that "it should be understood, however, that for most of the categories the diagnostic criteria are based on clinical judgement" (8). Nevertheless, the discussion of schizophrenia's operational definition refers frequently to its supposed basis in referenced empirical research. But it has been suggested here that to search for correspondence rules for an existing construct, as DSM-III's devisers have done for 'schizophrenia', is likely to be incompatible with claims for scientific status. The results of the search and the methods used therefore deserve detailed consideration.

Chapter five

The official correspondence rules for inferring schizophrenia –
2: DSM-III and 'schizophrenia'

The correspondence rules which DSM-III suggests as the source of schizo-phrenia are listed in Table 5.1. In suggesting these, DSM-III is claiming that they represent a pattern of regularities, a group of phenomena which co-occur above chance and which justify inferring the construct of schizophrenia. In support of this claim, it is stated that:

> This manual utilises clinical criteria that include both a minimum dura-tion and characteristic symptom picture to identify a group of conditions that has validity in terms of differential response to somatic therapy; presence of a familial pattern; and a tendency towards onset in early adult life, recurrence and deterioration in social and occupational func-tioning.

> (APA, 1980: 181)

This claim can be reworded to state that when individuals display particular behaviours in combination for a certain length of time, this is reliably associ-ated with: (1) people of certain ages; (2) a different response to drugs (different, presumably, from instances where the same behaviours are dis-played for a shorter period); (3) the presence of the same pattern in their family; (4) the recurrence of the same set of behaviours; and (5) deterioration in social and occupational functioning. It is this claim to predictive power which apparently justifies the assumption that the rules for inferring schizo-phrenia refer to a pattern. The arguments for and against the use of each of these five validating criteria are to some extent similar. But because they are complex and not identical, they are best discussed separately. It is important to emphasise that DSM-III is, in fact, making two claims about each of the validating criteria. First, that its correspondence rules for schizophrenia are reliably associated with them and, second, that the criteria are appropriate for imputing meaningfulness to a proposed cluster. These two issues will be con-sidered separately for each criterion.

Table 5.1   DSM-III criteria for inferring schizophrenic disorder

A.   At least one of the following during a phase of the illness:
  (1)   bizarre delusions (content is patently absurd and has no possible basis in fact), such as delusions of being controlled, thought broadcasting, thought insertion, or thought withdrawal
  (2)   somatic, grandiose, religious, nihilistic, or other delusions without persecutory or jealous content
  (3)   delusions with persecutory or jealous content if accompanied by hallucinations of any type
  (4)   auditory hallucinations in which either a voice keeps up a running commentary on the individual's behaviour or thoughts, or two or more voices converse with each other
  (5)   auditory hallucinations on several occasions with content of more than one or two words, having no apparent relation to depression or elation
  (6)   incoherence, marked loosening of associations, markedly illogical thinking, or marked poverty of content of speech if associated with at least one of the following:
    (a)   blunted, flat, or inappropriate affect
    (b)   delusions or hallucinations
    (c)   catatonic or other grossly disorganised behaviour
B.   Deterioration from a previous level of functioning in such areas as work, social relations, and self-care.
C.   Duration: Continuous sign of the illness for at least six months at some time during the person's life, with some signs of the illness at present. The six-month period must include an active phase during which there were symptoms from A, with or without prodromal or residual phase, as defined below.
    Prodromal phase: A clear deterioration in functioning before the active phase of the illness not due to a disturbance in mood or to a Substance Use Disorder and involving at least two of the symptoms noted below.
    Residual phase: Persistence, following the active phase of the illness, of at least two of the symptoms noted below, not due to a disturbance in mood or to a Substance Use Disorder.
  Prodromal or Residual Symptoms
  (1)   social isolation or withdrawal
  (2)   marked impairment in role functioning as wage-earner, student, or homemaker
  (3)   markedly peculiar behaviour (e.g. collecting garbage, talking to self in public, or hoarding food)
  (4)   marked impairment in personal hygiene and grooming
  (5)   blunted, flat, or inappropriate affect
  (6)   digressive, vague, overelaborate, circumstantial, or metaphorical speech
  (7)   odd or bizarre ideation, or magical thinking, e.g. superstitiousness, clairvoyance, telepathy, "sixth sense", "others can feel my feelings", over-valued ideas, ideas of reference
  (8)   unusual perceptual experiences, e.g. recurrent illusions, sensing the presence of a force or person not actually present.
  Examples: Six months of prodromal symptoms with one week of symptoms from A; no prodromal symptoms with six months of symptoms from A; no prodromal symptoms with two weeks of symptoms from A and six months of residual symptoms; six months of symptoms from A, apparently followed by several years of complete remission, with one week of symptoms in A in current episode.
D.   The full depressive or manic syndrome (criteria A and B of major depressive or manic episode), if present, developed after any psychotic symptoms, or was brief in duration relative to the duration of the psychotic symptoms in A.
E.   Onset of prodromal or active phase of the illness before age 45.
F.   Not due to any Organic Mental Disorder or Mental Retardation.

Source: DSM-III (APA, 1980).
Reprinted with permission from the *Diagnostic and Statistical Manual of Mental Disorders*, 3rd edn. American Psychiatric Association.

The criteria for inferring schizophrenia are said to have validity in terms of:

(1)   ... a differential response to somatic therapy

Unfortunately, it is not clear from DSM-III what specific claim is being made here, far less what evidence is offered in support. A paper describing the development of the rules for inferring schizophrenia (Spitzer *et al.*, 1978a) is given in support of, apparently, all the alleged validating criteria; no specific reference is given for the claim to a differential response to somatic therapy. Spitzer *et al.* claim that DSM-III's diagnostic criteria were developed in order to relate diagnosis more closely to, amongst other things, treatment. They claim to have done this, however, only whenever possible. The possibilities for relating the criteria to 'treatment response' were apparently limited: reference is later made to a "vast literature" said to indicate that those called schizophrenic and who have a "poor prognosis" differ from a "good prognosis" group on a number of dimensions including *"perhaps* treatment response" (491; emphasis added). From this "vast literature", four papers are quoted. Two of these describe the same study, written up by different members of the research team for different journals, and none of the four discusses response to somatic intervention. It may be that the authors of DSM-III inferred response to somatic treatment from 'poor prognosis'. It appears that the diagnostic criteria are intended to identify a group which shows a 'poor prognosis' or tendency towards recurrence. The merits of this claim will be discussed later, but it is obvious that if certain phenomena persist or recur, i.e. 'have a poor prognosis', they have not been significantly altered by any intervention. Thus, DSM-III is apparently claiming two validating criteria for the price of one. Certainly, no direct evidence is offered about the response to somatic intervention of people who show the phenomena listed in the diagnostic criteria.

But this hardly matters beside the fact that 'response to treatment' is almost always an inappropriate criterion for claiming that a proposed cluster is meaningful. It is so because, as has so often been observed in medical practice, the same intervention is often appropriate for what are known to be different patterns as, for example, in the instance cited by Kendell (1975b) of aspirin being appropriate for rheumatism and toothache. If response to intervention is therefore often uninformative, then the *lack* of it, as apparently used by DSM-III, is even more so because the number of phenomena which do not change in response to a particular intervention is usually much greater than is the number which do. Taking this argument to its conclusion, it might as well be claimed that the phenomena referred to by, say, multiple sclerosis, flat feet and brain tumours form a pattern because none of them is changed by treatment with antibiotics. Given these problems, it is extremely unlikely that lack of response to somatic intervention, which is apparently implied by DSM-III, can help to identify a pattern.

(2)   ... the presence of a familial pattern

As with 'response to treatment' it is difficult to know exactly what is being claimed here. DSM-III, like its predecessors, includes a long statement purporting to represent what is known about schizophrenia. This sketch is organised under a number of headings, one of which is familial pattern. It is claimed that "All investigators have found a higher prevalence of the disorder among family members" (186). This claim is a curious one. No explanation is given of how it could be possible to have studied 'the disorder', to have charted its progress in families, in the absence of a reliable set of rules for inferring schizophrenia. The authors of DSM-III thus placed themselves in the paradoxical position (apparently advised by Stengel) of devising criteria for inferring schizophrenia using research which assumed that the task had been completed. The research to which DSM-III presumably refers will be discussed in detail in the next chapter, but some aspects of it need to be mentioned here.

First, because there were no agreed referents for schizophrenia, researchers have studied a variety of behaviours. Indeed, in many of the family studies it is impossible to know what was being studied because the specific criteria used to infer schizophrenia were not stated. Family members may well have resembled each other, but in what way is difficult to say. But even the conclusion that families resembled each other in some unspecified way is questionable, first, because researchers have not always reported the reliability of their inferences to schizophrenia, and, second, because researchers have rarely employed truly blind observation of subjects and their family members. Taken together, these problems make the data from family studies virtually uninterpretable. Although it is presumably this research to which DSM-III refers, it must be emphasised again that, in talking of a family pattern for the disorder, the authors of DSM-III are implying that *their* correspondence rules for schizophrenia have been found to run in families. Thus, the only admissible research for their purposes would be that which used the DSM-III criteria. There is no indication that any such research was carried out prior to the publication of DSM-III, far less that it supported its conclusions.

But even if it had been demonstrated that DSM-III's diagnostic criteria 'ran in families', this would not support the claim that the criteria denote a meaningful pattern. It is easy to show that this is the case by taking any physical features or behaviour where family resemblance might be expected. Take, for example, small eyes, large nose and small mouth. If researchers could reliably isolate a group showing all three features, then it is likely that the prevalence of *the group of three* would be higher in its family members than in the general population. It could not, however (and no doubt would not), be concluded that these three features formed a pattern which justified inferring a new construct. Rather, it would be correctly pointed out that each feature *independently* may show family resemblance and that their co-occurrence might therefore be by chance. It might, of course, be the case that people who have these features are called unattractive and mate with other 'unattractive' people who are also more likely to show them. Their families might therefore show a considerably higher prevalence of the group of features than would the general population, but this would still not justify the conclusion that the three features formed a pattern. The same reasoning could be used for any arbitrarily chosen group of behaviours – for example, playing a musical instrument, smoking and attending church regularly. The mode of transmission from generation to generation might be different from that for physical features, but the argument remains the same.

The authors of DSM-III have therefore reached two false conclusions: one, that family studies show familial resemblance in a specified group of behaviours, and two, that even if this had been shown, it would justify imputing meaningfulness to it. In referring to these family studies, DSM-III appears to be confusing the original demonstration that a proposed cluster is not a chance co-occurrence with later attempts to elaborate the theoretical network of a construct derived from it. The presence or absence of family resemblance in an *already-observed pattern* might help clarify the nature of its antecedents; they cannot themselves reliably indicate that a proposed cluster does form a pattern.

(3)   ... a tendency towards onset in early adult life

In its sketch, DSM-III merely claims that "Onset is usually during adolescence or early adulthood" (184). This statement, of course, raises the same problems as does the use of 'family resemblance' – onset of what? The claim implies that data exist which demonstrate that DSM-III's criteria first show themselves, as a group, during adolescence or early adulthood. The difficulties of using 'age of onset' as a criterion were discussed in relation to Kraepelin's work in Chapter 3, but no mention is made of these problems in DSM-III; indeed, no justification is given at all for the claim that age of onset is usually during adolescence or early adulthood. Spitzer *et al.*, however, do attempt to provide one: "experience in the DSM-III field trials forced us to re-consider the question of the appropriateness of a diagnosis of schizophrenia in an individual whose first episode of illness is diagnosed as Involutional Paraphrenia" (1978a: 492). The language of this statement makes it difficult to know what is being claimed. Presumably the claim is that people who show a particular set of behaviours before age forty-five are different *in some important way* from those who show the same or similar behaviours at age forty-six or later. They presumably differ, that is, in some way which, if the groups were separated on the basis of it, would aid the prediction of previously unobserved events, different for the two groups. This interpretation is supported by Spitzer *et al.*'s conclusion that "since it is likely that such conditions are fundamentally different from schizophrenia of early onset, we believe it advisable to limit the diagnosis of schizophrenia to individuals whose first episode of illness occurred before the age of 45" (1978a: 492). Unfortunately, Spitzer *et al.* provide no evidence that this is the case; indeed, they do not even say what this alleged fundamental difference might be. Rather, they resort to their personal beliefs and to unspecified experiences. That such a difference has never been reliably observed is attested to by the fact that no reference is made to it in the diagnostic criteria: the problematic 'age of onset' is used instead.

(4)   ... a tendency to recurrence

Spitzer *et al.* note that in selecting criteria for inferring schizophrenia, one of their goals was to "[limit] the concept [of schizophrenia] so that it is not applied to individuals likely to return to an adequate premorbid level of adjustment" (490). (This does not, apparently, mean that those called schizophrenic using DSM-III's criteria will inevitably run a 'deteriorating course'.) DSM-III's claim that its criteria are reliably associated with particular events at follow-up (prognosis, outcome) appears to be central to the assumption that they identify a group sharing *important* features and that they therefore allow the inference to a hypothetical construct. As with the other validating criteria, two separate issues need to be considered. The first is whether the correspondence rules *are* reliably associated with whatever is meant here by a tendency to recurrence or poor prognosis; the second is whether, even if they are, this amounts to a demonstration of a pattern of events and justifies inferring a hypothetical construct.

Do the correspondence rules indicate a 'poor prognosis'?

Support for the assumption that the diagnostic criteria predict the phenomena from which poor prognosis is inferred appears to be drawn from three sources. The first is a study (Kendell *et al.*, 1979) purporting to show that a set of criteria very similar to those of DSM-III were "the most predictive of incomplete symptomatic recovery and poor social outcome" (Spitzer *et al.*, 1978a: 490). The second source is research relating the initial persistence of deviant behaviour (i.e. the length of time the behaviour has been present before it is brought to the attention of a psychiatrist) and behaviour at follow-up. The third source is research purporting to investigate the relationship between 'prognosis' and the presence or absence of 'affective disorder' in those diagnosed as schizophrenic.

DSM-III's authors have assumed that this research has identified a pattern of behaviours which are reliably associated with their own persistence or recurrence and with other negative phenomena such as unemployment or poor social relationships. Thus, the correspondence rules are based on those said to have "most predictive power" in Kendell *et al.*'s study; they stipulate that certain deviant behaviours should have been "continuously present" for 6 months and, finally, require "absence of major affective disorder", before the inference to schizophrenia is made. Taken together, these phenomena are said to be associated with a 'poor prognosis'. The three sources of support for this assumption will be considered separately.

Kendell et al.'s study.   Between 1959, when Stengel first called for operational definitions of psychiatric concepts, and 1980, when the first 'official' set was published in DSM-III, a number of users of 'schizophrenia' published their own preferred sets of correspondence rules (for example, Astrachan *et al.*, 1972; Feighner *et al.*, 1972; Carpenter *et al.*, 1973a; Spitzer *et al.*, 1978b). No two of these sets were the same and, as Fenton *et al.* (1981) have pointed out, all were to some extent arbitrary and none had demonstrated validity. Nevertheless, attempts were made to assess their relative merits, and the Kendell *et al.* study is an example of one such comparison.

Using their own preferred criteria, Kendell *et al.* inferred functional psychosis from the behaviour of 134 inmates of a London hospital. Six to eight years later, 118 of these people were followed up and interviewed. On the basis of interview data and hospital notes, each of the 118 was rated on five variables, called: social isolation; persistent delusions or hallucinations; defect state; employment status; and proportion of follow-up period spent in hospital. Scores on a sixth variable, called incomplete recovery from index episode, were derived from "all the information available". This score was called a global outcome rating. (Little information was provided about the specific phenomena used to infer these variables and to derive scores; no information was provided on the reliability of the ratings.) Shortly after these follow-up assessments had been made, the original interview data on the subjects were examined to discover to what extent each subject matched the (different) correspondence rules for schizophrenia suggested by Schneider (1959), Langfeldt (1960), Astrachan *et al.* (1972), Carpenter *et al.* (1973a) and Spitzer *et al.* (1978b). Seventy-five subjects met none of these criteria; the remainder met between one and all of them (there is considerable overlap amongst the criteria). Kendell *et al.* then conducted a large number of paired comparisons to discover to what extent the application of each set of rules would separate subjects on each of the six outcome variables. Thus, all subjects who matched, say, Schneider's criteria were compared, as a group, with the group made up of all remaining subjects, on every outcome variable. The same procedure was followed for each set of diagnostic criteria. Kendell *et al.* were thus able to construct, for each outcome variable, a kind of league table of the diagnostic criteria in terms of their ability to separate the groups on each outcome variable. For example, 45 per cent of those subjects who matched Langfeldt's criteria were said to show incomplete recovery from index episode, versus 13 per cent of those not fulfilling the criteria. For Schneider's criteria, the figures were 31 per cent versus 17 per cent. Langfeldt's criteria were therefore placed higher on the 'league table', for this variable, than were Schneider's. For those outcome variables rated on a continuous scale, group mean ratings were compared.

It is from these data that Spitzer *et al.* (1978a) concluded that one of the sets of criteria used, the Research Diagnostic Criteria (RDC) (Spitzer *et al.*, 1978b), was the "most predictive of both incomplete symptomatic recovery and poor social outcome". For this reason, the RDC formed the basis of the DSM-III criteria. This conclusion is unwarranted because the data provided do not allow any comparisons *within each league table*, i.e. they do not indicate whether any set(s) of diagnostic criteria were 'better' at predicting outcome variables. Spitzer *et al.* appear to have drawn the false conclusion that a set of criteria which assigns 43 per cent of those who match it to 'persistent delusions or hallucinations', versus 8 per cent of those who do not, is "more predictive" of this variable than a set of figures of, say, 36 per cent versus 8 per cent. The conclusion is false because no data are provided on the significance of the difference between the first and second sets of figures.

But even if Kendell *et al.*'s data *had* allowed statements about the 'most predictive set of diagnostic criteria', the implicit claim that the RDC are reliably associated with 'poor prognosis' is still problematic. It is so first, because the RDC achieved the largest separation of groups on only two of the six outcome variables; on the remaining four, it achieved third, third, fourth and second places in the 'league table'. (It must be emphasised that all definitions of 'poor prognosis' are to some extent arbitrary; there is no question of Kendell *et al.*'s six variables necessarily being a 'better' definition than Spitzer *et al.*'s choice of two of these. The point is made merely to highlight the apparent arbitrariness of Spitzer *et al.*'s choice of the RDC as the basis of DSM-III's criteria for inferring schizophrenia.) The implicit claim that the RDC are predictive of 'poor prognosis' is problematic, second, because on every outcome variable, a large number of subjects who fulfilled the RDC nevertheless did not conform to the criteria for poor prognosis. On the two variables for which Spitzer *et al.* claim the RDC was "most predictive", 57 per cent and 35 per cent of subjects *failed* to show a 'poor prognosis', i.e. their delusions or hallucinations did not persist and their 'social outcome' was rated as good. On the remaining variables where either/or classifications were used, the figures were 57 per cent and 76 per cent. Thus, whatever definition of 'poor prognosis' is used, the RDC can hardly be claimed to identify a group which is homogeneous in terms of it. Spitzer *et al.* in fact claim that they "later concluded" that the RDC combined " 'good' and 'poor' prognosis schizophrenia" (491). They do not quote Kendell *et al.*'s study as having indicated this; they do not say what was the source of their conclusion. They do, however, claim that "There is a vast literature indicating that [good and poor prognosis schizophrenics] differ markedly not only in prognosis, but also in family history, phenomenology, mode of onset, and, perhaps, treatment response" (491). The argument being pursued by Spitzer *et al.* is not clear; apparently, it is assumed that these alleged correlates of 'good and poor prognosis schizophrenia' justify the claim that the groups differ in important ways and so should be separated *and* that each group represents a pattern, thus justifying two hypothetical constructs, in this case 'schizophrenia' and 'schizophreniform disorder'.

Whether 'prognosis' can be used as a criterion of important within-group similarity will be discussed later. The problem here is to clarify Spitzer *et al.*'s arguments as to why and how the RDC should be modified so that they identify a group homogeneous for/reliably associated with 'poor prognosis'. The solution – within Spitzer *et al.*'s framework – appears simple: if members of a group share some deviant behaviours but differ in prognosis and also differ *markedly* in family history, mode of onset and phenomolology, then the good- and poor-prognosis members can be identified using family history, phenomenology, and so on. Inexplicably, again within their framework, Spitzer *et al.* did not choose to discriminate between the two groups in this way, i.e. they did not use family history, and so on, in the rules for inferring schizophrenia. On the contrary, they claim that "At the present time there is no entirely satisfactory method of separating [good and poor prognosis schizophrenics] on the basis of cross-sectional evaluation" (491). But cross-sectional evaluation, as used by Spitzer *et al.*, apparently means phenomenology. They are thus arguing both that good- and poor-prognosis schizophrenics differ markedly on phenomenology *and* that they cannot be separated on the basis of it. Then, instead of using any of the variables which they claim markedly differentiate good and poor prognosis groups, Spitzer *et al.* suggest that DSM-III's criteria should include six months of symptoms because "Some evidence suggests that requiring 6 months of symptoms is among the most powerful diagnostic indicators" (491). This evidence, then, is the second source quoted in support of the association between a 'poor prognosis' and DSM-III's correspondence rules.

Prognosis and "6 months of symptoms".   Three references are quoted in support of the inclusion of 6 months of symptoms in DSM-III's correspondence rules. The first is a follow-up study by Astrup and Noreik (1966), the second a brief report (Sartorius *et al.*, 1978) on the International Follow-up Study of Schizophrenia (WHO, 1979) and the third a study by Tsuang *et al.* (1976). The three studies will be considered separately.

Astrup and Noreik claimed to have studied "the natural course of illness in an unselected sample" because of "varying diagnostic practices and diagnostic uncertainty" (12). In fact, their sample was pre-selected in two ways – in consisting of "mental hospital cases" and of people to whom the term functional psychosis had been applied but by unspecified criteria. Astrup and Noreik reported follow-up data on two such groups, one admitted between 1938 and 1950 and one between 1951 and 1957. All were followed up at least five years after their first admission. Using information from a variety of sources –

interviews with subjects, their relatives or public-health officers, question-naires completed by subjects and hospital notes – subjects were placed in one of five 'outcome' groups called: (1) Severe schizophrenic deterioration; (2) Characteristics of slight deterioration; (3) Schizophrenic personality changes (1, 2 and 3 were together called schizophrenic outcome); (4) No schizophrenic personality change but have had psychotic relapses during the last five years or reduced social adaptation because of neurotic or psychopathic traits; (5) Well for at least five years (together called non-schizophrenic outcome). As well as being rated on 'outcome', subjects were also rated on a number of vari-ables using information recorded at admission and called, for example, symptomatology, intelligence, age of onset, body type, pre-psychotic person-ality and marital status.

There are a number of serious methodological weaknesses in Astrup and Noreik's study. They did not, for example, report on the reliability of outcome ratings nor on how the different sources of information – and these were dif-ferent for different subjects – were combined to give the global rating. They did report the extent of agreement on ratings of admission information. For some variables, for example marital status, this was obviously high; for others it was unsatisfactorily low. For the variable of interest here – 'duration of symptoms prior to first assessment' – raters disagreed on 29 per cent of sub-jects. Spitzer *et al.* (1978a), however, make no mention of these problems and have apparently taken Astrup and Noreik's data at face value. The discussion here will therefore also do so to examine the extent to which these data, what-ever their merits, justify Spitzer *et al.*'s conclusion that "6 months of symptoms is among the most powerful prognostic indicators".

Astrup and Noreik examined the relationship between the ratings made from admission information and outcome ratings using univariate and then multivariate analyses. In the first stage they calculated, for each admission variable, the distribution of subjects on the five-point 'outcome' scale. Table 5.2 shows this distribution for the variable 'prior duration of illness'. No sig-nificance levels were reported; apparently on the basis of visual inspection, Astrup and Noreik chose a number of admission variables said to be related to "favourable or unfavourable outcome" and used these in their multivariate analyses. Two aspects of the analyses are relevant here. The first is the way in which the variable 'prior duration of illness' was quantified and the second its fate in the multivariate analyses.

As can be seen in Table 5.2, Astrup and Noreik divided 'prior duration of illness' into five categories – < ½ year, ½–1 year, 2–5 years, 5–10 years and > 10 years. If Spitzer *et al.*'s conclusion is reasonable, it would be expected that the outcome distribution for the < ½-year group would be strikingly different from that for *all* other categories *and* that these would not differ significantly from each other. This last point is crucial: if two different constructs are in-ferred from 'less than 6 months' symptoms' and 'more than 6 months'

Table 5.2 Outcome by prior duration of illness

Outcome	Duration before admission (years)						Total
	$<1/2$	$1/2-1$	$1-2$	$2-5$	$5-10$	>10	
Recovered	93	12	10	4	2	0	121
Improved	138	35	18	22	9	9	231
Schizophrenic personality change	34	10	16	28	11	1	100
Slight schizophrenic deterioration	24	21	37	57	22	16	177
Severe schizophrenic deterioration	9	10	14	23	13	8	77
TOTAL	298	88	95	134	57	34	706

Source: Astrup and Noreik, 1966

symptoms' (as is the case in DSM-III) because their prognosis is said to be significantly different, it follows, using DSM-III's reasoning, that if '½–1 year of symptoms' is associated with a significantly different outcome distribution from, say, '2–5 years of symptoms', then a third construct should be inferred from this 'cluster'. This is exactly what emerges from an analysis of Astrup and Noreik's data. The outcome distributions for the $<$½-year and ½–1-year groups are indeed significantly different ($\chi^2 = 32.46$, df 4, p $>$ .001) but those for the ½–1-year and the 2–5-year groups are even more dissimilar ($\chi^2 = 144.4$, df 4, p $>$ .001). It can also be seen from Table 5.2 that the majority of those rated 'prior duration of symptoms ½–1 year' were rated as having recovered or improved. These figures hardly allow the conclusion that '6 months of symptoms' is reliably associated with a tendency to recurrence or a poor prognosis. Astrup and Noreik in fact chose to include 'prior duration of illness' in their multivariate analyses not because of differences between the $<$½-year and ½–1-year groups but because of the contrast between the $<$½-year and 2–5-year groups. It must be emphasised that it is not therefore being suggested here that Spitzer *et al.* should have chosen '2 years or more of symptoms' as part of the rules for inferring schizophrenia; to have done so would have been to ignore both the complexities of Astrup and Noreik's multivariate analyses and, more important, the problematic status of 'prognosis' as a validating criteria.

Having chosen admission variables said to be associated with favourable or unfavourable outcome, Astrup and Noreik performed a number of mutivariate analyses using, as is customary, different combinations of variables and different methods of analysis. As might be expected, their analyses showed that the power of the variable 'prior duration of illness' to predict 'outcome' varied from significant to non-existent, depending on which variables were included in the analyses – a point Astrup and Noreik emphasised. In one analysis, the independent contribution of each of seven admission variables, including 'prior duration' ½–2 years and >2 years, to an 'unfavourable outcome' was reported. For subjects admitted between 1938 and 1950, the relative contribution of the two duration variables was 12.7 per cent (½–2 years; sixth highest out of seven) and 27.9 per cent (>2 years; second highest out of seven). For those admitted between 1951 and 1957, the corresponding figures were 19.1 per cent (third out of seven) and 31.3 per cent (first out of seven). The analyses were carried out again but now included thirteen variables, all said to be associated with an unfavourable outcome. For the 1938–50 sample (results were not given for the other group), the figures for the same two duration variables were 10.5 per cent (fifth out of thirteen) and 29.9 per cent (first out of thirteen). Although Spitzer *et al.* do not indicate from which of Astrup and Noreik's many analyses they drew their conclusion, it was probably from these. In doing so, however, they apparently overlooked not only the fact that it was 'more than 2 years' prior duration' and not 'more than 6 months' which made the *relatively* large contribution to the variance of 'outcome'; they overlooked also the remainder of Astrup and Noreik's analyses *and* their conclusions.

In eight later analyses (four each for the two samples), Astrup and Noreik used different combinations of variables to produce listings of the best predictors of 'unfavourable outcome'. For each set of subjects, 'prior duration more than 2 years' was included in two of three listings (listings were not given for the fourth analysis). As would be expected, its predictive power varied depending on which variables had been included in the regression equation. Astrup and Noreik concluded from these analyses that the best predictors of unfavourable outcome in their data were clinical variables, i.e. ratings of initial symptoms, and not prior duration.

The role of 'prior duration' was further examined in another series of analyses. These used a maximum likelihood method (Maxwell, 1961) which predicted the outcome rating which was most frequent for each paired combination of five 'symptoms' said to be displayed at admission. Astrup and Noreik's conclusions from this series of analyses are worth quoting in detail:

the inclusion of duration of illness enhances the predictability to some extent (5.3 per cent in the 1951–57 sample, 2.1 per cent in the 1938–50 sample) but the number of symptoms predicts nearly as well as non-linear combinations of the five clinical symptoms....Though the inclusion of duration in a non-linear formula increases predictability for each of the original samples, these gains are not retained in cross-validation. It appears that the additive prediction based on the number of symptoms (excluding duration) leads to predictions that are about as good and more stable than the non-linear equation with or without duration.

(125; 128)

Three main conclusions can be drawn from Astrup and Noreik's study (ignoring its methodological problems) First, that Spitzer *et al.*'s conclusion that "6 months of symptoms is among the most powerful prognostic indicators" is, to say the least, an oversimplification of Astrup and Noreik's data. Second, the predictive power of 'prior duration' varies, depending on which variables are included in the analyses, from significant to non-existent. When it does emerge, it is as 'more than 2 years' prior duration' and not as 'at least 6 months'. Third, those variables which most consistently emerged as predictors of 'unfavourable outcome' were 'clinical symptoms at admission'. Because Astrup and Noreik rated the continued presence of these 'symptoms' as an unfavourable outcome, their data apparently suggest that one of the best predictors of extent of deviancy at point B was extent of deviancy at point A.

The second source of support quoted for Spitzer *et al.*'s conclusion that "6 months of symptoms is among the best prognostic indicators" is a brief report (Sartorius *et al.*, 1978) of the International Follow-up Study of Schizophrenia, a study conducted under the auspices of the World Health Organisation (WHO, 1979). This research was similar to that of Astrup and Noreik in that it examined the relationship between admission variables and outcome variables in a group to whom the term functional psychosis had been applied. It is difficult to understand how Spitzer *et al.* reached their conclusion from the Sartorius report; certainly, it was not drawn by the report's authors. Sartorius *et al.* in fact concluded that "no single factor and no combination of a small number of factors appear to be strongly associated with the course and outcome of schizophrenia" (107), and that:

> the three classes of predictor (i.e. admission) variables [(1) *sociodemo-graphic:* social isolation, social status and marital status; (2) *past history:* history of psychiatric treatment, poor psychosexual adjustment and unfavourable environment; (3) *factors relating to the initial psychotic episode:* length of episode before initial evaluation, insidious onset, presence of precipitating factors, presence of derealization, affective symptoms or flattening of affect] were found to be about equal in their predictive power.

(108)

It was also noted, however, that the 'length of the psychotic episode before the patient's entrance in the study' was amongst the best (albeit weak) predictors of every outcome measure in both "developed" and "developing" countries. It may be that it was this last point which encouraged Spitzer *et al.* to draw their conclusion about 6 months of symptoms. The actual data reported by

WHO, rather than Sartorius *et al.*'s report, will therefore be reviewed briefly here to assess the validity of Spitzer *et al.*'s conclusion.

The 1979 WHO report forms part of a larger study, divided into three phases – preliminary, initial evaluation and follow-up. Subjects were drawn from psychiatric centres in nine countries. Diagnostic terms were applied to them in the second phase of the study, using the guidelines for Section V of the ICD-8 and the Present State Examination (Wing *et al.*, 1974). Forty-seven independent (predictor) variables were chosen for investigation in the third, follow-up, phase. These were rated from information collected at initial evaluation. The forty-seven predictor variables were divided into the three classes mentioned earlier – sociodemographic, past history and factors relating to the initial psychotic episode. Some 1,202 subjects were evaluated initially; 906 were included in the multivariate follow-up analyses. Some 609 had received a diagnosis of schizophrenia.

Subjects were assessed by interview at 2-year follow-up using four assessment instruments – the Present State Examination (PSE) to assess 'symptoms', a Psychiatric History Schedule, a Social Description Schedule and a Diagnostic Assessment Schedule. With the exception of the PSE, no data were reported on the reliability of these instruments. Follow-up information from the Psychiatric History and the Social Description Schedules was converted, by a different set of raters, to five 'outcome' measures; ratings on these served as the dependent variables in the multivariate analyses. The five measures were called social functioning, length of episode of inclusion, percentage of time spent in psychotic episodes during follow-up period, pattern of course and overall outcome. The relationships between the forty-seven predictor variables and the five outcome categories were calculated mainly by multiple regression. In some analyses, the results for the whole sample were reported with 'country' included as a predictor variable. In other analyses, results were reported separately for "developed" and "developing" countries; in yet others, they were reported separately for each country. The results can be summarised briefly. First, the proportion of variance accounted for by the five best predictors of any of the 'outcome' measures in either type of country was always small, with a range of 8 to 22 per cent. Indeed, WHO emphasised the weak relationship between its predictor and outcome variables. Second, the best predictors were different for the different outcome measures and for different countries. Third, although 'prior duration' appeared frequently amongst the five best predictors, it did not appear for every outcome measure. Nor did it appear for every country as a predictor of 'overall outcome'.

There is little in these results to support Spitzer *et al.*'s and DSM-III's assumption that the inclusion of '6 months of symptoms' in the correspondence rules for schizophrenia will reliably identify a group homogeneous for 'poor prognosis/tendency to recurrence'. Its inclusion becomes even more puzzling when two additional factors are taken into account. First, the variable 'social isolation' also emerged frequently amongst the best predictors of 'outcome';

like 'prior duration', it emerged on every outcome measure in both groups of countries. It is difficult to understand why DSM-III's authors did not therefore follow their own reasoning and include this variable in the correspondence rules for schizophrenia. Second, in all of these analyses, the predictor variable 'prior duration' was *continuous* with a range from 'less than one week' to 'five years or more'. It is therefore impossible, as with Astrup and Noreik's data, to draw any conclusions about the predictive power of a specific 'prior duration', in this case '6 months or more'. Indeed, WHO mentioned 'more than or less than 6 months prior duration of symptoms' only to point out that dividing subjects in this way could not explain the fact that almost twice as many of those from the "developed" as from the "developing" countries were placed in the 'worst outcome' category.

A third source of support is quoted by Spitzer *et al.* for the inclusion of '6 months of symptoms' in the criteria for inferring schizophrenia. This is a study by Tsuang *et al.* (1976) which compared three groups of subjects, given different diagnostic labels, on five variables. The three groups were called: schizophrenia, atypical schizophrenia and primary affective disorder; the five variables were called family history of psychiatric illness, precipitating factors, outcome, age at admission and sex. None of these had been used as a criterion for assigning the diagnostic labels.

Tsuang *et al.* chose a sample which had originally, between 1935 and 1944, been given a diagnosis either of schizophrenia or primary affective disorder, using unspecified criteria. This population was then re-divided by the authors, using hospital records, into 'schizophrenia', 'atypical schizophrenia' and 'primary affective disorder (unipolar or bipolar)' using the criteria based on those of Feighner *et al.* (1972). Spitzer *et al.* appear to have drawn their conclusion that "6 months of symptoms is among the most powerful prognostic indicators" from the fact that on follow-up, 44 per cent of the 'atypical schizophrenia' group were rated as recovered compared with only 8 per cent of the 'schizophrenia' group. An examination of Tsuang *et al.*'s criteria, however, shows that this conclusion is, once again, questionable. The 'atypical' group could differ from the 'schizophrenia' group in many ways apart from '6 months of symptoms'. They could, for example, have differed on social variables such as marital status (which appeared frequently in the WHO study discussed earlier, amongst the best predictors of 'outcome'). On the other hand, subjects in the two groups were not even required to differ on 'at least 6 months of symptoms' and data on subject characteristics were not reported. It is thus impossible to deduce from Tsuang *et al.*'s data whether 'at least 6 months of symptoms' made *any* contribution to outcome ratings, far less how powerful its effect might have been. Certainly, the authors of this study drew no conclusions about '6 months of symptoms'.

None of the three studies quoted by Spitzer *et al.* justifies the conclusion that including 'at least 6 months of symptoms' in the correspondence rules for schizophrenia will identify a group which is reliably associated with a 'poor prognosis/tendency to recurrence'. What may cautiously be concluded (bearing in mind the considerable methodological weaknesses of all three studies) is that, depending on the variables included in the analysis and on the culture in which subjects live, there may be a relationship amongst the prior duration (unspecified) of some behaviours, their persistence and other variables such as employment and social activities. How this conclusion might be interpreted will be discussed later.

Prognosis and affective disorder. The third source of support for the assumption that DSM-III's diagnostic criteria are reliably associated with a 'poor prognosis' appears to be the claim that those who display *both*, whatever behaviours are called symptoms of schizophrenia *and* behaviours called symptoms of affective disorder, have a more 'favourable prognosis' than do those who display only the first set of behaviours. It is, in fact, extremely difficult to know what DSM-III's authors *are* claiming. Spitzer *et al.* (1978a) claim that the controversy over the relationship between affective disorder and schizophrenia is part of the good versus poor prognosis controversy. Unfortunately, they do not say in what way the two controversies are related. They claim also that good-prognosis and poor-prognosis groups of schizophrenics "differ markedly ... in family history, phenomenology, mode of onset and perhaps treatment response" (490); but, as was pointed out earlier, they do not say what these differences are.

DSM-III's reasoning is further obscured by the fact that the correspondence rules for schizophrenia do not stipulate an absence of whatever behaviour is used to infer affective disorder; they merely state that such behaviours "if present [should have] developed after any psychotic symptoms or [should have been] brief in duration relative to the duration of the psychotic symptoms" (190). There is certainly no piece of research quoted in DSM-III which compares the 'prognosis' of two or three groups – one which displayed behaviours A, B and C ('schizophrenia') and then behaviours D, E and F ('affective disorder') and one which displayed behaviours D, E and F and then A, B and C or one which displayed both sets, in any order, but with D, E and F displayed for a shorter period. Yet it is difficult to see how DSM-III's authors could have reached their conclusions about this part of the correspondence rules without the benefit of such research.

Of the studies which are quoted, none even allows the conclusion that simply the absence of whatever behaviour is the source of the construct of affective disorder is reliably associated with a 'poor prognosis' or its presence with a 'good prognosis'. Vaillant (1964), for example, followed up a group of people who had been admitted to hospital between 1947 and 1950 and given, by unspecified criteria, a diagnosis of schizophrenia. These subjects were rated on a 'prognostic scale' of seven variables claimed by Vaillant to be highly correlated in the literature with remission in schizophrenia. These were called: acute onset, confusion, depressive heredity, non-schizoid pre-morbid adjustment, clear symptoms of an affective psychosis, precipitating factors and concern with death. Seventy-seven per cent of those said to have achieved full remission were rated as showing clear symptoms of an affective psychosis; but so too were 49 per cent of those said not to have achieved full remission. From a correlational analysis, Vaillant concluded that "the diagnosis 'schizo-affective' attained prognostic significance only when the six other criteria were also applied to those schizophrenics who showed any depressive features" (i.e. those rated as showing clear symptoms of an affective disorder) (514).

Stephens (1970) reported a follow-up study of 349 subjects previously given a diagnosis of schizophrenia, reactive psychosis or cycloid psychosis. Forty-three variables "thought to have possible prognostic significance" were correlated with ratings of 'outcome' as recovered, improved or unimproved, in two samples followed up for less than or more than ten years. In the first sample, the correlation between 'depressive features' and 'outcome' was 0.25 ($p < 0.01$); in the second it was 0.19 ($p < 0.05$). These figures did not apparently reflect the independent relationship of 'depressive features' to 'outcome'; it is likely to be lower than that reported here if the prognostic variables are correlated with each other. And Vaillant noted that in his data "every favourable prognostic factor is positively correlated with every other favourable factor" (514). As would be expected from these low correlations, positive ratings of 'depressive features' did not identify a group homogeneous for 'good' or 'poor prognosis'; 43 per cent of those rated unimproved were said to have shown depressive features.

Three studies not quoted in DSM-III likewise cast doubt on the validity of its (apparent) conclusion that the presence of whatever behaviour is used to infer affective disorder is associated with 'good prognosis' when it appears in conjunction with the 'symptoms of schizophrenia'. Carpenter et al. (1978), as part of the WHO International Pilot Study of Schizophrenia, found no relationship between those behaviours whose absence or 'secondary presence' DSM-III apparently requires, and ratings of 'outcome'. Vaillant (1978) found no differences in admission ratings of 'affective symptoms' amongst those subjects whose 'schizophrenic' behaviour had persisted or recurred and those who no longer displayed this behaviour. And Gift et al. (1980) found a complex series of relationships between 'affective symptoms' and 'outcome' which depended on the criteria used both for diagnosis and for ratings of 'outcome'. (DSM-III criteria were not used.) In particular, higher ratings of 'depression' at admission, in conjunction with a diagnosis of schizophrenia according to Schneider's (1959) or Carpenter et al.'s (1973a) criteria, were associated with *lower* ratings of 'quality of work' at follow-up. This result is the opposite of that implied by DSM-III's criteria.

The authors of DSM-III appear to have accepted as methodologically sound those research studies quoted in support of their claim that DSM-III's concept of schizophrenia is valid in terms of a 'tendency to recurrence' or 'poor prognosis'. However, as the analysis here has shown, even when meth-odological problems are ignored, the available data are not consistent with DSM-III's claim. On the contrary, the data here suggest that the correspond-ence rules are likely to be reliably associated with considerable heterogeneity in 'prognosis', however this is defined.

Can 'prognosis' define a meaningful pattern?

It was emphasised earlier that, as with the other validating criteria, two separ-ate issues were raised by DSM-III's implication that their correspondence rules for schizophrenia are reliably associated with 'poor prognosis'. The first is the extent to which this is in fact the case; the second is whether *even if it were* it could be concluded that the correspondence rules represent a pattern of regularities or events which co-occur above chance. It has already been shown that the correspondence rules do not appear to be reliably associated with any particular 'prognosis'. The discussion will, however, ignore that con-clusion for the moment and assume that they are.

It would be tempting to conclude that the diagnostic criteria therefore rep-resent a pattern of regularities, especially in the face of assertions such as that of Gift *et al.* that "prognosis has often been used as a validating criterion for identifying disease entities" (1980: 580). The conclusion would, however, be false as, indeed, is Gift *et al.*'s claim. Many of the problems of using 'prognosis' or 'outcome' as criteria for assigning meaningfulness to a cluster have already been discussed in detail in Chapters 2 and 3. Only some additional points of particular relevance to DSM-III will be mentioned here.

In the research quoted by DSM-III's authors, 'prognosis/outcome' has been defined in a number of different ways. The various definitions have in com-mon that they reduce to statements about the *persistence* of various odd behaviours and to statements about their personal and social correlates (em-ployment, social relationships, self-care, and so on). But the fact that behaviours persist does not indicate that they co-occur above chance; the be-haviours could develop and persist independently, under the control of quite different antecedents and maintaining factors. Nor would the greater persist-ence of behaviours which had already been displayed for at least 6 months indicate anything other than that past behaviour predicts future behaviour. The same effect would be expected for many behaviours which may co-occur – smoking, learning a new language, taking up a sport, and so on; we should hardly be surprised to find that a greater proportion of those who have per-sisted at these activities for 6 months or more are likely to continue with them than is the case for those who started yesterday. Certainly, no conclusions can be drawn about the relationship of the behaviours to each other nor assump-tions made about common antecedents. It would also be unremarkable to find that behaviours which represent considerable deviation from social norms, as do the so-called symptoms of schizophrenia, are associated with other social and personal difficulties. But neither this association, which is common to much socially deviant behaviour, nor its persistence, allows the conclusion that these 'symptoms' form a meaningful pattern. Because social and personal difficulties may increase as the number of deviant behaviours increases, the spurious impression may be given that the 'symptoms' cluster together, simply because they become more noticeable in combination. To draw this conclusion, however, is rather like concluding that the phenomena from which, say, multiple sclerosis, Parkinson's disease and rheumatoid arthritis are inferred form a pattern because the presence of all three sets is more likely to be associated with social and personal difficulties than is the presence of only one. Similarly, the 'outcome' of 'multiple sclerosis' may in some cases be identical, in social and personal terms, to that of 'rheumatoid arthritis', while two cases of 'multiple sclerosis' might have quite different 'outcomes'. But if the social and personal correlates of 'symptoms of schizophrenia' are omitted from a definition of outcome, all that remains is the persistence of the 'symptoms'; it has already been noted that mere persistence cannot indicate that the behaviours in question form a pattern.

(5) ... deterioration in social and occupational functioning

The authors of DSM-III claim that its concept of schizophrenia is valid, finally, in terms of a deterioration in social and occupational functioning. No attempt is made to provide evidence that this is the case. Instead, DSM-III states simply that "Schizophrenia always involves deterioration from a previous level of functioning during some phase of the illness in such areas as work, social relations and self-care" (181). The implication here is that a pattern of phenomena, from which schizophrenia can be validly inferred, has been found invariably to be associated with whatever is meant by a deterioration in social and occupational functioning. It is therefore difficult to understand why this 'deterioration' has been included in the correspondence rules for schizophrenia in DSM-III. If 'schizophrenia' is invariably associated with such phenomena, then it follows that, whenever it is inferred, 'deterioration' will invariably be found.

Spitzer *et al.* fail to clarify the problem. As before, they offer nothing more than their personal beliefs in relation to this validating criterion:

> Central to our concept of Schizophrenia is the notion that the disorder
> interferes with normal social and occupational functioning. Yet occasion-
> ally one encounters individuals with one or more of the characteristic
> schizophrenic symptoms, such as bizarre delusions of longstanding, with-
> out any apparent disruption of their functioning. We believe that in such
> problematic cases the diagnosis of Atypical Psychosis is preferable.
>
> (1978: 493)

It must be said that this use of 'deterioration in social and occupational functioning' as a validating criterion is unique in the history of medicine and it is not difficult to see why. Negatively valued changes in these areas, which is presumably what DSM-III means by 'deterioration', are common to so many physical and behavioural problems, and may be the product of so many idiosyncratic factors, such as the level of skill needed for an occupation or the presence of a supportive partner, as to be useless as indicators of whether any of the problems co-occur above chance. Where such changes are found in association with a cluster of behaviour, they may be a result of just one of the behaviours in the cluster or the result of the simple accumulation of independent problems. To these difficulties with the criterion has to be added that of reliably describing this 'deterioration', free of value judgements as to how people *should* behave in their working and social lives.

DSM-III's correspondence rules for schizophrenia – an overview

Relatively little attention has been paid here to the considerable methodological problems of the research quoted in DSM-III in support of its criteria for inferring schizophrenia. This is for two reasons. First, the authors of DSM-III have ignored most of them and the discussion here has sought simply to compare its conclusions with the available data, whatever its merits, in order to indicate that even these do not allow the conclusions. Second, to have concentrated on methodological issues might have created the false impression that DSM-III's authors simply needed to find or commission 'better' research. This might have distracted attention from the three major issues raised by the development of diagnostic criteria for schizophrenia – the inappropriateness of the task, the question-begging approach used and the use of inappropriate criteria to assign meaningfulness to a cluster of behaviour.

It is clear that DSM-III's authors have tried to create an impression of similarity between their work and that of medical and other scientists. They have suggested that certain phenomena co-occur above chance because their co-occurrence is reliably associated with other events – family history, age of onset, tendency to recurrence, treatment response, deterioration in social and occupational functioning. In doing so, however, they have ignored the fact that they have worked in a direction, from construct to correspondence rules, opposite to that of the researchers they have sought to imitate *and* that they have used inappropriate criteria to impute meaningfulness. They have also argued, in a circular fashion, that DSM-III's concept of schizophrenia is valid in terms of some of the phenomena from which it is inferred. In addition, with the exception of deterioration in social and occupational functioning, not one of the events said to be reliably associated with schizophrenia can be measured *independently of the cluster from which schizophrenia is inferred*. The use of each of these criteria therefore implies that a valid set of correspondence rules already exists for the construct, otherwise it is nonsensical to talk of family history (of schizophrenia), age of onset (of schizophrenia), and so on. But it is axiomatic that in any attempt to demonstrate that a set of phenomena co-occur above chance, the cluster, and the event(s) said to be reliably associated with it, must be capable of being measured independently. Medical researchers do, of course, investigate family resemblance, 'prognosis', and so on, but do so *after* a pattern has been observed and in order to elaborate a construct's theoretical network. The question arises, of course, of why DSM-III's authors used inappropriate criteria to impute meaningfulness. The answer, presumably, is that had they adopted appropriate criteria, they would have been forced to the conclusion that no set of regularities which would justify inferring schizophrenia had ever been observed. An appropriate criterion in this case would have been the reliable observation of an association between a cluster of behaviours and a reliably observable biological event or process which was thought to be an antecedent.

A syndrome?

It was pointed out in Chapter 1 that the term schizophrenia is said to refer to a syndrome. This usage is also adopted by DSM-III. It is clear that DSM-III's correspondence rules for schizophrenia do not refer to such a pattern. There is no event included in them which can claim the status of a sign. Alpert (1985) has suggested that diagnosticians should give more weight to those events which can be reliably observed in the cluster from which schizophrenia is inferred; these, he has suggested, should be called signs. It is, of course, true that in medicine, signs are, by definition, events which can be reliably observed. Alpert, however, is also suggesting that whichever of DSM-III's criteria can be reliably observed should be called signs of schizophrenia. In doing so, he is ignoring the important fact that the second part of the requirements for a sign, used in this sense, is that it be reliably associated with whatever events are called symptoms in such a way as to support the assumption that the whole cluster forms a pattern. It is not sufficient to take, as Alpert has done, a suggested cluster like DSM-III's for which this demonstration has not been made, and arbitrarily choose to label as signs whichever of its constituents clinicians can be trained to reach agreement about. It might as well be suggested to diagnosticians that they should give more weight to someone's height or weight, both of which can be reliably measured, in making a diagnosis of schizophrenia. If the analogy seems absurd, it is only because of the strong *a priori* belief that certain phenomena, which do not happen to include height or weight, are symptoms of schizophrenia.

Finally, two more aspects of DSM-III should be mentioned here – its description of 'subtypes of schizophrenia' and its use of 'multi-axial classification'. These are apparently seen as attempts to improve the classification system and to describe those to whom it is applied in more useful ways. But both of these 'improvements' are dependent on the assumption that the 'overall' correspondence rules for schizophrenia refer to a meaningful pattern. Thus, the grouping of this supposed pattern into subtypes is an attempt to specify patterns within the larger pattern, while multi-axial classification groups people simultaneously on several axes, the major one of which, in DSM-III, is the diagnosis. If, as appears to be the case, no larger pattern has been observed, and, therefore, no diagnosis can be made, then it is meaningless to talk either of subtypes or of DSM-III's type of multi-axial classification. Given the lack of evidence that those called schizophrenic share important features, it is not surprising that Stephens (1978) should conclude that the subdivision of schizophrenia into various subtypes had not proved particularly useful.

DSM-IIIR

In 1987, the APA published a revision of DSM-III based on the consensus or majority vote of various committees over the previous three or four years. The criteria for inferring schizophrenia underwent a few minor changes for which no clear justification is offered. For example, it is no longer required that "major depressive or manic syndrome", if present, should have developed after any "psychotic symptoms", merely that "the total duration of all episodes of a mood syndrome has been brief relative to the total duration of the active and residual phases of the [schizophrenic disturbance]" (194). The only major change is, apparently, the deletion of the age criterion, i.e. the diagnosis of schizophrenia can now be applied to people whose behaviour changes after the age of 45. It is noted that the proposal to change this criterion "came from a review of several studies in which that distinction was found to lack validity" (p. xx). It is unfortunate that no references are cited, given that the review here suggests that DSM-III's authors were selective in their research reviews, that they misrepresented some of the research they did review and that they used highly questionable criteria for making decisions about validity.

'Schizophrenia's' theoretical network

Three main conclusions have been drawn in the discussion here. First, before the publication of DSM-III in 1980, there was no officially agreed set of correspondence rules for inferring schizophrenia. Second, the responses to this state of affairs – a call to 'find' correspondence rules and the appointing of committees to do so – were inappropriate and incompatible with claims to scientific status for 'schizophrenia'. Third, the official criteria suggested for inferring schizophrenia in DSM-III and DSM-IIIR do not denote a set of regularities which would justify inferring any hypothetical construct.

It was emphasised in Chapter 1, however, that correspondence rules which denote a set of regularities are a prerequisite, a necessary condition, for examining the fate of predictions from a construct and, therefore, for developing its theoretical network. But if the conclusions drawn here are valid, then it is extremely difficult to understand how a construct without, so to speak, this benefit could have developed the kind of rich theoretical network said to surround 'schizophrenia' (for example, Neale and Oltmanns, 1980; Gottesman and Shields, 1982; Cutting, 1985). Central to this network is the claim that schizophrenia has a genetic basis – in other words, that the construct has enabled researchers to make predictions and to gather supporting data which imply genetic antecedents of a particular cluster of behaviour. Kety (1974), for example, has asserted that "If schizophrenia is a myth, then it is a myth with a large genetic component" (961). Kendell (1975b) has claimed that there is "incontrovertible evidence that genetic factors are involved in the transmission of [schizophrenic illness]" (185). Neale and Oltmanns (1980) believe that "The genetic literature certainly provides the most solid information available concerning the etiology of schizophrenia" (458); DSM-III states that "genetic factors have been proven to be involved in the development of [schizophrenia]" (186); while an editorial in the *Lancet* (14 January 1989) declares that "An impressive body of evidence ... suggests that inheritance plays an important part [in schizophrenia]" (79). This paradox – of a construct without, apparently, an empirical base, nevertheless being surrounded by a strong theoretical network – will be examined in the next chapter.

Chapter six

Genetic research

✳ It is interesting to note that before any empirical literature existed, the belief that 'schizophrenia' or 'dementia praecox' had a genetic basis was apparently strong. Kraepelin (1899) claimed, without providing any data, or even indicating how he had researched the question, that "An inherited predisposition to mental disturbances was apparent in approximately seventy per cent of those cases in which data could be evaluated" (203). Some clues as to what these data might have been were provided by Kraepelin's comment that "Bodily signs of degeneracy were often found – a small or deformed skull, childlike appearance, defective teeth, misshapen ears, strabismus, massess of warts on the chest, general feebleness and indications of an easily excited brain" (203). Bleuler shared Kraepelin's beliefs, and his lack of data:

✳ if an adherent of an "infectious theory" of this disease should choose to say that there is no hereditary factor in schizophrenia but merely an infection from some common source ... we would be unable to produce any proof to the contrary. Such skeptics could observe that in many cases, · even after the most thorough study, no evidence of any hereditary *anlage* and no individual predisposition has ever been proven. And yet heredity does play its role in the etiology of schizophrenia.

(1950: 337)

Thus, before any attempt at systematic data collection was ever made, the two ✳ most prominent users of the concepts of dementia praecox and schizophrenia were disseminating the view that whatever phenomena they included under these terms were largely inherited.

✳ The subsequent empirical genetic literature to which Neale and Oltmanns referred can be divided into two parts. The first consists of studies of unseparated families; of particular interest here is a series of twin studies in which the prevalence of schizophrenia diagnoses in the monozygotic and dizygotic co-twins of 'schizophrenics' has been examined. The second set of studies is usually referred to as the adoption studies. Their major aim was to study the prevalence of schizophrenia diagnoses in the biological relatives of adopted children who had been diagnosed as schizophrenic and in the 'adopted away' children of 'schizophrenic' mothers.

Twin studies

Although, as will be seen, a variety of methods has been used to study 'schizophrenics' and their twins, the aim of all studies is to locate a reasonable number of people diagnosed as schizophrenic and who are also members of a ✱ twin pair. The zygosity of the twin pairs is then investigated and the prevalence of 'schizophrenia' in identical and same-sex fraternal co-twins is examined. It is assumed that monozygotic (MZ) twins are genetically identical and that dizygotic (DZ) twins, like siblings, share, on average, half their genes. It is apparently taken for granted (Gottesman and Shields, 1972, 1982) that, if the prevalence of schizophrenia diagnoses is significantly different in the MZ and DZ co-twins and if no plausible environmental factors are suggested to explain this, then we can assume that genetic factors are important in schizophrenia. The extent to which a group of MZ and DZ twins resemble ✱ each other in terms of diagnoses of schizophrenia is usually expressed by a concordance rate. There are a number of ways of calculating and interpreting these rates which will be discussed in more detail later. Table 6.1 presents rates derived from a number of twin studies using what is usually known as pairwise concordance. This rate expresses the proportion of the MZ or DZ group in which both twins have received a diagnosis of schizophrenia (or probable schizophrenia or schizoaffective disorder, and so on, depending on the diagnostic criteria used). It is, in fact, virtually impossible to present the results of twin studies in tabular form without giving a misleading impression of what actually went on. Table 6.1, however, simply presents the pairwise concordance rates reported by researchers using broad criteria for inferring schizophrenia or probable schizophrenia.

The question of interest here is how this disparate set of results, from ✱

Table 6.1 Reported pairwise concordance rates from some earlier and later twin studies using broad diagnostic criteria

Author	Date	MZ rate (%)	DZ rate (%)
Luxenburger	1928	58	0
Rosanoff et al.	1934	61	13
Essen-Möller	1941	71	17
Kallmann	1946	69	11
Slater	1953	65	14
Kringlen	1966	38	10
Allen et al.	1972	27	5
Gottesman and Shields	1972	50	19
Hoffer and Pollin	1970	14	4
Fischer	1973	48	20
Tienari	1975	15	7.5

studies with, as will be seen, considerable methodological and conceptual problems, has come to be presented as part of the "incontrovertible evidence" that schizophrenia has a genetic basis. Clearly, in order to support this view two points must be argued: first, that the data can be interpreted as support for a genetic view rather than being interpretable in other ways; and second, that the results are consistent across studies and thus lead to similar and reliable conclusions. The methods by which writers on this topic have succeeded in drawing from twin data conclusions which support the genetic hypothesis can be roughly divided into two types. The first involves ignoring or underemphasising serious methodological and conceptual problems which cast doubt on the validity of the data. The second involves presenting, or re-presenting data in such a way as apparently to achieve some conformity to genetic theory and to give an impression of consistency across studies. The two types of method are not, of course, independent: it is in part by ignoring methodological and conceptual problems that the data can be made to seem consistent.

Methodological and conceptual problems

The type of study which will be reviewed here is usually conducted over a number of years and can be divided into several stages. First, the sampling frame is selected, i.e. the geographical and residential confines within which the 'schizophrenic' twins will be sought. Second, when this group has been selected, efforts are made to trace their co-twins. Third, the twins' zygosity is investigated. Fourth (or concurrently), information is collected from the twins themselves and from other sources, and diagnoses are made. Fifth, concordance rates are calculated and interpreted. Problems can – and do – arise at any or all of these stages.

Sample selection

Subjects initially selected for study are usually called probands or index cases. They must satisfy two criteria: they must conform to the researchers' idea of a schizophrenic and they must be a twin. Rosenthal (1962a) has discussed some of the problems which might arise in trying to find subjects who belong to both of these relatively infrequent groups. Because many twin studies used hospitalised samples, then only those who had come to psychiatric attention could become probands. It is not unreasonable to suppose that two people whose behaviour is disturbing are more noticeable, and more of a burden to their family, than is one and that one or both are more likely to be admitted to hospital. Thus, the use of a hospitalised population may result in an excess of concordant pairs. Leonhard (1980) has suggested that both twins are more likely to be admitted in a concordant MZ than in a DZ pair, thus spuriously heightening the MZ concordance rate of a hospitalised sample. Of course, once admitted, MZ twins are extremely striking, so that some early twin-researchers' practice of asking staff to help identify twins for study would exacerbate this bias.

Kringlen (1976:430) has clearly demonstrated another way in which concordance rates may be inflated by the use of hospitalised subjects and, in particular, by the use of a small and unrepresentative sampling frame. His argument runs as follows:

If the probability of being hospitalised and reported to a twin researcher is 80 per cent, and members of a concordant pair are admitted and reported independently, then the probability of being included in the sample = 0.8 for a discordant pair.

For a concordant pair, p = 0.96 (the probability that either of two outcomes will occur = the sum of their independent probabilities minus the probability that both will occur together).

If the probability of being hospitalised and reported = 50 per cent (i.e. the sampling frame is smaller) then:

p (discordant pair)   = 0.5
p (concordant pair)   = 0.75

If the sampling frame is reduced further, and the probability of being hospitalised and reported = 10 per cent, then:

p (discordant pair)   = 0.1
p (concordant pair)   = 0.2

Thus, with a very small sampling frame, using hospitalised subjects, the probability of concordant pairs being reported may be double that of discordant pairs. This bias should, of course, influence both MZ and DZ pairs unless, as Leonhard has suggested, concordant MZ pairs are more likely to be admitted or more likely to be noticed by hospital staff.

The later studies listed in Table 6.1, with the exception of that of Gottesman and Shields, have avoided some sampling biases by using a national twin register. Unfortunately, comprehensive registers exist only in Scandinavian countries but they have enabled researchers to conduct twin studies with more representative samples than was ever the case with the older twin studies. Hoffer and Pollin's US study also began with a twin register – that of the National Academy of Science/National Research Council's Panel of all Veteran twins. Some of these later studies have cross-referenced twin registers with records of psychiatric hospitalisation (again, central registers exist only in Scandinavian countries).

Zygosity determination

Having chosen a proband sample and traced their partners, it is relatively easy to decide whether a same-sex pair is fraternal; it is much more difficult to know if they are identical. Even reports that the twins shared one chorion (the membrane surrounding the foetus) cannot be taken as strong evidence of identity; it appears that some pairs, which by other criteria are obviously fraternal, were monochorionic (Tienari, 1963). Similarly, a number of apparently MZ pairs were reportedly dichorial (Price, 1950). It is, however, generally agreed (see, for example, Tienari, 1963; Fischer, 1973) that identity can be established with a satisfactorily high probability by comparing twins on eight or nine serological systems. (This method may be superseded by the introduction of DNA matching.) It is notable that none of the twin studies listed here applied the serological-systems technique to all twins eventually called MZ, and some did not employ it at all. In the early studies, for example Luxenburger's, as Kringlen (1966) has pointed out, decisions as to zygosity were often made only by supposed similarity of appearance. Kallmann also appears to have used this method: he claimed that zygosity was decided by personal investigation and by extended observation by the author. Essen-Möller (1941) also used personal examination supplemented "if possible" by blood groupings and fingerprinting.

It is not difficult to see how such methods could lead to inaccurate conclusions. Researchers' judgements as to similarity of appearance may have been influenced by personal biases, not the least of which was their opinion about diagnoses and knowledge of whether one or both twins had been hospitalised. If twins were not seen simultaneously then judgements might have been influenced by poor or biased memory of the first twin's appearance. In MZ pairs where only one twin had been hospitalised, the appearance of the pair may have become dissimilar. Thus, discordant MZ pairs might have been judged to be DZ, and the MZ concordance rate inflated.

Personal observation was often supplemented or replaced by questioning twins' relatives about confusion of identity, similarity of appearance, and so on. Hoffer and Pollin made extensive use of this method and themselves presented data which query its accuracy. They noted that in a number of cases only one twin of a pair returned the questionnaire and commented that when this was the schizophrenic twin, a much higher number claimed to be monozygotic than when the non-schizophrenic co-twin answered. And when other relatives were asked about twins, it is not unreasonable to suppose that similarity or dissimilarity in behaviour might have led to over- or underestimations of similarity in appearance.

Slater (1953) made extensive use of the similarity method. He also, however, took fingerprints from 62 per cent of pairs eventually called MZ, but reported that he used a method of quantifying similarity which had never been used before and whose accuracy was therefore unknown. The only evidence he produced as to its accuracy was data demonstrating greater print similarity within MZ than DZ pairs but where similarity scores had already been used as one of the criteria for the zygosity decision. Slater did provide more, albeit sparse, detail than did the authors of some of the other older twin studies, about the information on which zygosity decisions were based. Rather than reassuring the reader, the information in fact emphasises the apparent arbitrariness of some decisions and the fact that they may have been influenced by knowledge of diagnoses. All of the subjects described below were included by Slater, and by those who have reported his study, in the concordant MZ group:

> The family told them apart by a difference about the eyes, but they were often mistaken by others....It was not possible for me to make contact with M owing to family obstruction....In hospital records, M's eyes are recorded as hazel, C's as blue but no great reliance can be placed on this and it does not appear that any direct physical comparison between the twins was made. Their past history strongly suggests uniovularity. Their psychotic states bear many resemblances....
>
> (150–1)

> They were not mistaken at school as L was fatter and not clever.... M says she is the taller by 1 or 2 inches....Despite the history of no close resemblance, either physically or in personality in early years, there can be little doubt that these twins are uniovular. Both have paranoid illnesses coming on at the time of the menopause and within two years of one another, and with many clinical resemblances.
>
> (127–9)

> A photograph taken of the twins at about fourteen shows close but not startling facial resemblance. P's hair looks rather darker.
>
> (144)

The use of blood and serological testing is more common in recent twin studies but, in spite of the importance of accurate zygosity determination, it has never been extended to whole samples. Fischer used these tests in only 39 per cent of pairs, Gottesman and Shields in 50 per cent and Kringlen in 71 per cent. Tienari used them in all but one of the pairs eventually called MZ. The problem of establishing zygosity is confounded by the fact that subjects included in a research sample may actually be dead at the time the research is carried out. For example, 43 per cent of Fischer's sample were dead; one partner was already dead in 27 per cent of Slater's MZ group; 29 per cent of Kringlen's sample had either died, left the country, could not be traced or refused to co-operate in zygosity determination; 15 per cent of Kallmann's sample were dead while Hoffer and Pollin reported that 1.5 per cent of their sample had committed suicide, but not how many had died from other causes.

Collecting information about the twins

The ways in which data have been collected by twin researchers have at times

123

been as haphazard and incomplete as the methods used to determine zygosity. The methods used have included talking to twins and their relatives (sometimes for only short periods and sometimes only after considerable pressure had been exerted on the reluctant), searching case records and asking questions of family doctors, relatives or even family friends. Each of these methods could clearly result in inaccurate reporting whether through biases or problems in recall. There is, moreover, no twin study in which those who collected the information were definitely blind as to the twins' possible zygosity or to the diagnoses of the proband subjects. Nor are there any reports of the reliability or accuracy of the information. There is by now sufficient evidence available on the biases which operate when we make dispositional judgements about others (see, for example, Mischel, 1968; Ross, 1977; Shweder, 1977; Jones, 1979; Kahneman *et al.*, 1982) to cast considerable doubt on the usefulness of information collected in these ways. (And it must be emphasised that in spite of the medical and pseudo-scientific language in which these studies tend to be reported, they are all concerned with making dispositional judgements.) It is remarkable that even modern twin researchers have shown so little apparent knowledge of or interest in these problems. The methods used by twin researchers to obtain information, and the problems they present, can perhaps best be illustrated by quoting from the accounts which some of them have provided and which, apparently, contain the total amount of information on which a diagnosis was based:

> X (co-twin) replied to an enquiry, but he died before a follow-up examination could be made. He stated that he was well. A friend of the family related that X was "eccentric", living entirely alone in a small house, but no further details were known.
> (Fischer, 1973: 123; diagnosis: nervous, odd, neurotic or
> ?normal; MZ group)

> [Co-twin] had no psychiatric history. Family unwilling for him to be contacted ... neither twin was seen by us.
> (Gottesman and Shields, 1972: 140; diagnosis: normal; DZ group)

> [Co-twin] refused to be seen for the Twin Investigation, remaining upstairs out of sight, but his wife was seen at the door and an MMPI [Minnesota Multiphasic Personality Inventory] form left for B. He did not consider completing the MMPI and his wife reported, "... once his mind is made up, nothing will make him change". He was regarded as a healthy, level headed, solid, happy person who got on well with others, had few close friends and was something of a home bird.
> (Gottesman and Shields, 1972: 170; diagnosis: normal; DZ group)

> [Co-twin] had a nervous breakdown at 27 in which she could not concentrate and could not work. She is said to have had periods of confusion and to have thought she would go mad. She did not have any hospital

treatment ... after the birth of her third child in 1938 her husband ... was killed in an accident. D developed mental symptoms and was transferred to a mental hospital in the West Country which it has proved impossible to trace....She was seen again (by a psychiatric social worker) for a few minutes in 1948, when she refused all information. She spoke of the past with little feeling. She said she suffered badly with her nerves, but would not say more about them than that she felt so tired. She seemed withdrawn and apprehensive.

(Slater, 1953: 135, 136; diagnosis: psychosis/?schizophrenia; MZ group)

About 20 [co-twin] started to lie late in bed in the mornings and was so often late at the office that he was eventually fired.... He joined the army as a private, went to India and about 3 years later his uncle heard that he had committed suicide, by swallowing poison. No other details were provided by the authorities but some unposted letters found at his death were returned to the family and showed no suicidal intention or possible reason for such an act.

(Slater, 1953: 143; diagnosis: ?schizophrenic; MZ group)

Making a diagnosis

It is worth noting that no twin researcher apparently doubts the validity of the concept of schizophrenia. Certainly, a naive reader of the studies, and reports of them, would receive the impression that neither the concept nor the business of inferring it presented any serious problems. There are occasional references to validity (for example, Gottesman and Shields, 1972, 1982) or to low reliability (for example, Fischer, 1973), but the implications are not pursued. In fact, it is difficult to know if any two twin studies have used the same diagnostic criteria. Indeed, many of the studies listed here did not even state what criteria were used. Slater, for example, simply reported that "Our material divides itself conventionally into four main diagnostic groups. By far the largest of these is formed by the schizophrenic psychoses" (33). In those studies which did provide criteria, they are so vague as to make it impossible to know what specific phenomena were used to infer schizophrenia. Fischer (1973), for example, stated that:

The criteria used were: A psychiatric disorder with disintegration of personality and affect, associated with impaired relation to reality, disturbance of thought, hallucinations and/or delusions. There should be no clouding of consciousness, no marked disturbance of mood and no major signs or symptoms of organic defects.

(11)

Kallmann did not provide any diagnostic criteria in his 1946 paper, but did so elsewhere:

our diagnosis of schizophrenia rested on the constellative evaluation of basic personality changes observed in association with a whole group of possible psychopathological mechanisms, rather than on the presence of any particular type of symptomatology. As a general principle, greater diagnostic importance was attached to the demonstrable effect of a "bending" curve of personality development than to any surface similarities to pathognomic textbook descriptions, especially when this bend was found in conjunction with such malignant features as xenophobic pananxiety, loss of capacity for free-association, inability to maintain contact with reality (autistic and dereistic attitude towards life), or a compulsive tendency to omnipotential thought generalisations.

(1950; Kringlen, 1964: 22)

With such non-specific, or with no stated, criteria, it might be supposed that researchers would at least report on the reliability of their inferences. Reliability has, in fact, been fully reported in only one study, that of Gottesman and Shields (1972). This study differs from the others in having had diagnoses made by a panel of six judges, from written material. The judges were asked "to apply his personal criteria in his own way" (211). Of those subjects eventually called schizophrenic by consensus, 66 per cent had been independently called this by six judges and 90 per cent by five or six. The problem is compounded by the fact that in many twin studies, diagnoses were made by the researchers who had themselves collected the sometimes extremely limited information on which they were based, and who apparently knew of, or at least suspected, the twins' supposed zygosity. Even in those studies where zygosity judgements were made quite independently of the researchers, it is difficult to believe that in the course of collecting information, the researchers did not pick up strong clues as to zygosity. In two studies – Gottesman and Shields' (1972) and Hoffer and Pollin's – diagnoses were made independently. In Gottesman and Shields' study, however, the written material on which judgements were based was prepared by the authors, who reported that "Of course, when we prepared the summaries, we knew about both twins and tried to do justice to both similarities and differences" (210). It can only be assumed here that they were referring to zygosity, as well as to other details; certainly, they did not reassure readers to the contrary. Given that Gottesman and Shields' bias in favour of genetic explanations of twin data is so strong as to invite comment even from a fellow twin researcher (Kringlen, 1976), it is difficult completely to share their confidence. In Hoffer and Pollin's study, diagnoses were made by a variety of army doctors. There is, however, no way of knowing to what extent they were aware of whether their patients' MZ or DZ twins had also been diagnosed as schizophrenic. In the later extension of this research (Allen et al., 1972), these diagnoses were accepted or rejected by the authors after examination of case material. Unfortunately, the case material was arranged in twin pairs and included details of assumed zygosity.

Once diagnoses, however problematic, have been made, it is a relatively simple matter to calculate the concordance rates which are generally presented as data in primary and secondary sources. As will be seen in the next section, however, the ways in which these data have been calculated and reported have served to obscure the considerable methodological and conceptual problems presented by the twin studies.

The presentation of twin studies and their data

It is clear that the inadequacies both of the concept of schizophrenia and twin researchers' methods make the conversion of their subjective judgements into numerical data and the interpretation of such data very problematic. Nevertheless, the conversion and interpretation have both been achieved and in such a way as apparently to leave beyond doubt the fact that schizophrenia has a genetic basis. The two most prolific commentators on twin studies have been Irving Gottesman and James Shields. They have also produced the only textbook devoted to reviewing genetic research on 'schizophrenia'. Their comments will therefore be considered in some detail, along with those of the authors of a standard and extremely detailed academic text on 'schizophrenia'.

The uncritical road from judgements to numbers

Gottesman and Shields (1982) have presented the results of twin studies apparently as a series of straightforward 'findings', in two tables (here Tables 6.2 and 6.3). Indeed, they had earlier (1972) referred to some of these as forming part of a 'network of basic facts'. There is no detailed discussion of the problems described here, although they do mention some of them: Kallmann's concordance rates, for example, may have been "rather high" because he used a resident hospital population; it is reported that 35 per cent of Fischer's sample were dead; that Rosanoff's series was "obviously incomplete", and that

Table 6.2 Simple pairwise concordance in older schizophrenic twin series (reported by Gottesman and Shields, 1982)

Investigator	MZ pairs		SS DZ pairs	
	Total	% concordance	Total	% concordance
Luxenburger	19	58	13	0
Rosanoff	41	61	53	13
Essen-Möller	11	64	27	15
Kallmann	174	69	296	11
Slater	37	65	58	14
Inouye[a]	58	59	20	15
Total	340	65	467	12

Note: [a] Updated with 1972a final report and using schizophrenic plus schizophrenic-like psychotic disorders in co-twins.

Table 6.3 Concordances in newer schizophrenic twin series (reported by Gottesman and Shields, 1982)

Investigator/locus	MZ pairs			SS DZ pairs		
	Total	Pair-wise[b] % concordance	Proband-wise %	Total	Pair-wise[b] % concordance	Proband-wise %
Tienari[c]/Finland	17	0–36	35	20	5–14	13
Kringlen/Norway	55	25–38	45	90	4–10	15
Fischer/Denmark	21	24–48	56	41	10–19	27
Pollin et al.[c]/USA	95	14–27	43	125	4–8	9
Gottesman & Shields/UK	22	40–50	58	33	9–19	12
Weighted total			46			14

Notes:

[a] At the level of functional schizophrenic-like psychoses in co-twins.

[b] Value or range reported by investigators.

[c] Only male twins were studied. Results for 1971 tabled for Tienari because 1975 summary data adding 3 MZ and 22 DZ new pairs lack details; he reports MZ rate 15%, DZ 7%.

he made no personal investigations. In general, however, the problems are either overlooked or, in some cases, mentioned and then excused. Kallmann, apparently, laid himself open to criticism because he unfortunately never found the time to report the details of his study (Shields *et al.*, 1967). Similarly, it is admitted that methods of establishing zygosity often left much to be desired but, although Gottesman and Shields cannot possibly know, they have claimed that "[early researchers'] clinical judgements, when based on the simultaneous examination of both twins, were not likely to be much in error" (1972: 24). Unfortunately, they omitted to mention that even this crude method was not always used by early twin researchers.

Neale and Oltmanns (1980) have adopted a rather different approach and include a more detailed critique of the methodology of older twin studies. They concentrated, however, on sampling and zygosity determination and ignored the issues of information collection and the status of the concept of schizophrenia. And, like Gottesman and Shields, they are apparently willing to excuse Kallmann his methodological foibles (172). They are thus able to claim, wrongly, that the later studies offer significant methodological advances. There is no mention of the haphazard way in which information was collected and diagnoses made. Nor is there mention of the fact that the very restricted sampling frame employed by Gottesman and Shields may have heightened concordance rates. On the contrary, one of the reasons why Neale and Oltmanns' readers are urged to take more note of later twin studies is because of improvements in sampling techniques. Gottesman and Shields' study is then highlighted as being amongst the best of these later studies because it reported consensus diagnoses. The fact that its sampling technique was quite unlike that of the Scandinavian and American studies is not mentioned.

The search for consistency

Gottesman and Shields' major concern, like that of Neale and Oltmanns, appears to be with the creation of an impression of *consistent* support for genetic theories amongst the twin research data. It is, of course, important that such an impression be created if the research is to look credible. A consistent impression demands, first, that concordance rates for MZ twins be relatively high and obviously higher than those for DZ twins and, second, that the rates be roughly similar across studies. It seems obvious, however, that rates ranging from 69 per cent to zero are neither consistent nor always particularly high. The question of interest is therefore how Gottesman and Shields have presented the data in order that they should appear to support their conclusion. The methods discussed below, together with an examination of Tables 6.2 and 6.3, will show some of the ways in which this goal has been achieved.

The use of the 'schizophrenia spectrum'

Gottesman and Shields report two sets of pairwise rates obtained using narrow and broad criteria for inferring schizophrenia, i.e. less or more relaxed criteria for calling twins concordant. The use of broad criteria will tend to inflate concordance rates.

In some studies the inflation is apparently greater for MZ than for DZ pairs. Although this might be predicted by genetic theory, it is difficult to know to what extent it might be a function of more information being available about MZ co-twins, or more of them being seen, or more effort being expended in tracking them down. In most studies (Gottesman and Shields' is an exception), the use of broad criteria also accentuates the differences between MZ and DZ concordance rates so that, in a simplistic way, 'schizophrenia' may be made to 'look' more genetic. The extent to which concordance rates may be changed by broadening diagnostic criteria is shown in Table 6.4.

The use of broad criteria has been justified by the concept of the schizophrenia spectrum (Gottesman and Shields, 1972). This concept, in turn, has been justified by the claim that, although some relatives of schizophrenics have not behaved in such a way as to earn the label themselves, they nevertheless deviated from normality in ways that were more or less similar to the proband subjects. It is thus assumed that there is a spectrum of schizophrenic disorders and that those who are genetically related to a schizophrenic may show not full-blown schizophrenia but some lesser variant. At first glance, this argument may appear reasonable and, indeed, in principle, it is reasonable.

Table 6.4 Pairwise concordance rates for MZ twins using the authors' broad and narrow criteria

Author	Narrow criteria %	Broad criteria %
Essen-Möller (1941)	14	71
Tienari (1963)	0	19
Kringlen (1968)	27[a]	38[b]
Fischer (1973)	24	48

Notes:
[a] Based on "registered hospitalised cases".
[b] Based on "personal investigations".

Applied to 'schizophrenia', however, it has two major problems. First, there is, not surprisingly, no agreement about the referents of the spectrum. This means that there is no way of knowing just how similar – or dissimilar – are the twins who are called concordant. It also makes comparisons across studies, already a difficult task, virtually impossible. In their tables, Gottesman and Shields present a misleading picture of orderliness by implying that the figures are comparable across studies.

The second, more important, problem stems from the status of the parent concept of schizophrenia. The problem is perhaps best understood by drawing an analogy with the familiar concept of diabetes, particularly as this is a comparison favoured, in another context, by Gottesman and Shields. There have been a number of studies of concordance for diabetes in MZ and DZ twins (for example, Cerasi and Luft, 1967; Pyke *et al.*, 1970). These, however, have looked at concordance for signs and symptoms or for *signs* and not simply at concordance for loosely defined symptoms. If we found a twin pair where one had an abnormal response to a glucose-tolerance test, sugar in the urine, severe thirst, weight loss, tiredness, and so on, while the other had recently lost some weight or sometimes felt 'a bit tired', it would be absurd to call them concordant for diabetes in the absence of signs in the second twin and because weight loss and tiredness are so overdetermined. But this is exactly how twin researchers have proceeded but without, of course, the presence of any phenomena in the proband twin which would merit the term 'sign'. It will be recalled that the variable cluster from which schizophrenia is inferred contains no sign, but only a number of presumably overdetermined behaviours called symptoms and which have never been shown to be systematically related. To use another analogy, if we call a pair of twins who share one or two of these vague 'symptoms', concordant for schizophrenia, it is almost like calling concordant for cancer a pair of twins where both report that they sometimes get headaches or feel nauseous. There is, in fact, no exact analogy for the absurdities of the schizophrenia spectrum; the major point to be made is that it is impossible to have 'lesser varieties' of a non-existent pattern.

The error made by twin researchers is not simply that of confusing a pattern of signs and symptoms with an arbitrary cluster of supposed symptoms. They assume that, if a co-twin shows any similarity to the partner in the behaviours of interest, then the antecedents must be the same. They may, of course, be quite different and they have certainly not been systematically investigated by twin researchers. The behaviour of twin researchers who use the spectrum concept is, in fact, similar to that of medieval medical men who tried to group physical complaints in ignorance of their antecedents and who created classificatory chaos. It must be added that in 'schizophrenia' research the error is compounded because concordance is not judged by degree of similarity between twins but by the extent to which each twin independently satisfies the researchers' criteria for 'schizophrenia' or the 'schizophrenia spectrum'. Because these criteria are so broad and ill-defined, it is quite possible to call concordant a twin pair who have none of the behaviours of interest in common.

The presentation of concordance rates

Once diagnostic judgements have been made, then the pattern of concordance across pairs can be expressed in a number of ways. Until recently, the most popular way of expressing concordance was by the pairwise method. As was mentioned earlier, this expresses the percentage of pairs where both twins have received a schizophrenia or schizophrenia-spectrum diagnosis. More recently, however, Gottesman and Shields have shown a marked preference for concordance rates calculated in a different way – by the proband method; indeed, by 1982, they were talking of this as the "standard, appropriate" method (107), although it must be said that it is they who have set the standard and who have argued most volubly for its appropriateness.

The use of the term 'proband method' reflects the fact that it depends on counting not pairs but *probands*. Probands are those 'schizophrenic' twins found in the original search for subjects (i.e. independently) rather than during the later process of tracing co-twins (i.e. dependently). It is possible that some of these proband subjects, though found independently, will actually be each other's twins. If this were true of five pairs in a sample of thirty pairs, then the researcher would talk not of thirty probands and their co-twins but of thirty-five probands and their co-twins. Thus, the use of the pairwise and probandwise methods imply different questions: the pairwise method asks, In what proportion of pairs are both called schizophrenic?, while the probandwise method asks, In what proportion of probands is there a 'schizophrenic' co-twin? It is obvious that the use of the proband method will result in some subjects being counted twice, because if twin A and twin B are both found during the original search for subjects, then A will be said to be concordant

Table 6.5 Methods of calculating concordance in twin studies

Pairwise	Probandwise
100 pairs	100 pairs
30 with both 'schizophrenic'	30 with both 'schizophrenic' *but* 10 of the 30 'schizophrenic' co-twins found in the original search
Concordance = 30/100 = 30%	Concordance = 30 + 10/100 + 10 = 36.4%

with B and B with A, making, in effect, two concordant pairs. The way in which these rates are calculated is shown in Table 6.5.

Clearly, the probandwise rate will vary depending on the number of 'schizophrenics' who are found independently of their twins. At first glance, the use of a 'counting twice' method might appear suspect. It is, however, not so *provided certain sampling requirements are met and the appropriate conclusions are drawn*. If the sampling is exhaustive – if a researcher, in the original search for subjects, managed to trace every person in a very large population who was a twin and who fulfilled criteria for inferring schizophrenia, then it follows that every subject would have been located independently. If the researcher again produced 100 twin pairs, in thirty of whom both partners were called schizophrenic, then the probandwise concordance rate would be 30 + 30/100 + 30 = 46.1 per cent. This rate, however, equals what is known as the *casewise* rate, which is calculated in answer to the question, How many cases in the sample have a schizophrenic co-twin? In calculating this, every member of concordant pairs is counted twice – the term casewise reflects the fact that all 'cases of schizophrenia' are counted, regardless of how they were found. Thus, when all 'cases' are found independently, the probandwise and casewise rates are identical. Marshall and Pettitt (1985) have demonstrated that the casewise rate is in fact not an expression of concordance as the term is usually understood, but of the prevalence of the diagnosis of schizophrenia amongst the co-twins of 'schizophrenics'. It can thus only be compared meaningfully with the *population* prevalence of schizophrenia diagnoses.

If the pairwise rate expresses the proportion of concordant pairs and the casewise rate is comparable to a population statistic, where does this leave the probandwise rate as a measure of concordance? The simple answer is nowhere, or, as Marshall and Pettitt point out, as an arbitrary and uninterpretable figure somewhere between pairwise and casewise rates. Probandwise rates are arbitrary because they are completely dependent on the vagaries of sampling. Neale and Oltmanns (1980), following Slater and Cowie, have noted that the probandwise method is appropriate *"only if the probability of ascertaining an index case (proband) is independent of the condition of the co-twin*" (182; emphasis added). It is extremely unlikely that this condition could be met by any twin study of 'schizophrenia' or that it could ever be possible – short of investigating every twin in an exceptionally large population – to know whether it had been achieved. It is challenging credulity to suggest that, if both partners in an MZ twinship are behaving strangely, and one has been reported, then the other has no more chance of being noticed (and therefore ending up as an index case) than has a single person. Whether or not both twins are noticed may depend on such factors as the attitude and tolerance of the family, the curiosity of the psychiatrist, the age gap between the twins becoming deviant, the age at which one was reported and the geographical mobility of the population. These last two are important because twins living close together or even in the same house are surely both more likely to be reported than are twins who live far apart. It may be that any bias towards joint reporting is greater for MZ than for DZ twins in the same way that concordant MZ pairs may both be more likely to be admitted to hospital. Allen *et al.* (1967) have argued that probandwise rates can be used provided the twin sample is representative of a defined population. They have suggested that, if this condition is met, then the 'double ascertainment' of concordant pairs in a hospital sample will be balanced by pairs in which neither twin is ascertained as an index case. The problem with this argument is that it is virtually impossible to demonstrate that such a research sample *is* representative of the population of interest – in this case MZ and DZ twins where one or both are behaving strangely – because the parameters of the population are unknown. Certainly neither Gottesman and Shields nor Neale and Oltmanns, all of whom favour probandwise rates, have demonstrated that the twin samples discussed here are representative. It may be that Gottesman and Shields, like Neale and Oltmanns (188), believe that a sample is representative if its ratio of MZ to DZ pairs approximates the population rate. But this is not the only criteria which must be fulfilled here. It must also be shown that twin-study samples – many of whom are drawn from *hospital* populations – are the same samples which would result from a representative selection of the appropriate ratio of MZ and DZ pairs from the total population of all deviant twins whose behaviour – whether reported or not – might earn them the labels 'schizophrenia' or 'schizophreniform' or whatever.

It can be seen from Table 6.3 that probandwise rates are higher than pairwise rates in later twin studies; the use of probandwise rates will almost certainly inflate concordance rates. It is also not unreasonable to suggest that double ascertainment may be more probable for MZ than for DZ pairs because MZ pairs are more remarkable, because physical identity may heighten an impression of behavioural identity and because MZ twins may live closer together.

Selective criticism of low-rate studies

The two studies which have obtained the lowest pairwise rates are those by Tienari and by Hoffer and Pollin. These rates have been inflated by the use of the probandwise method but Gottesman and Shields have further altered the rates from these studies by the selective presentation of their data.

In 1975, in an extension of his 1963 study and using broad diagnostic criteria, Tienari reported an MZ pairwise concordance rate of 15 per cent. This low figure, however, does not appear in Gottesman and Shields' table because, they claim, the report lacks case details. To be fair, the results are mentioned in a footnote but it is curious that they were not tabled because studies whose (higher) rates *were* tabled also lack case detail. Kallmann (1946), for example, presented no case detail; Fischer reported information only for MZ twins and Slater only for concordant MZ pairs and for DZ pairs which he considered to be of special interest. Gottesman and Shields are also peculiarly critical of Tienari's sample, in claiming that his 1963 zero per cent concordance rate "[was] mitigated by the fact that some of the pairs seemed to us to be organic psychosis from the detailed case histories Tienari provided" (1982: 103). It is not clear why Tienari's research should be singled out in this way, given the haphazard and often unreported information on which other researchers based their diagnoses. In addition, Fischer mentioned clear organic problems in some of her sample and the fact that some cases had had head injuries; Allen *et al.* (1972) apparently included subjects with histories of chronic alcoholism, head injuries, febrile convulsions and tuberculosis, while Gottesman and Shields themselves admitted of one of their probands that "The role of organic factors in A's personality development and eventual somewhat atypical schizophrenia is unclear" (1972: 179). Nevertheless, A remained in the sample as part of a discordant DZ pair. Tienari's supposedly organic discordant MZ subjects were, however, omitted in Gottesman and Shields' presentation of the maximum pairwise concordance rate, and they later explicitly drew attention to the fact that Tienari's study had now been 'brought into the fold': "The possible use of some kind of age correction together with the probandwise method of calculating rates makes the Finnish study no longer so much of an odd-man-out in the literature" (1982: 105). Although Gottesman and Shields have not made this age correction, it is strange that they should even suggest it, given that they had earlier rejected the idea for Kallmann's data, that they have not suggested it for other studies and that Tienari's later figures were derived from a sample all of whom were 40 and over, thus virtually eliminating the need for any age correction. If, however, Gottesman and Shields wished to be consistent themselves, they could have applied age corrections to some older studies and compared Tienari's results with those. Had they done so, however, they would have been forced to compare Tienari's age-corrected (and probably little changed) 15 per cent with, for example, an age-corrected rate (however inappropriate) of 86 per cent for Kallmann and 76 per cent for Slater.

Gottesman and Shields' treatment of Hoffer and Pollin's study offers further support to the idea that they have tried to create an impression of consistency where none exists. Using a very large sampling frame, one of the largest samples in this research area and diagnoses made independently of the authors, Hoffer and Pollin reported a pairwise MZ concordance rate of 13.8 per cent. Two years later, Allen *et al.* (1972) reported a rate of 27 per cent obtained by presenting themselves with Hoffer and Pollin's case material *but arranged as twin pairs of known zygosity* and by widening diagnostic criteria. Clearly, these two studies, carried out in very different ways by different people, should have been presented separately. As can be seen from Table 6.3, however, Gottesman and Shields have presented them as one study by Pollin *et al.*. The way in which the data have been presented could create the impression that Hoffer and Pollin's 13.8 per cent was obtained using narrow criteria and Allen *et al.*'s (1972) using broad. But this was not the case. Hoffer and Pollin's sample had been diagnosed by military psychiatrists who apparently used the broad and rather vague criteria of DSM-I or DSM-II and it is impossible to know to what extent the rise to 27 per cent was a result of Allen *et al.*'s broad criteria or of their extremely flawed methodology. Nevertheless, Hoffer and Pollin's data have been effectively ignored, while Allen *et al.*'s were apparently used to calculate the probandwise rate. Gottesman and Shields merely commented that Allen *et al.*'s results are "not very different from other samples but quite different from the first reports of these data by the investigators" (1982: 101).

Although Gottesman and Shields have thus created some impression of consistent results across later studies, the problem remains of the discrepancies between the results of older and later studies. Gottesman and Shields have dealt with this partly by offering comparisons between the *pairwise rates* from older studies with the *probandwise* rates from the later work and declaring them to be similar. They did not offer the appropriate (from their point of view) comparisons between the *probandwise* rates of earlier and later studies. This is curious because not only are pairwise and probandwise comparisons meaningless even within their framework, but they have, in another context (Shields *et al.*, 1967), provided estimated figures which easily allow the calculation of a likely probandwise rate from Kallmann's data: for his MZ twins, the figure is around 77 per cent, which is hardly consistent with their figure of 35 per cent for Tienari's study or 43 per cent for Allen *et al.*'s. Instead, having compared pairwise and probandwise rates, they reached the conclusion that:

> Allowing as we have for the small sample sizes in some of the twin
> studies and for certain key dimensions, many of the alleged discrepancies
> among all twin studies are attenuated. We feel quite comfortable in con-

cluding that the twin studies of schizophrenia as a whole represent variations on the same theme and are, in effect, sound replications of the same experiment.

(1982: 115)

This conclusion appears to have been reached by three simple devices: first, by the use of probandwise rates for the later studies which both inflated concordance rates and possibly attenuated the presumed effects of improved sampling; second, by the comparison of pairwise with probandwise rates; and third, by the claim that these consistent results must be taken note of because the newer data, which replicate the old, were obtained using improved sampling techniques. (Incidentally, as far as can be seen, Gottesman and Shields have made no allowances for small sample sizes. And, since the highest and lowest pairwise rates come from the two largest samples – Kallmann's and Hoffer and Pollin's – it is difficult to know what allowances could be made.)

Interpreting the results of twin studies

It is assumed, virtually without question (see, for example, Kendell, 1975b; Clare, 1976; Wing, 1978b; Neale and Oltmanns, 1980; Strauss and Carpenter, 1981), that the twin studies reported here support the idea that schizophrenia has a strong genetic component. Obviously, this conclusion is partly based on a disregard for the considerable conceptual and methodological problems discussed here. It is also based, however, on the assumption that any difference in the concordance rates between MZ and DZ twins must be explained by invoking genes. It is apparently assumed, in other words, that the environments of MZ twins are, on average, no more similar than are those of DZ twins. Gottesman and Shields, for example, have commented that: "MZ and DZ co-twins of schizophrenic probands *despite sharing virtually the same ecology with their twin siblings...*" (1972: 9; emphasis added). But not only is there no evidence to suggest that MZ and DZ twins are usually exposed to highly similar environments, there are good reasons to suggest that they are not. Any greater similarity in the environments of MZ pairs may be the result of many factors but two of the more important are likely to be the greater amount of time they apparently spend together (Rose *et al.*, 1984) and their striking physical similarity; indeed, they may have their identity fostered by being dressed alike. There is abundant evidence that appearance is an important factor in impression formation (Berscheid and Walster, 1978). When we add to this the fact that MZ twins are frequently mistaken for each other, it becomes highly likely that they will be 'behaved towards' in very similar ways by others. Sarbin and Mancuso (1980) have highlighted one aspect of this process. They point to the strong evidence that the age at which boys reach puberty is an important determinant of when and whether they are seen as leaders. Boys who mature early are apparently more likely to be seen as behaving like adult males and to be given more responsible tasks, and assigned more authority, by their peers. Because MZ twins reach puberty at roughly similar times, this series of roles and expectations is likely to be more similar for them than for DZ twins. By contrast, Gottesman and Shields appear to see 'the environment' as being rather like the decor – something that is there and reacted to, rather than a complex series of interactions.

An afterword on the twin-studies' population

It was suggested in Chapter 3 that Kraepelin's and Bleuler's descriptions of 'cases of dementia praecox/schizophrenia' were often virtually identical to von Economo's later descriptions of 'encephalitis lethargica' and its Parkinsonian sequalae. It was also suggested that there followed considerable diagnostic confusion, not least because of the erroneous assumption that 'schizophrenia' had been described as a separate and valid pattern. It can reasonably be suggested that this confusion is reflected in the data provided by twin researchers, i.e. that at least some of their subjects were undiagnosed cases of encephalitic infection, for two reasons. The first is that the vast majority of subjects in these studies lived at a time when 'encephalitis lethargica' and other infectious diseases were, apparently, much more common than is the case today; indeed a great many subjects lived through the great European epidemic of encephalitis lethargica: all but two of those for whom Slater (1953) and Fischer (1973) give birth dates, for example, were born before the epidemic began in 1916–17; the remaining two were born during it. The second, and more direct reason is that parts of many subject descriptions show a strong similarity to von Economo's and little resemblance to modern descriptions of 'schizophrenia'. The descriptions of Slater, Gottesman and Shields, and Fischer, for example, contain references to phenomena said by von Economo to be the result of infection. These include jerky movements of the limbs, dramatic weight changes, sleep disorders, profuse sweating, cyanosis of the extremities, convulsions, 'attacks' of total rigidity, chronic constipation, difficulties in swallowing, peculiarities of gait, tics and facial twitches. In addition, many of Slater's and Fischer's samples, and some of Gottesman and Shields', are described as slipping into stuporous or semi-stuporous states from which they might sometimes 'awake' only to indulge in 'maniacal' behaviour such as screaming, howling, running, and so on. Again, these descriptions are similar to von Economo's. It is interesting to note that Slater occasionally appears to have used the virtually identical motor and other physical phenomena shown by some twin pairs (including, in one pair, cyanosis of the extremities) to support his more uncertain judgements of monozygosity. He also mentions one case in which a shuffling gait and (unspecified) ocular symptoms suggested a diagnosis of post-encephalitic Parkinsonism. This, however, was apparently rejected in favour of schizophrenia because tremor and other (unspecified) ocular neurological signs were absent. Sacks (1982), however, has pointed out that tremor was very often absent as a sequelae to the infection while von Economo commented on the variability of ocular disturbances.

Although the likelihood seems high, it is, of course, impossible in retrospect to know whether many of these subjects should have received diagnoses of post-encephalitic Parkinsonism, or of some other organic disorder. But whatever the antecedents of the phenomena described in twin studies, their methodological and conceptual problems remain.

Adoption studies

Although twin researchers have apparently been reluctant to draw attention to the fact, it is obvious that in studies of unseparated families the genetic endowment and, in part, the rearing environment are provided by the same people. It was in an attempt to avoid this problem that Kety, Rosenthal and their colleagues designed what have become known as the adoption studies. Kety et al. (1976) have claimed that:

> Studies of adopted individuals and their biological and adoptive families offer a means of disentangling the genetic and environmental contribution to a disorder such as schizophrenia and permit an examination of the effects of one type of influence while the other is randomized or controlled.
>
> (1976: 413)

(As with twin studies, the complexities of the nature/nurture debate and the naivety of assuming that it is ever possible to disentangle the effects of genes and environment on behaviour are not issues here. What is of interest, again, is how these studies have come to be seen as supporting the view that schizophrenia has a genetic basis.)

The claims made for the adoption studies are, if anything, even stronger than are those made for twin studies. Gottesman and Shields (1976), for example, have called them "the straw that broke the environmentalist's back" (402). Neale and Oltmanns (1980) claimed that they "[have] provided almost irrefutable confirmation of the importance of genetic factors" (142) while Revely and Murray (1980) have called their methodology exemplary.

The adoption studies have been designed in three ways. First, there is a series where the focus of interest is the biological and adoptive relatives of a group of adoptees who had been diagnosed schizophrenic; second, a series where the focus was on the adopted-away children of mothers who had been diagnosed schizophrenic; and third, a study of the adopted children of 'normal' mothers but one of whose adoptive parents had been diagnosed schizophrenic. This last type is known as the 'cross-fostering' strategy.

Studies with 'schizophrenic' adoptees as index subjects

The first of these studies was reported by Kety *et al.* (1968). The research was made possible by the existence in Denmark of excellent records not only of the general population and its geographical movements, but also of all adoptions granted by the state, including details of biological mother, putative father and adoptive parents. Records are also kept, as was noted earlier, of admissions to psychiatric hospitals and of diagnoses. Subjects were drawn from the records of all adoptions in Copenhagen between 1924 and 1947. Cross-referencing of the adoption and psychiatric registers yielded 507 subjects whose hospital records were examined by two Danish psychiatrists, one of whom knew the purpose of the research. One of them classified subjects as: definitely schizophrenic, definitely not schizophrenic or probably schizophrenic. A summary was also prepared by the second psychiatrist, who was ignorant of the purpose of the research, giving details such as 'symptoms', judgements of work performance, 'sexual adjustment', 'intellectual ability', 'age of onset', marital status and most probable diagnosis. This summary was sent to the American collaborators – Kety and Wender – who independently rated each subject as definitely, definitely not or probably schizophrenic. Where all three psychiatrists rated an adoptee as definitely schizophrenic, the adoptee became a subject. Those unanimously called definitely not schizophrenic were dropped. Where there was disagreement, the first Danish psychiatrist prepared and forwarded a summary from the hospital records. Where a consensus on 'definitely schizophrenic' was reached by the Danish and two American psychiatrists, the adoptee became a subject. By this method, thirty-three subjects (called index cases) were selected. The control subjects were selected from a pool of adoptees who had no record of admission to a psychiatric hospital or unit. Index and control groups were matched for age, age at transfer, social class of adoptive parents and time spent with biological relatives, in institutions or with foster parents.

Having selected index and control subjects, Kety *et al.* began the daunting task of searching for their relatives, both biological and adoptive. The searches were made by people who did not know which were index and which control subjects. Relatives were traced through the population register – 150 and seventy-four biological and adoptive relatives respectively for index subjects and 156 and eighty-three for the controls. Information about these relatives was gathered from Psychiatric Registers, police and military records and the Mothers' Aid organisation. The records of those relatives with a psychiatric history were obtained and summarised mainly by a psychiatrist unaware of the research design; some (the exact number was not given) were

Table 6.6 Diagnostic classification system used in adoption studies

A.   Definitely not schizophrenia (specify diagnosis).

B.   Chronic schizophrenia (chronic undifferentiated schizophrenia, true schizophrenia, process schizophrenia).
Characteristics: (1) Poor prepsychotic adjustment; introverted; schizoid; shut-in; few peer contacts; few heterosexual contacts; usually unmarried; poor occupational adjustment. (2) Onset: gradual and without clear-cut psychological precipitant. (3) Presenting picture, presence of primary Bleulerian characteristics; presence of clear rather than confused sensorium. (4) Post-hospital course: failure to reach previous level of adjustment. (5) Tendency to chronicity.

B2.   Acute schizophrenic reaction (acute undifferentiated schizophrenic reaction, schizoaffective psychosis, possible schizophreniform psychosis, (acute) paranoid reaction, homosexual panic).
Characteristics: (1) Relatively good premorbid adjustment. (2) Relatively rapid onset of illness with clear-cut psychological precipitant. (3) Presenting picture: presence of secondary symptoms and comparatively lesser evidence of primary ones; presence of affect (manic-depressive symptoms, feelings of guilt); cloudy rather than clear sensorium. (4) Post-hospital course good. (5) Tendency to relatively brief episode(s) responding to drugs, electroshock therapy, and so on.

B3.   Borderline state (pseudoneurotic schizophrenia, borderline ambulatory schizophrenia, questionable simple schizophrenia, "Psychotic character", severe schizoid individual).
Characteristics: (1) Thinking; strange or atypical mentation; thought shows tendency to ignore reality, logic and experience (to an excessive degree) resulting in poor adaptation to life experience (despite the presence of a normal IQ); fuzzy, murky, vague speech. (2) Experience; brief episodes of cognitive distortion (the patient can, and does, snap back, but during the episode the idea has more the character of a delusion than an ego-alien obsessive thought); feelings of depersonalisation, or strangeness, or unfamiliarity with or towards the familiar; micropsychosis.
(3) Affective: anhedonia – never experiences intense pleasure – never happy; no deep or intense involvement with anyone or anybody. (4) Interpersonal behaviour: may appear poised, but lacking in depth ("as if" personality); sexual adjustment – chaotic fluctuation; mixture of heterosexuality and homosexuality.
(5) Psychopathology: multiple neurotic manifestations that shift frequently (obsessive concerns, phobias, conversion, psychosomatic symptoms, etc.); severe widespread anxiety.

C.   Inadequate personality.
Characteristics: A somewhat heterogeneous group consisting of individuals who would be classified as either inadequate or schizoid by the APA (1968) Diagnostic Manual. Persons so classified often had many of the characteristics of the B3 category, but to a considerably milder degree.

D1, 2 or 3.   Uncertain B1, 2 or 3 either because information is lacking or because even if enough information is available, the case does not fit clearly into an appropriate B category.

Source: Kety *et al.*, 1968.

summarised by one of the authors. The summaries were then edited to delete diagnostic opinions and any information which might have indicated whether the relative 'belonged' to an index or control adoptee. Unfortunately, although Kety *et al.* concede the importance of this strategy, they made no check

on its success by, for example, asking independent raters to guess
which relatives belonged. An edited summary for each relative
the four authors who independently 'diagnosed' the relative.
the twin researchers, made use of the concept of the schizoph
the concepts they included in this term, and the criteria for inferring
shown in Table 6.6.

Interpreting the results

Kety *et al.* analysed their data in several ways. They showed, first, that 8.7 per
cent of biological relatives of index adoptees (i.e. those called schizophrenic)
had been assigned a spectrum diagnosis, while the figure for control subjects
was 1.9 per cent. Second, they showed that this significant difference remained
when only biological relatives of 'early separated' index and control subjects
were compared (10 per cent versus zero per cent). They showed, third, that
there was a significant difference in the number of biological families of index
and control subjects in which at least one member had received a spectrum
diagnosis. Kety *et al.* commented that: "this study found little to support the
importance of environmental transmission of schizophrenia between family
members" (359).

A closer analysis of their data, however, suggests that both their analyses
and their conclusions are questionable. Before a re-analysis of their data is
presented, two points must be emphasised. First, some of the criticisms centre
on Kety *et al.*'s use of the 'schizophrenia spectrum'. This is not to suggest that
there is some proper usage or that their B1 and B2 diagnoses were more accurate. Second, part of the re-analysis involves comparing Kety *et al.*'s data
with those of family studies. Again, it is not being suggested that data from
these family studies are accurate. What is of interest here is the way in which
Kety *et al.* have analysed and presented their data and the extent to which they
have ignored analyses which, within these authors' own framework, would
have been more appropriate. Kety *et al.*'s analyses and conclusions ignore four
major factors which could influence the results and their interpretation. First,
there is the issue of the type of adoptive homes in which subjects were reared
and the extent to which they were matched; second, the weakness of their diagnostic concepts and in particular their spectrum concept; third, the
different genetic loadings which must be given to first and second degree relatives; and fourth, the fact that a significant difference in the prevalence of
spectrum diagnoses between index and control biological relatives could arise
in different ways. Two of these are of particular interest here: if the index biological relatives had a higher than expected prevalence of schizophrenia
diagnoses and the control relatives were indistinguishable from the general
population *or* the index relatives resembled the general population and the
control relatives were exceptionally free from diagnoses, then significant differences, but carrying very different interpretations, could appear.

The adoptive homes of index and control subjects

Kety *et al.* have apparently assumed that index and control subjects' adoptive family homes were virtually identical and that any supposed similarity between subjects and their biological relatives was mediated by genetic factors. In order to foster similarity amongst adoptive families, index and control groups were matched in various ways but this does not indicate how well individuals were matched; Kety *et al.* reported only that out of four possible controls who matched each index on age and sex, one was chosen "who matched best in respect of socioeconomic status of adoptive family and time spent with biological mother or father, in a children's home or with foster parents" (1976: 422).

Rose *et al.* (1984), however, have presented data which suggest that this matching process may have been inadequate. Using unpublished data supplied to them by Kety *et al.*, Rose *et al.* demonstrated that in 24 per cent of the adoptive families of index subjects, an adoptive parent had been in a psychiatric hospital, while not one adoptive parent of a control subject had been admitted. It is interesting to note also that the rate of admission of a parent (6 versus 24 per cent) was significantly lower ($\chi^2 = 6.9$ df1 $p < 0.01$) in the biological than in the adoptive families of index subjects. There is, of course, the possibility that the adoptive parents were driven to the psychiatric services by the behaviour of their child, but it remains interesting that Kety *et al.* did not publish this potentially important data, although it was apparently easily retrievable from data sheets. Rose *et al.* have suggested that this apparently greater deviance amongst index subjects' adoptive families might reflect the operation of 'selective placement', and thus have created a spurious impression of similarity between adoptive subjects and their biological relatives. It is common practice to attempt to match the backgrounds of biological and adoptive families. Obviously, the matching must be limited because adoptive parents have to conform to certain standards. But a selective placement effect does seem to have operated in the Danish samples, because Kety *et al.* (1976) and Wender *et al.* (1973, 1974) have reported a significant correlation between the social class of the biological and adoptive families. More seriously, Kety *et al.* have never satisfactorily demonstrated that their choice of index subjects was not influenced by knowledge of some characteristics of biological relatives. (They have, apparently, satisfied themselves that this was not the case, but that is not quite the same thing.) If selective placement factors were operating, and if the biological parents of index subjects were known deviants, then, within limits, so too might have been the adoptive parents.

Diagnoses and the schizophrenia spectrum

Some of the problems of the spectrum concept were discussed in the last section but they are sufficiently important and so often ignored as to justify brief repetition here. Kety *et al.* made no attempt to justify empirically their spectrum concept; rather, they appear to have fallen into the same trap as have twin researchers, of assuming that just because some relatives show behaviours which seem vaguely similar to those of the index subjects, then they must be 'suffering from related disorders' (and the sheer breadth of Kety *et al.*'s concept emphasises just how tenuous this similarity may be). Some of the problems of Kety *et al.*'s use of the spectrum concept can be highlighted by drawing a similar analogy to that used in the last section. If their strategy were to be used by, say, cancer researchers, we should hardly consider them justified in including in a 'cancer spectrum' biological and adoptive relatives who had ever complained of nausea, abdominal pain, or of passing blood or even of 'growths' such as warts, bunions or cysts. If the analogy seems absurd, it does so only because it is known *in advance of the research* that the antecedents and 'behaviour' of the phenomena of interest, in this case malignant tumors, are quite different from those of warts, and so on and that there are many antecedents of nausea, etc. apart from cancerous tumours. It was, however, in total ignorance of the antecedents or of any other aspects, of the long and disparate list of phenomena in Table 6.6, and in ignorance of whether any of them form a meaningful pattern, that Kety *et al.* decided on their criteria for their schizophrenia spectrum. The arbitrariness of their spectrum classification is suggested by Kety *et al.*'s own report (1968) that it "was worked out largely by Dr. Wender" (353). In the face of criticism of the width of their spectrum concept, Kety *et al.* (1976) protested that it had merely been a "hypotheses or group of hypotheses on which we hoped our continuing studies might cast some light" (417). But Kety *et al.* made no such reservations in their earlier reports of this work and, as will be seen, have relied heavily on some or other version of their spectrum concept in their attempts to secure apparently significant results. But it is not simply the width and arbitrariness of Kety *et al.*'s spectrum which should give cause for concern. The criteria for inferring many of its concepts are extremely vague. Nor have Kety *et al.* indicated how many of the characteristics on the list people must show in order to be called borderline schizophrenic or whatever.

No data were provided on the reliability of diagnoses made from these criteria. Kety *et al.* stated simply that:

> those cases in which there was a disagreement among the raters were discussed at a conference of all four authors where an effort was made to review additional edited information which it was possible to obtain and to arrive at a consensus diagnosis.
>
> (1968: 351)

Unfortunately, Kety *et al.* did not say what this additional information was, where it had been obtained and whether it was likely to 'identify' a relative. It is notable also that some of the diagnoses were apparently made on the basis of very little information, as Kety *et al.* pointed out. Some of those for whom information was lacking were assigned to one of the D (uncertain) groups.

These presumably already highly heterogeneous categories were therefore made up of those who were not assigned to a B category because information was lacking and of those for whom a good deal of information was available but who did not, in the raters' opinions, match the B groups.

Analysing the data – genetic weighting of relatives and population comparisons

The major analyses carried out by Kety *et al.* involved grouping together all biological relatives (parents, sibs and half-sibs) of index and control subjects and comparing the frequency of spectrum diagnoses in the two groups. As Benjamin (1976) has pointed out, however, this kind of analysis assumes that all relatives stand in the same genetic relationship to the index and control subjects. It fails to acknowledge that the predictions made about the occurrence of any genetic phenomena in biological relatives will depend on their degree of closeness. Half-sibs, of whom there were many in Kety *et al.*'s study, are particularly problematic because predictions depend, as Lidz and Blatt (1983) have noted, on whether the common parent shows the phenomena of interest, whether the other parent is known and 'affected' and on the genetic model used. Similarly, as has already been pointed out, a simple comparison of two groups of biological relatives does not indicate how similar is each to the general population. In the case of the 'schizophrenic' adoptees, it would be predicted from a genetic theory that the prevalence of schizophrenia diagnoses in their first- and second-degree relatives should be higher than that in the general population and similar to that of unseparated relatives, although even this latter finding would not preclude non-genetic explanations.

A much clearer picture of Kety *et al.*'s data could therefore be obtained by separating first- and second-degree relatives and comparing the prevalence of schizophrenia diagnoses with population rates (and see also Lidz and Blatt, 1983). Kety *et al.* (1976) in fact claimed that they "toyed with the idea of giving [half-siblings] half the weight as soon as we recognised how many were being identified but rejected it as being too pretentious" (416). It is difficult not to wonder whether the idea was also rejected because it leads to a quite different set of conclusions; but to Kety *et al.*'s credit, they have made it easy for others to perform a more appropriate analysis.

Kety *et al.*'s data for first- and second-degree relatives can be compared both between experimental and control groups and with two sets of population figures: the prevalence rates for diagnoses of schizophrenia in the general population and the rates for unseparated relatives of those already diagnosed as schizophrenic. There are, of course, problems with these population comparisons. As would be expected, the prevalence rates for the general population vary from study to study, even when the same measure is used (for example, lifetime risk or prevalence at a particular point). So too do the rates for relatives. For example, as Rosenthal (1970) has shown, the risk for parents of 'schizophrenics' in one study is sixty times that in another, while the risk for sibs in one study is twenty-eight times larger than that for parents but in another the risk for parents is 1.5 times larger than that for sibs. One of the reasons for this is presumably that researchers have used different criteria for inferring schizophrenia and that they have gathered different kinds of information, sometimes about people who had been dead for many years. It is acknowledged, moreover (see, for example, Gottesman and Shields, 1972, 1982; Cooper et al., 1972), that the criteria used by European psychiatrists are generally narrower (sometimes much narrower) than are those used by American psychiatrists. Many of the studies for which prevalence rates have been derived are European and would almost certainly have excluded Kety et al.'s D3 and C categories and possibly their B3. To add to the difficulties, the rates quoted for relatives or for the general population are sometimes for an age-corrected lifetime risk of being diagnosed schizophrenic and different researchers have used different risk periods. Kety et al.'s data do not allow such calculations, although it can reasonably be assumed that many of the biological parents, who make up almost the whole sample of first-degree relatives, were close to or had passed the so-called risk age of around 45.

Because of the difficulty of determining an appropriate numerical base for the population figures, direct statistical comparison of these with Kety et al.'s data will not be attempted. The best that can be done is to offer a range of figures obtained for the general population and for relatives of 'schizophrenics' and to compare these with Kety et al.'s figures for first- and second-degree relatives (see Tables 6.7–6.9). The comparisons may be made somewhat more meaningful by taking only the B (definite and borderline schizophrenia) categories and, so as to give Kety et al. the benefit of the doubt,

Table 6.7 Estimated risk of being diagnosed schizophrenic in the general population and in relatives of 'schizophrenics'

General population	Parents	2nd-degree relatives
0.7 – 1.5%	0.2 – 12%	0.3 – 6.5%

Sources: Rosenthal, 1970; Gottesman and Shields, 1982.

Table 6.8 Prevalence of B and D1 & 2 diagnoses in first-degree relatives of index and control S's [a]

	Biological %	Adoptive %
Index	1.5	0
Control	2.9	2.4

Note: [a]Because so few sibs were traced, the figures for parents and sibs have been combined. The figures for biological parents only are 1.5 per cent and 1.6 per cent.

145

Table 6.9 Prevalence of B and D1 & 2 diagnoses in second-degree relatives of index and control S's

	Biological %	Adoptive %
Index	8.2	0
Control	0	0[a]

Note: [a] None identified.

the D1 and D2 categories, which may resemble the 'probable schizophrenia' of European psychiatrists. Even so, these criteria may be broader than those used in many population and family studies.

These figures reveal patterns in Kety *et al.*'s data which were obscured by their 'unpretentious' analysis. They show, for example, that the rates of B and D1&2 diagnoses in the first-degree biological relatives of index subjects are not clearly different from the population rate and that the rates for index and control relatives are not significantly different from each other ($\chi^2 = 0.002$ df1). The comparison remains non-significant even when D3 and C categories are included, i.e. when the full width of the spectrum is used, and when only data from parents are analysed. Kety *et al.*'s statistically significant results appear to be derived from the relatively high rate of spectrum diagnoses in biological half-sibs of index subjects combined with their non-existence in the half-sibs of control subjects. Unfortunately, Kety *et al.* have provided no information on the backgrounds of these half-sibs, whether they were from 'broken homes', institutions or what. It is notable that the rate of spectrum diagnoses is higher – though not significantly so – in the second-degree than in the first-degree relatives of the index subjects, a result which even genetic researchers have called 'genetically meaningless' (Gottesman and Shields, 1976; Kringlen, 1976).

An extended study, using interviews

In a later report, Kety *et al.* (1975) described an extension of this study in which some biological and adoptive relatives were interviewed. Diagnoses were then based on interview data rather than on hospital records. Kety *et al.* reported that the results of this extended study "confirm results previously obtained only from institutional records" and that their data are "strongly suggestive of the operation of genetic factors" (163). As with the previous study, however, closer inspection of their methods and data shows that these conclusions are untenable. There are three major problems with this extension study (quite apart from those associated with 'schizophrenia'): first, the methods by which the interview data were collected; second, the criteria used to assign spectrum diagnoses; and third, the data analyses.

Data collection by interview

Kety *et al.* secured the co-operation of an independent psychiatrist to conduct interviews with as many biological and adoptive relatives as could be traced and agreed to be interviewed. Because he knew the design and purpose of the study, and because clues to subjects' status may have been given during the interview, Kety *et al.* asked the interviewer to guess the status of his subjects. His guess was correct for 17 per cent of interviews. Although Kety *et al.* then re-analysed their data to exclude these interviews, this hardly amounts to a demonstration that the data collection was completely uncontaminated. The interviewer, after all, knew why he was being asked to guess the subjects' status. It is, perhaps, not unreasonable to suppose, and without accusing him of lying, that his guesses might not have been an accurate reflection of what actually took place during the interview. Of more concern, however, is the way in which some of the interviews were conducted. Kety *et al.* reported that about 10 per cent of relatives refused to co-operate and that:

> Even though a subject refused initially, Dr. Jacobsen would telephone and try to persuade him and, occasionally, when he passed his door, would knock and attempt personally to obtain his co-operation, and with considerable success. In addition, in twelve instances, even though the individual persistently refused to give an interview, Dr. Jacobsen nevertheless obtained considerable information in the process.
>
> (150)

We are thus asked to believe that the diagnosis of a serious mental disorder can be based on the behaviour of someone either distressed or annoyed at being persistently asked, in spite of refusals, to give personal information to a stranger.

From the way in which Kety *et al.* described the data collection, there is nothing to suggest that 'an interview' was not just that – an interviewer talking to someone (however reluctant) and recording the results. Kety *et al.* then recorded the diagnoses in one of their data tables with a clear indication of whether this was based 'on an interview'. The term interview, however, was apparently used by Kety *et al.* in a quite different way from the usual usage. Rose *et al.* (1984) contacted the psychiatrist who had conducted the interviews and asked him what had happened when relatives were dead or unavailable. The psychiatrist reported that, in an unspecified number of these cases, he had prepared a 'pseudo interview' using hospital records. In effect, he had conducted an interview with himself by asking how (he thought) this person might have responded had he actually conducted a personal interview.

Making a diagnosis

The procedure for making diagnoses in this extended study was similar to that of the earlier research: edited transcripts of the interviews and pseudo-inter-

views were read independently by Kety, Rosenthal and Wender and a diagnosis recorded. Later, the raters met and discussed each subject in order to
reach a consensus diagnosis. As before, no information was given about reliability, although it was promised elsewhere. Kety *et al.* merely remarked that
"In formulating the consensus diagnoses we were constantly impressed with
the agreement among our independent diagnoses" (157). It is difficult to
know how the raters could have been impressed by their agreement if they did
not know its extent or, if they knew enough about it to be impressed, why they
did not share the information with their readers.

Although Kety *et al.* do not discuss the fact, they adopted different criteria
for diagnosing the schizophrenia spectrum in this extended study. Previously,
the spectrum had included the B, D and C categories described in Table 6.6.
Now, however, it included only the B and D categories because, on analysing
their data, Kety *et al.* discovered that the C category diagnoses did not distinguish between the biological relatives of the index and control subjects. At
least, we must assume that this was the reason, for none was given. Kety *et al.*
thus behaved like a researcher who hypothesises that men are more intelligent
than women but who refuses to accept as a test of intelligence any task on
which men and women perform equally well.

This elasticity of the spectrum concept is particularly interesting when considered alongside the information which Rose *et al.* uncovered about the
'interviews'. They reported that one subject – a biological relative of an index
subject – had twice been given a diagnosis of manic depressive psychosis by
hospital doctors and that this had been recorded in the notes used by Kety *et
al.* to make their diagnosis. In the first study, this woman had been given a 'C'
diagnosis – inside the spectrum – and had therefore contributed towards the
supposedly significant results. In the extended study, she was recorded not, as
would be expected, as outside the spectrum, now made up only of B and D
diagnoses, but as still inside, with a diagnosis of 'uncertain borderline schizo-
phrenia/severely schizoid individual' (D3) *based on an interview*. The woman,
however, was dead and had never been interviewed; the interviewing psychiatrist had made up an interview from her hospital notes. The fact that a woman
who had twice been called manic depressive should consistently be included
in Kety *et al.*'s spectrum is interesting in view of their comment that
"Manic-depressive illness was never thought to be in the schizophrenia
spectrum by us" (417).

Analysing the data

Once again, Kety *et al.* produced significant results by grouping together all
biological relatives of index and control subjects and showing a significant difference in spectrum diagnoses between the two groups. Again, however, a
rather different picture emerges when the data are split into first- and second-
degree relatives and comparisons made between them and with population

rates. (The problematic D3 is again removed.) These figures can be seen in Tables 6.10 and 6.11.

Several important points emerge from this presentation of the data. First, the rates of B and D1&2 diagnoses are not significantly different for first-degree biological relatives of index and control subjects ($\chi^2 = 0.0004$ df1) and the differences remain non-significant when D3 diagnoses are included ($\chi^2 = 0.76$ df1). Second, in these relatives, all but two of the diagnoses are B3 or D3 (borderline or uncertain borderline state) and the majority were reportedly obtained by interview. It will be recalled that the population rates are derived from studies which probably excluded D3 and possibly B3 behaviours from a schizophrenia category and which usually used hospital records, rather than population interviews. There is no known population rate for B and D diagnoses made by interview, but it is likely to be considerably higher than 1.5 per cent. Kety, Rosenthal, Wender, Schulsinger and Jacobsen (1978) in fact claimed a prevalence of 4 per cent for B and D diagnoses from interview, using adoptive relatives and biological control relatives. It cannot therefore be claimed confidently that the rate of spectrum diagnoses for first-degree biological relatives of index subjects is above the expectation for the general population. Third, as with the previous study, it is the apparently high and difficult-to-interpret rate of B and D diagnoses in the second-degree biological relatives of index subjects, combined with a very low rate in control relatives, which appears to have contributed most to Kety *et al.*'s significant result.

Kety *et al.* (1975) emphasised the fact that there was a significantly higher rate of spectrum diagnoses amongst the paternal half-sibs of index adoptees than amongst paternal half-sibs of controls. Because these people did not

Table 6.10 Prevalence of B and D1 & 2 diagnoses in first-degree biological relatives[ab]

	Index S's %	Control S's %
	5.8	4.3

Notes: [a] Parents and sibs; figures for parents only are 4.5 per cent and 3 per cent.
[b] Diagnoses are counted if given after either interview or examination of hospital records.

Table 6.11 Prevalence of B and D1 & 2 diagnoses in second-degree biological relatives[a]

	Index S's %	Control S's %
	11.5	1

Note: [a] See Table 6.10.

share an intra-uterine environment with the adoptees, Kety *et al.* considered this to be "compelling evidence that genetic factors operate significantly in the transmission of schizophrenia" (1975: 156). But what Kety *et al.* did not mention, and which is very difficult to explain by their genetic theory, is that the frequency of spectrum diagnoses does not differ between *maternal* half-sibs of the index and control subjects (for B and D1&2 diagnoses, $\chi^2 = 0.49$ df1; for B and D diagnoses, $\chi^2 = 2.4$ df1 p > 0.05).

Kety *et al.* also provided an analysis of their data by family, rather than individual; that is, they compared the number of index subjects' biological families in which at least one member had been given a spectrum diagnosis with the corresponding number for control subjects. It was claimed, in a summary table derived from a more detailed table of data, that fourteen families of index subjects contained someone given a B diagnosis compared with only three for control subjects. The difference was highly significant. In fact, the figure for index relatives is incorrect and should be *eight*. The difference between index and control families is then not significant ($\chi^2 = 1.89$ df1 p > 0.05). It is difficult to understand why this mistake (acknowledged as such by Kety *et al.*; see Paton-Saltzberg, 1982) has apparently not been corrected. Seven years after the wrong figures first appeared Gottesman and Shields (1982) reported and claimed significance for them. And thirteen years later, these figures were quoted again ('The Mind Machine'; BBC2, 18 October 1988), although by now they had been transformed to the claim that 14 per cent of biological relatives and 3 per cent of adoptive relatives of schizophrenic adoptees had received a diagnosis of schizophrenia.

An extension of the adoption study to the whole of Denmark has been reported (Kety, 1978; Kety, Rosenthal and Wender, 1978). This will not be discussed in detail here as it repeats many of the errors of the earlier work.

Studies of adopted-away children of a 'schizophrenic' parent

Rosenthal *et al.* (1968) began with the same pool of adoptees as had Kety *et al.*, but their interest focused on their biological parents. (The biological father was unknown in about 25 per cent of cases and may well have been incorrectly recorded in others.) As before, names were cross-referenced with psychiatric records in order to find those parents who had given a child up for adoption and who had received a psychiatric diagnosis. The records were read and summarised by psychiatrists who then made a diagnosis according to the criteria used by Kety *et al.* and described in Table 6.6. The summaries and diagnoses were then reviewed by Rosenthal *et al.*, who also recorded diagnoses. No data on reliability were given, but Rosenthal *et al.* reported that "In each case where we have a full consensus that the parent is in the schizophrenic range (coded B1, B2 or B3) the child he or she gave for adoption is selected as an index case" (379). Fifty-six parents (2.5:1 mothers to fathers) were selected by this method. Information about the children of each of the index parents was then recorded (name, sex, birthdate, age of transfer to adoptive parents, age at formal adoption, adoptive parents' occupation, income and 'fortune'). To obtain control subjects, i.e. adopted children whose biological parents had no psychiatric record, Rosenthal and one other person ranked adoptees close to each index adoptee in the relevant characteristics. The subject with the highest summed rank was chosen as a control. If any refused to participate, the adoptee with the next highest summed rank was chosen; if they refused, then the next highest, and so on. Fifteen potential control subjects refused, but no information was provided on how well index and control adoptees were eventually matched. Information on index and control adoptees (i.e. those with and without a 'schizophrenic' biological parent) was sent to Copenhagen but without identifying information. Subjects were then contacted by a social worker who, without revealing the purpose of the study, attempted to persuade them to participate.

The researchers were then faced with the problem of what to do with these subjects as, by their own admission, they lacked a clear-cut theory. Perhaps predictably, Rosenthal *et al.* again fell into the same trap as had the twin researchers in assuming that any vague similarity between adopted children of 'schizophrenics' and the researchers' idea of a schizophrenic meant that they were 'showing signs of the same disorder'. Indeed, their reasoning was, if anything, even more confused:

> [Our] strategy was based on the idea that we should find the same kinds of traits and aberrations in our index groups as in the premorbid personality of known schizophrenics. Of course, those who become schizophrenic must be different in some way from those who do not, and since we could expect only a few of our subjects to become schizophrenic, we might be focusing on the wrong traits. Moreover, the literature on the premorbid personality of schizophrenics was hardly exciting. It was based on retrospection, or on past clinical records in service settings for reasons not necessarily coinciding with ours. Formulations thus derived emphasised traits such as shyness, timidity, passivity, sex difficulties, introversion and others. We would, of course, look for such traits, but we hoped for a more fine grained description of the inherited diathesis than that. We included a self-assessment procedure whose items were based on such literature and on our own clinical observations or impressions as well.
>
> (380–1)

Rosenthal *et al.* also included three sets of test procedures. First, a "conditioning procedure" and a "habituation and a demandingness" procedure claimed to discriminate between schizophrenic and control groups, though with what reliability and for what purpose was not discussed; second, an unnamed set of projective and cognitive tests based on the work of Singer and Østergaard; and third, "a few tests" included on the basis of "hunches" and "which would take much too long to describe" (381). Thus, it is not at all clear what information was actually collected from subjects, how reliable it was or even why some of it was collected.

Rosenthal *et al.* assessed a total of 155 subjects (some of whose parents had been diagnosed as manic-depressive psychosis). The assessors' impressions, which may or may not have included test data, were somehow converted to spectrum diagnoses. No information was provided on how, by whom, with what reliability or using what criteria this was done. Instead, readers were offered the information that "Dr. Welner made a carefully formulated diagnostic evaluation of each case examined" and the claim that "Both he and Dr Schulsinger, who pinch hit [*sic*] for him when Dr. Welner was ill, have an appreciation of the nuances of diagnosis which is too often discounted in the United States. In addition, both have had training and supervision in psychoanalysis and both have been psychoanalysed" (386). Although the arbitrariness of Rosenthal *et al.*'s procedure means that it hardly matters, readers might be misled here into thinking that Welner and Schulsinger actually decided whether each subject was in or out of the spectrum. Private enquiries by Rose *et al.* (1984), however, have indicated that this was apparently not the case. Who made the decision and how remains unknown.

Some 155 adopted subjects, sixty-nine index and eighty-six control, were investigated. Eighty-six subjects, thirty-nine index and forty-seven controls were examined in detail. Only one of the 155 had ever been hospitalised with a diagnosis of schizophrenia, a rate at the lower end of the expectation for the general population. This subject was an index case, so that the rate for this group was 1.4 per cent. This contrasts with a pooled 'morbid risk' of 12.8 per cent quoted by Gottesman and Shields (1982) for children of a parent diagnosed as schizophrenic. Rosenthal *et al.* in fact made no attempt to analyse their data on the distribution of spectrum diagnoses in index and control adoptees, but simply reported on the number of these diagnoses in index and control groups (thirteen versus seven). The thirteen, however, included two children whose parent had been diagnosed as manic-depressive psychosis, which the same authors were later to state, as was pointed out earlier, was never thought by them to be in the schizophrenia spectrum (Kety *et al.*, 1976). In fact, these authors appear to be in some confusion about this as, two years earlier, Rosenthal *et al.* had claimed that they were "tentatively including" manic-depressive psychosis in the schizophrenia spectrum (1974: 153). It may be that Rosenthal *et al.* did not elaborate on the figures they presented because, with or without 'manic-depressive' parents, there were no significant differences in the rate of spectrum diagnoses in index and control adoptees ($\chi^2 = 3.09$ df1 p > 0.05; $\chi^2 = 1.89$ df1 p > 0.05).

Rosenthal *et al.* also reported on the results of subjects' self-assessments on supposedly pre-schizophrenic traits and on their MMPI scores. From a genetic point of view, the results of the self-assessments were extremely disappointing. Group means for both index and control subjects were within the average range on all items. In between-group comparisons, three items differentiated groups in the predicted direction and three in the opposite direction. Without providing any evidence in support, Rosenthal *et al.* claimed that these latter scores suggested that index subjects "may have a distorted self-image or are over defensive with respect to these traits" (390). The MMPI results were equally disappointing: there were no significant differences between groups on any of the so-called pathology scales including the schizophrenia scale. It is perhaps hardly surprising that Rosenthal *et al.* should have said that they "[did] not want to spend too much time with possible explanations of these findings" and that they "[did] not want to dwell on these findings" (390). They gave as their reason the fact that they intended to collect data from more subjects, but it is difficult not to wonder whether the data would have been dismissed so readily had it been in line with their expectations. What happened to the data from the remaining tests was not reported.

Adopted-away children of 'schizophrenics' – an extension

Ten years after the first report had been published, Haier *et al.* (1978) reported on the results of an MMPI assessment of a larger sample of adoptees (sixty-four index and sixty-four control). In this report, however, the analyses were more extensive. The authors first looked at the 'overall configuration' of scores on the MMPI but found no significant differences between index and control groups. It was noted also that no scale mean for either group exceeded seventy, the cut-off point for supposed psychopathology. Thus, both index and control groups appeared to be remarkably 'normal', according to MMPI criteria. The test data were then analysed scale by scale, using thirty-four univariate tests (seventeen scales × two sexes). Of these, four comparisons yielded significant differences: index males scored higher (but still within the 'normal' range) than did control males on scales purporting to measure masculinity/femininity and schizophrenia. Index females achieved higher scores (but still within the 'normal' range) on 'hysteria' and 'psychopathic deviance'. As the authors point out, however, "these ... differences are not powerful statistically and should be interpreted with the caution implied by the use of multiple univariate tests" (172).

Haier *et al.* conducted three further analyses, each looking at the scoring patterns of the index and control groups. It is notable that the concept of the schizophrenia spectrum had apparently been abandoned and that the authors were now arbitrarily searching for anything which would discriminate index and control groups. The search was unsuccessful: the number of index and control subjects who had 'generally elevated MMPI profiles' (i.e. 4 or more

T = > 70 scales, either clinical or masculinity/femininity) was not significantly different. Nor were the 'profile types' for the two groups (this involves a comparison of the two highest scales). The final analysis involved combining various scale scores to derive what was claimed to be a composite index of psychological disturbance, psychotic signs and schizophrenia signs. These methods had been developed by other researchers and no details were provided by Haier et al. For reasons they did not explain, Haier et al. did not take the obvious step of comparing index and control-group scores on each of these indices. Instead they conducted a curious statistical analysis by calculating a mean score for index and control groups combined and then comparing the percentages of index and control subjects who scored more than one standard deviation above this mean. The analysis showed no significant differences between either male or female index and control groups on the 'psychotic' or 'schizophrenia' indices; on the 'psychological disturbance index', significantly more index than control subjects scored one standard deviation or more above the combined group mean. The problem with this technique is that it is easy to construct examples where the attainment of a significant or non-significant result depends on the criterion adopted for a high score. Figure 6.1 shows a possible distribution of high scorers, based on

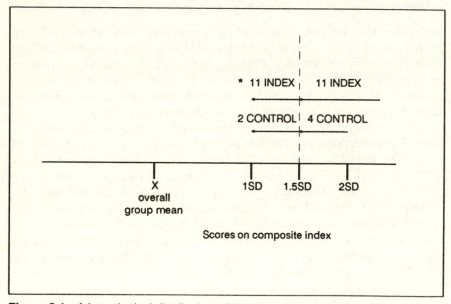

Figure 6.1   A hypothetical distribution of data from adopted-away children of 'schizophrenic' and 'normal' parents

* Haier et al. report that 22 index and 6 control subjects scored 1SD or more above the overall group mean.

Haier *et al.*'s figures, in which the choice of 1SD above the mean as the criterion would produce a significant effect, but the equally arbitrary choice of 1.5SD would not. Even if these authors could reassure us that their analysis was valid, however, the result would still be a long way from supporting their original genetic hypothesis.

It will be recalled that in their 1968 report, Rosenthal *et al.* did not say how or by whom the spectrum diagnoses had been made. Embedded in Haier *et al.*'s 1978 report, but not indicated in the title, are the results of consensus diagnoses of the index and control adoptees but again with no information about criteria or reliability. There was no significant difference in the proportion of index and control children who were assigned spectrum diagnoses by consensus. It is interesting to note, as an indication of the breadth of the diagnostic criteria, that 25 per cent of *control* subjects were assigned spectrum diagnoses. Perhaps in the face of this weight of insignificant results, Haier *et al.* again lost sight of their original hypothesis and of the spectrum concept. Instead, they introduced another new criterion in an attempt to discriminate index and control groups – a spectrum diagnosis plus a score of $T = >70$ on any one of the nine MMPI clinical scales *or* the masculinity/femininity OR the social introversion scale. But even criteria as lax as these still did not discriminate female index and control groups. In the male groups a higher proportion of index than control subjects fulfilled one of the criteria. It is interesting to note that these arbitrary and *post hoc* 'anything will do' MMPI criteria described in the text had become "MMPI criteria for schizophrenia spectrum disorders" by the time they reached the table of results (174).

In the face of this theoretical chaos, and lacking any systematic evaluation of the subjects' backgrounds or information on the success of the matching procedures, Haier *et al.* still felt able to conclude that their combination criteria "continue to support a genetic hypothesis" (175). Quite what, by now, this genetic hypothesis might be – given that at various points in this research both independent and dependent variables had been abandoned – they did not say.

Cross-fostering studies

A further strategy which has been used by the adoption researchers is that of comparing the prevalence of schizophrenia diagnoses in groups of children said to have the characteristics shown in Table 6.12. The number of children adopted by someone who will later be diagnosed as schizophrenic is clearly small, because adoptive parents are screened. Wender *et al.* (1974) reported that they were unable to find a sufficiently large sample of adoptees whose adoptive parents had received a diagnosis of chronic or borderline schizophrenia and so included subjects whose adoptive parent had been called chronic schizophrenic; certain or doubtful acute schizophrenic or schizoaffective; borderline schizophrenic; doubtful schizophrenic or schizoaffective.

Table 6.12 Sample characteristics of cross-fostering studies

Biological parent	Adoptive parent
'normal'	'schizophrenic'[a]
'schizophrenic'	?[b]
'normal'	?[b]
'schizophrenic'	[c]

Notes: [a] Cross-fostered group.
[b] Refers to the groups described earlier in the adoption studies.
[c] Non-adopted group.

They did not say how or by whom these diagnoses were made. These criteria produced twenty-eight 'cross-fostered' subjects. As in the Haier *et al.* report, however, the concept of schizophrenia spectrum appears to have been abandoned by Wender *et al.* in favour of global ratings of psychopathology made from the recorded brief impressions of an interviewing psychiatrist. The global ratings were made from one to twenty. Wender *et al.* compared the percentage of subjects in each of the three groups (cross-fostered; adoptee with 'normal' biological parent; adoptee with 'schizophrenic' biological parent) who had been assigned scores of sixteen and above. It was claimed, although there is no way of knowing if it was the case, that this corresponded to Kety *et al.*'s B and D categories. There were no significant differences amongst the three groups. Wender *et al.* then combined the cross-fostered and 'normal' parent adoptee groups and compared this group with that of the 'schizophrenic' parent adoptees. The justification for this *post hoc* comparison was that it represented a test of genetic versus non-genetic effects. In the absence of information on the success of matching procedures or on the subjects' environments, not to mention the possibility of contaminated ratings and the obscurity of their meaning, it clearly may mean nothing of the sort. The final analysis also reflects a quite different prediction from that originally made by Wender *et al.* and it allows the combination of chance differences in the two groups and the inflated size of the new comparison group to produce an apparently significant effect from data which was previously shown not to support the main hypothesis.

In the same year Paikin *et al.* (1974) published a report concerned with the personal characteristics of those who refused to participate in the adoption studies. Embedded in this paper, and neither analysed nor commented upon, is a table crucial from the adoption researchers' point of view. It shows not only the prevalence of spectrum diagnoses in the three adoptee groups but also their prevalence in a new group – of children reared with their biological 'schizophrenic' parent. No details were given of the procedures used to collect these data, of the diagnostic criteria or their reliability (the diagnoses were apparently made by Wender), or of where the considerable number of additional subjects came from. But the table does show that there was no significant difference in the prevalence of spectrum diagnoses between the cross-fostered group, with their 'normal' biological but 'schizophrenic' adoptive parent, and the non- adopted group, reared by their 'schizophrenic' biological parent ($\chi^2 = 0.04$ df1).

Genetic-linkage studies

The data from twin and adoption studies have recently been supplemented by the results of what are known as genetic-linkage studies. This research examines family patterns of genetic markers and of particular diagnoses. If the markers show a similar family pattern to the diagnoses, then it is assumed that there is 'linkage' between the marker(s) and a putative gene assumed to determine the diagnosis. A genetic marker is the biochemical product of a gene locus and it is assumed, as the name implies, to 'point to' the gene locus, although it may still, in genetic terms, be a considerable distance away. The data from these studies are usually expressed as lod, or logarithm of odds, scores. These are described by Watt *et al.* (1987) as "an estimate of the relative likelihood that linkage at distance θ is occurring between the two locii against the alternative that linkage is not occurring" (365). Particular lod scores are associated with particular probabilities of linkage, although these may vary depending on the genetic model assumed to be operating for a given diagnosis.

Linkage studies of 'schizophrenia' have been of two main types. In the first, the inheritance pattern of a number of genetic markers, presumably from different chromosomes, has been examined and compared, in groups of families, to the pattern of schizophrenia and schizophrenia spectrum diagnoses. The data from these studies have been inconclusive (Turner, 1979) or negative (McGuffin *et al.*, 1983; Watt *et al.*, 1987). The second type of study is one which concentrates on a particular chromosome. In this case, it is chromosome 5, or particular sections of it, which has been selected for study, although for reasons which Lander (1988) has described as "quite flimsy" (105). Nevertheless, the first major report of such a study claimed to have localized "a susceptibility locus for schizophrenia on chromosome 5" and to have provided "the first strong evidence for the involvement of a single gene in the causation of schizophrenia" (Sherrington *et al.*, 1988: 164). The report, however, was accompanied by the report of a study of a more extensive area of chromosome 5 and which claimed to find "strong evidence against linkage between schizophrenia and ... seven loci" (Kennedy *et al.*, 1988: 167). These two studies used different populations, one Icelandic with a few English subjects, and one Swedish. Sherrington *et al.* also used three diagnostic groupings: schizophrenia, schizophrenia spectrum and a group with other, unspecified diagnoses. Kennedy *et al.* used only one group, probably similar to Sherrington *et al.*'s schizophrenia group. St Clair *et al.* (1989), however, have since reported data from a Scottish sample, with similar diagnostic groupings to the Sherrington *et al.* study. They found "no evidence for linkage, regardless of how broadly or narrowly the schizophrenia phenotype is defined" (305) in the chromosome 5 area they studied and which included that studied by Sherrington *et al.*

These reports have excited considerable media and professional interest. It is dismaying, however, to see the subtle, and sometimes not so subtle, ways in which the weight of negative evidence is being undermined. There seem to be four main ways in which this is being achieved. First, it is apparently assumed that a 'schizophrenia gene', or genes, exist(s), that it (they) will one day be reliably detected, and that these conflicting results reflect the complexity of the search and the possibly genetic heterogeneity of 'schizophrenia'. Perhaps not surprisingly, the twin and adoption studies reviewed earlier have been uncritically cited in support of the belief that schizophrenia has a genetic basis (Watt *et al.*, 1987; Lander, 1988; *Nature* Editorial, 10 November 1988; *Lancet* Editorial, 14 January 1989). Second, the specifics of Sherrington *et al.*'s results, and the considerable problems of interpretation which they present, have not always been clearly reported. Sherrington *et al.* cited three maximum lod scores for their three diagnostic groups, the third of which, it will be recalled, had never been given schizophrenia or schizophrenia spectrum diagnoses. The lod score cited for the schizophrenia group was just below the acceptable level for 'good evidence of linkage' set by these authors; the scores for the other two groups were above it, with the "fringe" group 3 achieving the highest score. This latter result suggests – to put it bluntly – that strong evidence for linkage of genetic markers and diagnoses can best be obtained when any old diagnoses are lumped together. Given the very weak theoretical foundations of the schizophrenia and schizophrenia-spectrum diagnoses and the lack of any theoretical justification for combining these with unspecified diagnoses, the result is a curious one. In fact, Sherrington *et al.* caution that it may have been obtained by chance. These details, however, have not been clearly presented in secondary sources. On the contrary, there are indications of 'language slippage', with the diagnostically extremely heterogeneous sample studied by Sherrington *et al.* being transformed to 'schizophrenia' (Lander, 1988; *Nature* Editorial, 10 November 1988; Sherrington *et al.*, 1988).

The third method by which the negative results may be undermined can perhaps best be dubbed the 'flight of ideas' around Sherrington *et al.*'s results. These include the ideas that the research offers the prospect of "cloning and sequencing the chromosome 5 schizophrenia gene" (Gurling, 1989: 277), of "a systematic route to an understanding of the mechanisms of schizophrenia", of more effective drugs, of settling outright the "contentious side issue" of the relativistic definition of madness, of discovering the familial advantages which must account for the fact that 'schizophrenia' remains extremely common in spite of the reproductive disadvantage to 'schizophrenics' (*Nature* Editorial,

10 November 1988: 95–6), of "identifying non-penetrant carriers as well as fetuses at risk with a reasonably high level of probability" (Gurling, 1989: 217) and of considering "genetic counselling in families where chromosome 5 linkage can be reliably established" (Sherrington *et al.*, 1988: 167). To say the least, this does seem to be going beyond the data. Finally, perhaps the most popular way of reconciling these conflicting results has been to see them as confirming the idea that schizophrenia has many causes, or that only some types of schizophrenia are genetically determined. These arguments have the same weakness as those surrounding the idea of schizophrenia as an infectious disease: given the status of 'schizophrenia' and the 'schizophrenia spectrum' it makes no sense to talk of some types of schizophrenia having particular causes. As with the infection theory, however, there is no objection in principle to the idea that some instances of bizarre behaviour now said to be symptomatic of schizophrenia may show a particular pattern of inheritance, although it must be said that the kind of direct and rather simplistic relationship apparently sought in these studies is unlikely to be found (Rose, 1984).

The social context of genetic research

There is clearly a considerable gap between the original data from family studies and the claims made for them. Severe methodological and conceptual weaknesses (not all of which have been mentioned here) have often been overlooked, while researchers in the twin and adoption studies have shown a dismaying tendency to omit important procedural details, to define variables in ways which support their hypotheses, to engage in strange statistical practices and to gloss over non-significant results or to report them without comment in papers where they might well be overlooked. The obvious question arises as to why researchers should behave in this way. Although there is no clear answer to this question (which will be considered in more detail in Chapter 8), it can be considered in terms of the functions which genetic theories of deviant behaviour have served since Kraepelin introduced the concept of dementia praecox. It was mentioned earlier that the belief that 'schizophrenia' was 'a genetic disorder' was held strongly by Kraepelin and Bleuler. Although we have no way of knowing how they reached this conclusion, it clearly could have served to support the claim that many types of deviance were a medical matter; as was seen in Chapter 2, the credibility of the claim was by no means taken for granted at the end of the nineteenth century.

Later, however, one function which could be served by genetic theories was to become apparent with the development of the Eugenics Movement in the USA and Western Europe (see, for example, Haller, 1963; Gould, 1981). Gottesman and Shields (1982) have described what they call an era of scientific genetics in psychiatry, as beginning with the work of Ernst Rudin and they discuss his work relatively uncritically. They did not mention the fact that Rudin, who was a committed supporter of Nazism and of Hitler, had founded a School of Racial Purity and Hygiene. He spoke of Hitler as enabling "our more than 30-year dream [to] become reality and racial hygiene principles [to be] translated into action". He went on to emphasise his "deep gratitude" to his Führer (Marshall, 1985: 107). Rudin also served on the panel, chaired by Himmler, which drew up the 1933 sterilisation laws.

Kallmann's work has also been rather uncritically presented by Gottesman and Shields (who have gone to considerable lengths to defend it) and by other commentators. While not showing Rudin's zeal for racial purity, Kallmann, by his own admittance, was a strong supporter of eugenic policies (Kallmann, 1938). He expressed his strong belief in the genetic basis of schizophrenia before he started his own extensive studies – of which he wrote in a rather exasperated way, as if they were a bothersome but necessary method of convincing sceptics.

There is no suggestion that modern genetic researchers share Rudin's and Kallmann's ideas, although they are strangely reluctant to report the enthusiasm with which they were espoused by those whose work modern researchers support and to consider the effect this might have had on research practice. Nevertheless, it would be naive not to acknowledge the importance of genetic theory for the credibility of the modern concept of schizophrenia. Neale and Oltmanns' claim that "The genetic literature certainly provides the most solid information available concerning the etiology of schizophrenia" (1980: 458) illustrates the point well, as does Gottesman and Shields' comment that "Our case for the role of genetic factors in the etiology of schizophrenia is built on clinical-population genetics data, *but it implies a biochemical and/or biophysical cause for the maladjustment of the brain that leads to the development of schizophrenia*" (1982: 235; emphasis added). In the continuing and predictable absence of consistent biochemical or neurological data in support of the assertion that schizophrenia is a brain disease, claims such as these and results such as those of Sherrington *et al.* assume considerable importance because they create the impression that the brain abnormality which causes bizarre behaviour is waiting to be discovered. It is notable, too, that it has been suggested that the genetic-linkage studies will benefit the psychiatric profession. The *Nature* Editorial, for example, asserts that "It goes without saying that psychiatry, for too long one of the Cinderella specialities of medicine, will profit enormously from the availability of objective tools for study" (95), while Lander (1988) declares that "psychiatrists have now joined the ranks of experimental geneticists" (106). These claims may then justify the assumption that the behaviour from which schizophrenia is inferred is a medical matter and should be dealt with using the language and techniques of medicine. Thus, if the genetic research is discredited, then the concept of schizophrenia and the practices it allows become more obviously vulnerable.

Chapter seven

An analysis of arguments used to support 'schizophrenia'

It might be supposed, given 'schizophrenia's' claim to scientific status, that it would be substantiated by the presentation of empirical data. It is generally admitted, however, that crucial data which would directly support the concept are missing and that existing data are somewhat 'messy' (see, for example, Neale and Oltmanns, 1980; Gottesman and Shields, 1982; Spaulding and Cole, 1984; Cutting, 1985). But it is apparently assumed that stongly supporting data will soon appear (Gottesman and Shields give it until the end of the century) and that the major assumptions now made about schizophrenia will turn out to be correct. One result of this lack of empirical data is that 'schizophrenia' is now defended by a series of non-empirical arguments and it is these which will be examined here. Not all of them are concerned with supporting the concept directly; as will be seen, many of their proponents seem to take for granted that the concept refers to a pattern of behaviour and therefore seek only to support the assumptions and practices which surround it.

Schizophrenia as a mental illness

It was pointed out in Chapter 4 that the subject-matter of psychiatry is usually depicted as being mental illnesses, mental disorders or mental diseases. It was also emphasised that these terms are social constructions of unwanted or distressing phenomena and that all definitions of the terms are arbitrary. This does not mean, of course, that adopting one definition might not have systematically different consequences from adopting another; it does mean, however, that no definition can in any sense be more 'correct' than another or be used to demonstrate anything about the phenomena to which it is applied. Nevertheless, attempting to show that 'schizophrenic', and many other, behaviours are 'manifestations of mental illness' is one of the most popular ways of defending the assumption that they represent some kind of brain dysfunction or, at the very least, that they should be dealt with using the language and techniques of medicine. By definition, these arguments are bound to be false, but it is interesting to see how they have been set out.

Kendell (1975a) and Kräupl-Taylor (1971, 1976, 1979) consider psychiatric constructs in general but their ideas are relevant to 'schizophrenia', as Kendell makes clear. Both attempt to set out the referents of the term disease in such a way as to justify its application to various behavioural phenomena. They also see their arguments as justifying the application of medicine's theoretical models to deviant behaviour. Kendell presents his task as one of 'defining' or 'setting out the meaning of' the term disease. Kräupl-Taylor, however, is careful to avoid the potentially problematic terms definition and meaning and instead places his arguments within the framework of modern set theory. Kendell suggests that the defining characteristics of 'disease' are that it represents a deviation from some normative standard *and* confers a biological disadvantage in the form of a reduction in fertility. Because those called schizophrenic clearly deviate from normative standards of behaviour and have fewer than average children, Kendell concludes that schizophrenia is therefore "justifiably regarded as illness" (314). Kräupl-Taylor looks for the common attributes of those to whom the label 'patient' is applied and suggests that they consist of a statistically significant deviation of an attribute from a norm and therapeutic concern for a person felt by that person and/or the social environment. He calls the intension composed of these two attributes 'morbidity'. In turn, this set of 'morbid' attributes is seen as characterising all diseases.

It is interesting to note that Kendell (1975a, 1975b) and Kräupl-Taylor (1979) have provided critiques of the other's definitions but unfortunately without acknowledging the futility of the attempts at definition. Both Kräupl-Taylor and Toon (1976) have pointed out that Kendell's definition encompasses phenomena such as sterilization, celibacy via religious vocation or just by choice, and homosexuality (since defined as not a disease by the American Psychiatric Association). Kendell, in turn, has pointed out that Kräupl-Taylor's analysis allows the medical profession and society free rein to label all deviants as ill and suggests that "any definition of disease which boils down to 'what people complain of' or 'what doctors treat' or some combination of the two, is almost worse than no definition at all" (1975a: 307).

Clare (1976) and Sedgwick (1982) have taken a rather different, but no less fallacious, approach to the problem of the term mental illness. Clare's major point appears to be that critics of the term mental illness have assumed that the term disease is used in a straightforward and non-problematic way in medicine (to mean organic pathology) and that it therefore cannot be used to describe behavioural or psychological phenomena. Sedgwick, too, makes this point and it is a valid one. Their conclusions, however, are not. Clare points out that the way in which the word disease has been used in medicine has changed considerably over the last few centuries and that older usages, which emphasised specific organ pathology, and assumed that psychic disease was brain disease, were based on a now outmoded dualistic view of the relationship between mind and body. A rather similar argument has been suggested by Roth and Kroll (1986). The problem with these arguments is that they assume some logical connection between the idea that the psychological may influence the physical, and the *implied* conclusion: that we are justified in adopting specific theoretical models and concepts in dealing with certain deviant behaviour. We cannot, of course, assume any such connection, any more than we could argue the validity of gas laws merely by asserting that the physical and the chemical interact. Arguments about dualism are simply a means of avoiding the crucial issue of the lack of empirical support for certain theories and concepts applied to disturbing behaviour.

Sedgwick's argument is more straightforward than Clare's. He points out that the concepts of illness and disease are always social constructions, whether applied to physical or behavioural phenomena. It might reasonably be concluded from this that they should therefore be abandoned by both medicine and psychiatry – that we should abandon futile attempts to prove that such and such a behaviour is or is not 'a disease'. But Sedgwick appears to conclude the exact opposite – that because 'illness' as applied to physical phenomena is a social contruction, then we are justified in applying it to behaviour, where it is also a social construction. How and by what authority 'the mentally ill' are to be recognised is apparently not an issue; Sedgwick appears simply to take it for granted that there are such people as the mentally ill or infirm or deranged, who are victims of mental illness and who can presumably be recognised without difficulty.

Apart from their failure to recognise the implications of illness as a social construct, there are two notable points about these arguments. The first is that their proponents always proceed by begging the question: while purporting to examine the concept of mental illness, they talk of the mentally ill and of mental illnesses, apparently in ignorance of the fact that these terms cannot be admitted in this way to any discussion of the concept of mental illness, because these usages pre-empt the conclusion. The second notable point is that questions are rarely asked about the *usefulness* of the terms in constructing what are supposed to be scientific theories of behaviour. In fact, it is rarely made explicit why we should bother with the concepts at all, although the implicit message is clear: they are used to defend the application of medical language, theoretical structures, techniques and personnel to behaviour in the absence of good empirical data to justify this.

There is an exception to the practice of not clarifying why it should be necessary to use words like illness and disease outside of everyday discourse. Sedgwick claims that:

> Without the concept of illness – including that of mental illness since to exclude it would constitute the crudest dualism – we shall be unable to *make demands* on the health service facilities of the society we live in.
>
> (40, emphasis in original)

and that:

> In trying to remove and reduce the concept of mental illness, tl
> sionist theorists have made it that bit harder for a powerful can
> reform in the mental health services to get off the ground.

These arguments can be criticised in two ways (quite apart from the fact
that they seek to blacken the critics). Sedgwick fails to distinguish between the
demands of administrators and the demands of theory construction. It was, no
doubt, easier for Victorian philanthropists to obtain money to 'help fallen
women' than to 'house whores' but this hardly means that we need to include
the idea of fallen women in theories of why women sell their bodies. Sedgwick
must be aware of the fact that the concept of mental illness is used to do far
more than provide services: it informs assumptions about the antecedents of
deviant behaviour and influences research questions. It is difficult to see how
research can progress if its concepts are mere administrative conveniences.
But there is more to Sedgwick's argument than this and three assumptions
underlie it: first, that there are people who are properly called mentally ill and
that they are readiliy recognisable; second, that they need help; and third, that
they need a particular kind of help, namely that provided by a health service.
There is no doubt that many of those presently said to be mentally disordered
are distressed and would like to change their behaviour and psychological
state. There is, however, no *a priori* reason to suppose that calling them ill,
taking them to hospital and administering drugs or other physical interventions is the best way of achieving this and Sedgwick provides no evidence that
it is. Sedgwick would no doubt deny that he believes that 'the mentally ill' need
a particular kind of help; indeed, he sees no reason why these people should
not be 'looked after' by social workers, social and clinical psychologists or
even by "a non-professional philanthropy responsive to professional advice"
(221). Unfortunately, Sedgwick is betrayed by his language: in talking of caring for the mentally ill and of the problem of being sure that we are talking
about a real illness, and not something that was the product of faulty family
handling, he makes clear that he holds certain beliefs about the behaviour of
whoever he calls mentally ill. These may, at best, be unnecessary for, and at
worst incompatible with, the kinds of interventions offered by psychologists,
social workers or philanthropists. And there remains the problem of those
people who are not, apparently, distressed but are distressing, whose behaviour is annoying not to themselves but to other people and who deny that
they need help of any description. It is hardly a good argument simply to pro-
claim them mentally ill according to convention and therefore in need of a
particular kind of help.

The confusion of observation and inference

It was noted in the last section that question-begging is a common feature of arguments about 'mental illness', that the arguments begin by taking for granted precisely what is being contested. Question-begging is, in fact, endemic to the literature on 'schizophrenia'; indeed it was shown in Chapter 3 that its precursor 'dementia praecox' was introduced by Kraepelin in a question-begging fashion which was subsequently taken up by Bleuler and Schneider. The fallacy also characterises virtually the whole of the literature quoted in Chapters 4 and 5 in which the search for an operational definition of schizophrenia is described as if it had already been successful. It may be that this taking for granted of what is in dispute – in other words, a failure to appreciate what *is* in dispute – is in part responsible for arguments which seem to assume that the use of the term schizophrenia is synonymous with a description of behaviour, rather than being an inference from behaviour. Once this assumption is made, it is easy to make critics look rather absurd by implying that they are denying the 'existence' of what self-evidently 'exists'. Clare (1976) provides an example of this confusion, using an analogy from medicine. He claims that:

> A patient intermittently troubled by severe gastric pain and nausea would hardly be reassured by a physician who told him that since there is considerable doubt as to the precise cause, pathology and prevalence of his condition it had been concluded that it does not exist! It is important to note that instead of drawing such a conclusion, physicians devote enormous energy and resources to developing more sophisticated tools of exploration.

(13)

The implication here is apparently that those who criticise 'mental illness' or 'schizophrenia' are denying the 'existence' of the behaviours and experiences from which those concepts are inferred. They are, of course, doing nothing of the sort. It is obviously the case that people claim to hear voices, speak incomprehensibly and show other disturbing behaviours. What is contested is the interpretation of these observations. Thus, critics of 'mental illness' or 'schizophrenia' would proceed in exactly the same way as the physicians Clare admires: they would acknowledge the person's behaviour and experiences and devote enormous energy and resources to trying to understand why these phenomena occur and what variables influence them, but without inferring unsupported concepts like schizophrenia. Indeed, the more correct analogy which a critic might use is to point out that dyspepsic patients would hardly be helped, and knowledge about the problem hardly advanced, by their being told that they were suffering from a disturbance in the black bile. A similar confusion is evident in Serban's comment that: "with all these diversified views of the meaning of the concept of schizophrenia ... it remains a clinical reality definable in terms of symptoms regardless of the degree of social acceptance of deviant behaviour" (1980: 10). By 'clinical reality' Serban presumably means that psychiatrists see people who behave in ways which textbooks *say* are symptoms of schizophrenia, an observation which has never been in dispute.

The confusion of observation and inference is apparent also in the idea that the claimed universality of certain bizarre behaviour is relevant to discussion of the validity of concepts such as mental illness or schizophrenia (see, for example, Roth and Kroll, 1986). The claim is usually made, not that particular behaviour, but that schizophrenia or mental illness, has been found in many cultures. But the mere observation of behaviour, no matter in how many cultures, does not tell us how it should be understood, or what theoretical models will be useful in accounting for it. And it certainly tells us nothing about the occurrence of the *patterns* of behaviour and biological events implied by the concept of schizophrenia.

The fact that the validity of concepts like schizophrenia and mental illness is so taken for granted, to the point of losing sight of their status as *inferences*, may well explain the apparent surprise with which criticisms have sometimes been greeted:

> I was amazed (as the expansion of radical or revolutionary groupings gathered force in the late sixties and the seventies) to discover on the left that the most popular attitude towards the mental illnesses was to deny their very existence.
>
> (Sedgwick, 1982: 4)

> Some people – unfortunately among them even a few professionals – insist that schizophrenia does not exist, that it is a myth, and they succeed in getting considerable attention from the public and from the press because of the sensational nature of their statements.
>
> (Arieti, 1979: 6–7)

The necessity-of-classification argument

There are a number of examples of this argument, which has been used to defend the activities of classification and diagnosis in psychiatry and, therefore, the inferring of concepts like schizophrenia. Their main theme is that classification is what scientists do; that psychiatrists develop and use classification systems, are thus behaving like scientists and therefore cannot be criticised for behaving unscientifically. It is also suggested that, presumably because of the supposedly scientific nature of classification, psychiatry cannot function without it:

> In any situation in which populations or groups of patients need to be considered ... some form of classification or categorisation is unavoid-

able....Without diagnosis, or some comparable method of classification, epidemiological research would be impossible. We would have no way of finding out whether mental illness was commoner in one culture than another ... without a criterion for distinguishing between sickness and health ... all scientific communication would be impossible and our professional journals would be restricted to individual case reports, anecdotes and statements of opinion....There is no point in defining a population unless its members possess something in common with one another which distinguish them from members of another population, and once this condition has been satisfied a classification has been created....I believe [this argument] to be irrefutable ... it will be taken as proven that psychiatry cannot function at all without classifying its subject matter.

(Kendell, 1975b: 6–8)

To discard classification ... is to discard scientific thinking.

(Shepherd, 1976: 3)

It is traditional to complain about the short-comings and the illogical nature of the various systems of nomenclature and classification; yet this writer knows of no psychiatry that can get along without them.

(Brill, 1974: 1121)

There are two major problems with these arguments. The first is that they fail to emphasise the crucial distinction between 'a classification system' and 'a classification system based on the observation of patterns and capable of predicting new observations'. This is achieved partly by the implication that it is only scientists who classify when in fact all of us categorise objects and people in our day-to-day lives but, as was pointed out in Chapter 1, according to rather different procedures from those generally adopted by scientists. Kendell's and Shepherd's claims are thus rather misleading in that they fail to make clear that to *adopt* certain classification systems could be to discard scientific thinking and that to fill journals with papers based on such systems would be to fill them with anecdotes and statements of opinion.

The second problem arises from the implicit assumption that a useful classification of disturbing behaviour will have the same *form* as the present psychiatric system, in the sense that it would be based on assumptions about dispositions or traits which people would be said to have, although, of course, the content would change over the years. Thus, the crucial point, that the structure and content of the present system and the diagnostic practices it generates are based largely on opinion rather than evidence, is avoided by the implication that it is an admittedly very imperfect step in the right direction. It is, of course, also assumed that the subject-matter of a useful classification system will be mental illnesses which need treatment. The idea that the subject-matter of psychiatry should be thought of as mental illnesses has already been criticised. Similarly, there is no *a priori* reason to suppose that the form or type of patterns which may be observed by the systematic empirical study of bizarre behaviour will show any resemblance to those suggested by psychiatrists. On the contrary, because psychiatric models of bizarre behaviour were suggested before the systematic study of behaviour existed, there is every reason to suppose that they will not.

These arguments are thus based on the untenable assumption that a defence of the *principle* of classification as it is practised in the empirical sciences allows, in some unarticulated way, a defence of psychiatric classification even in the absence of evidence of its validity (see also Wing, 1988). The arguments also show the same question-begging qualities of those discussed in the last section: they take for granted the nature of the subject-matter with which psychiatrists deal and the kind of patterns which may be observed there.

'Schizophrenia' could have a pathological basis ... or the 'it might be true' argument

Although it is readily admitted that direct evidence that 'schizophrenia' has a pathological basis is not available, it is still assumed that such evidence will eventually be found and that, in the mean time, we are justified in proceeding as if certain behaviours *had* a demonstrated pathological basis. A major justification for this has, of course, been the misrepresented genetic research reviewed in Chapter 6. Another set of arguments, which reaches the same conclusion, has been put forward by Kräupl-Taylor (1976) and by Kety (1974). Kräupl-Taylor's argument runs as follows:

> It seems to me that the illustrations [of Down's Syndrome and phenylketonuria] significantly undermine the psychologists' case ... against the medical model in the apparently non-organic psychiatric field ... morbi like PKU show clearly that one is not justified in assuming that failure to find structural pathological abnormalities in a morbus indicates their actual absence. They can still be present at a molecular level.
>
> (592)

Kety's argument is similar:

> Laing argued [that] 'There are no pathological findings *post-mortem*. There are no organic structural changes noted in the course of [schizophrenia]'....What he could have said is that none of these has yet been found.
>
> (958; emphasis in original)

Neither Szasz nor Laing denied the reality and validity of general paresis as a disease of the brain. This raises the interesting question of what it was before that was established. Was it a myth, a political judgement, a

creative adaptation to an evil society or simply a mental illness of unknown origin?

(958)

These arguments appear to be examples of induction gone mad: because some
behaviours in which doctors are interested turned out to cluster together in a
meaningful way and to have a clear biological antecedent, we are apparently
expected to accept that all (or, at least, certain other) behaviours that doctors
are also interested in will show the same features. Kety's second argument
demonstrates well his misunderstanding of the issues. 'General paresis' is not
a 'disease of the brain' but a construct inferred from a cluster which includes
behaviour and infectious organisms. Before this cluster was observed, it was,
simply, unobserved although many people showed it. The fact that it was later
observed has no bearing whatsoever on what we can assume about 'schizophrenic' behaviours. In fact, Kety's argument can easily be reversed,
apparently to demonstrate the opposite point although, of course, like the
original, it demonstrates nothing:

> Psychiatrists now do not doubt the reality of apathy, social withdrawal,
> etc. as a consequence of many years of monotonous institutional life, al-
> though these were once thought of as manifestations of illness. This
> raises the interesting problem of what institutionalisation was before
> that was established. Was it a brain disease, part of an illness, a medical
> diagnosis or simply a set of behaviours of unknown origin?

The fact that Kräupl-Taylor and Kety make no mention of the many instances
where doctors were *wrong* about the antecedents of behaviour is an interesting
example of the 'attributional error' well described by Ross (1977), of ignoring
the importance of negative instances.

But there is a more subtle problem with these arguments as, presumably,
Kräupl-Taylor and Kety would claim familiarity with the fallacious 'some
swans are white therefore all swans are white' argument. The problem lies in
their apparent assumption that there are important similarities between the
behaviours they have mentioned and, for example, 'schizophrenic' behaviours
and that it is therefore legitimate to generalise from one to the other. Neither
makes explicit what this similarity is or how it justifies such sweeping generalisation, but it would appear to be nothing more than the claim that both
types of behaviour are rightly called illness. In other words, the correctness of
the conclusion is taken for granted in formulating the premiss. But even a
more convincing claim that these behaviours were similar in some way still
would not justify the assumption that what is demonstrated for one holds for
another. That fallacy would easily be demonstrated by someone who assumed
that because iron and plutonium were both metals, they could be handled with
equal lack of harm. The only convincing argument that certain behaviours

cluster together meaningfully *and* have a 'pathological' biological antecedent is direct evidence that this is the case.

But although the arguments put forward by Kräupl-Taylor and Kety can be discounted, there is, of course, a sense in which all scientific research proceeds on an 'as if' basis. Indeed, the use of the words hypothesis and theory implies this. But to take an indiscriminate 'as if' attitude means that constructs and theories with little or no supporting evidence are eternally protected from criticism because they might at some unspecified future point turn out to be 'correct'. The important point is not that a theory might be 'true' (any theory *might* be 'true') but what evidence exists to support that idea.

Defence by comparison

A number of attempts have been made to defend psychiatric classification and diagnosis in general, and 'schizophrenia' in particular, by drawing comparisons between these and supposedly acceptable aspects of scientific constructs and medical diagnosis. As will be seen, these arguments founder on the fact that the comparisons are either false or, if reasonable, are irrelevant to the issue of scientific status.

Comparison with scientific constructs

The major comparison of 'schizophrenia' with scientific constructs has, of course, been made in attempts to develop an operational definition of schizophrenia. It will be recalled that this was attempted in response to Hempel's pointing out that scientific constructs, unlike psychiatric constructs, were characterised by the availability of clear rules for inferring them. Psychiatrists' attempts to develop these rules for schizophrenia have been criticised in detail in Chapters 4 and 5, where it was pointed out that scientific constructs are characterised by correspondence rules based on the *prior* observation of patterns and not on the *post hoc* deliberations of committees.

Arieti (1979) has put forward a rather different argument which attempts to compare 'schizophrenia' with the constructs of electricity and the atom:

> If we had waited ... to define electricity or the atom until we knew everything there is to know about them, science would have made no progress. Even now, as a matter of fact, many people can argue that we do not know what electricity is.

(7)

Arieti's comments are based on a misunderstanding of how scientific constructs are developed and used. It never will be possible to say that we 'know everything about a construct' (i.e. that its theoretical network is complete), so that to compare 'schizophrenia' and 'electricity' in this way is meaningless. Rather, the crucial difference between 'electricity' and 'schizophrenia' is not

171

that we 'know more about' one than the other but that 'electricity', unlike 'schizophrenia', was introduced following the observation of patterns and has proved extremely useful in predicting new observations which is, of course, why we say that we 'know a lot about it'. It is these characteristics which allow it to claim scientific status and the lack of them which disallow the claim for 'schizophrenia'. Similar attempts to invest 'schizophrenia' with scientific status have been made by comparing it with the construct of diabetes, by pointing out that the antecedents of diabetes (and schizophrenia) are unknown and that many centuries passed before the original observation of the syndrome was elaborated (Gottesman and Shields, 1972; Wing, 1988) The problem with these arguments is similar to those of the 'electricity' comparison: the concept of diabetes is derived from the observation of a pattern, that of schizophrenia is not. Any suggestion that 'schizophrenia' should be granted a sort of provisional scientific status, and that it will one day catch up, is therefore unjustified.

But in spite of the fact that users of the construct of schizophrenia wish to claim scientific status for it, they apparently also wish to claim special dispensations. Gottesman and Shields (1972), for example, claim that: "The syndrome of schizophrenia enjoys the status of an 'open concept' and need not be strictly defined operationally to retain its legitimacy as a concept" (12). Neale and Oltmanns (1980) make a similar claim:

> We believe that [schizophrenia] is most usefully thought of as being an *open scientific construct*....It is now thought that theoretical constructs can only be partially defined by reference to single measurement operations. Even a set of such operations may not exhaustively define the construct, which thus remains "open".
>
> (1980: 19–20; emphasis in original)

These comments, like Arieti's, are based on a misrepresentation of the development of scientific constructs. If we use Neale and Oltmanns' inappropriate language, then it is true to say that constructs can only be partially defined by reference to a single measurement operation. If we use more appropriate language, we can say that the correspondence rules and theoretical network of a scientific construct such as, say, diabetes, cannot adequately be conveyed by reference to one measurement operation such as the presence of sugar in the urine. But this does not make diabetes an 'open' construct in the way the term is used for 'schizophrenia'. It simply makes it a useful construct with a complex theoretical network any part of which we might use to characterise the construct. And as Carnap (1937) has pointed out, when constructs are 'defined' in these multiple ways, the statements are systematically related to one another, just as statements about sugar in the urine are systematically related to statements about blood-sugar levels or insulin secretion. By constrast, when the term 'open' is used for 'schizophrenia', it refers to the fact that there is no agreed set of correspondence rules for inferring the construct in the first place or, as Neale and Oltmanns euphemistically put it, the limits of the concept are unclear. Nor is there any systematic relationship between different 'definitions' of schizophrenia. The reason for this, as was pointed out in Chapter 4, is that the construct was introduced and has been maintained without evidence that it had been derived from the observation of relationships amongst various phenomena. Thus, its present 'openness' is an inevitable consequence of the failure to recognise the implications of this lack, and not a feature of other scientific constructs.

Comparisons with medical diagnosis

Two kinds of comparison have been made between psychiatric and medical diagnosis. In the first, attempts have been made to demonstrate that the reliability figures found in studies of psychiatric diagnosis are not dissimilar to those found in medical diagnosis, while the second seeks to show that psychiatric diagnosis (like medical diagnosis) is a careful and complex business and not the indiscriminate application of pejorative labels. Clare (1976), for example, reviews a number of studies which show sometimes low rates of agreement amongst physicians or laboratory technicians and concludes that "There are good grounds for believing that all varieties of the diagnostic process are at times subject to significant inter-observer (and, to a lesser extent, intra-observer) variation" (135). Meehl (1972) has put forward a similar argument in claiming that "The interjudge reliability of a diagnosis of *schizophrenia* ... is at least as high as typical diagnostic agreements in other branches of medicine" (385; emphasis in original).

It may, of course, be the case that diagnostic agreement for some medical constructs is as low (or lower) than that for 'schizophrenia'. This similarity, however, appears to have blinded Clare and Meehl to a crucial difference between the two processes: disagreements about some medical diagnosis may be resolved by appeal to independent criteria; disagreements in psychiatric diagnosis, and certainly in the diagnosis of schizophrenia, which rest only on opinion, cannot. It is not difficult to imagine circumstances where the reliability of judgements, even of something as straightforward as, say, the sex of a foetus, might be low (staff are overworked; equipment is faulty; staff are badly trained, and so on) but the judgements can be checked either with those of experienced staff using good equipment or, ultimately, when the baby is born. It must be emphasised, however, that disagreement in medical diagnosis might also stem from the use of problematic concepts whose claim to scientific status is as suspect as that of 'schizophrenia'. This point is important because of the implication in both Clare's and Meehl's argument that medical practice is automatically 'right', or, at least, acceptable, so that any similarities which can be drawn between it and psychiatric practice imply that the latter, too, is acceptable. These arguments are also, of course, examples of the fallacy discussed in Chapter 4 of the confusion of reliability and validity. The mere fact that reliability coefficients of 0.9 and above may be found in diagnostic judgements of schizophrenia demonstrates nothing about the construct's validity.

Clare (1976) and Wing (1978b) have compared psychiatric and medical diagnosis in a rather different way by portraying psychiatric diagnosis as a careful and thoughtful process by which, in the case of 'schizophrenia', the term is applied only to a small group of carefully evaluated people. Both Clare and Wing discuss Rosenhan's by now famous 1973 study in which 'actors' achieved admission to psychiatric hospitals by complaining of hearing voices saying the words 'empty', 'hollow' and 'thud'. The implication of their discussion is, apparently, that experienced psychiatrists acting properly would not have applied a diagnosis of schizophrenia in these cases, at least not without a much more thorough examination. The problem with these arguments is that it does not matter how carefully someone is examined or how narrow the criteria for inferring schizophrenia if the criteria are not derived from the reliable observation of regularities. The Catholic Church takes considerable care and uses very narrow criteria in deciding whether to call someone a saint but we should hardly consider this to be evidence of the scientific status of 'sainthood'.

These arguments attain their apparent plausibility by emphasising similarities between 'schizophrenia' and some positively valued activity or construct. It is then implied that 'schizophrenia' therefore shares other positive features such as acknowledged scientific status. The fallacy in the arguments is that they fail to acknowledge crucial differences between 'schizophrenia' and other constructs and the fact that it is precisely these differences, and not the similarities, which are relevant to the claim of 'schizophrenia' to scientific status. It might as well be argued that because both cars and planes have metal bodies, both can fly.

The arguments discussed so far are indirect attempts to support 'schizophrenia', either by supporting the assumptions and practices which surround it or by comparing it with other constructs. There are, in fact, few attempts to defend the construct directly, that is by claiming that the behaviours from which it is inferred form a pattern and/or that it has strong predictive power. The discussion of the concept in DSM-III and the claims made from genetic research are, of course, direct defences and these have already been evaluated. Two other direct arguments have been put forward: one seeks to show that the concept is useful in practice and the other that some of the behaviours used to infer it do cluster above chance level.

The usefulness of 'schizophrenia'

Clare (1976) has argued that a diagnosis of schizophrenia appears to have prognostic and therapeutic implications "even if these are somewhat crude" (140). By this he means that a diagnosis of schizophrenia can predict outcome and response to intervention. Wing (1978b) has put forward a somewhat similar argument about treatment, though not about outcome.

There are two problems with these arguments. The first has already been discussed in some detail and concerns the unsatisfactory status of 'outcome' and 'response to treatment' as criteria for assessing constructs, in the absence of other evidence of their predictive power. The second problem is that even if we accept these criteria for the moment, 'schizophrenia' still comes off very badly. It was shown in Chapter 5 that follow-up data collected from those previously diagnosed as schizophrenic show considerable variability in so-called outcome. Evidence gathered after 1980 and using DSM-III criteria cannot, of course, be used to demonstrate homogeneity of outcome as the criteria have specifically been chosen in the hope of reducing the variance in outcome. As to the specificity of 'treatment', there is considerable evidence not only of variability in response to drugs (usually phenothiazines) but also that 'schizophrenics' show behavioural changes following administration of drugs usually given to other diagnostic groups (notably lithium and minor tranquillisers). It has also been demonstrated that groups not diagnosed as schizophrenic may show reductions in disturbing behaviour following phenothiazine use (Tobias and MacDonald, 1974; Kendell, 1975b; Luchins, 1975; Beckman and Haas, 1980; Naylor and Scott, 1980; Delva and Letemendia, 1982; Crow *et al.*, 1986). Interestingly, Clare (1976) notes that "some depressed patients do respond to phenothiazines" but he considers that "this is probably as a result of a non-specific sedative effect" (140). It is unclear why he does not also apply this reasoning to 'schizophrenics'.

There is another way in which attempts have been made to argue for the usefulness of 'schizophrenia', and that is by claiming that it has 'clinical utility'. DSM-IIIR, for example, places the achievement of "clinical usefulness" as the first goal of DSM-III and DSM-IIIR. This usefulness is said to be in terms of "making treatment and management decisions in varied clinical settings" (xix), so that the argument may be similar to that put forward by Clare and Wing. The particular problem with this argument, however, is that the relationship between clinical usefulness and validity is never stated; they are certainly not the same, as "consistency with data from research studies bearing on the validity of different diagnostic categories" is listed as a separate goal, and achieves only eighth place out of ten goals. It is difficult to see how the utility of a concept which claims scientific status can be considered separately from its validity, or how an invalid concept can have any constructive use in making 'treatment' decisions. It is difficult to avoid the conclusion that what is meant here is clinicians' *beliefs* about whether a concept is of use to them in their work. There is by now sufficient evidence available on the biases and errors which may attend the kinds of judgements which clinicians are required to make to encourage us to be rather sceptical about claims to 'clinical utility' in the absence of independent evidence of validity (see, for example, Nisbett and Ross, 1980; Kahneman *et al.*, 1982).

Patterns by multivariate analysis

Various attempts have been made, using the techniques of factor and cluster analysis, to demonstrate that certain 'schizophrenic' behaviours cluster together above chance level. The data for these analyses are usually ratings of the presence or absence of supposed symptoms in unselected samples of psychiatric patients. It is argued that if these techniques 'reveal' groupings which correspond to diagnostic categories of schizophrenia, then it may be assumed that the construct does refer to a pattern. Trouton and Maxwell (1956), using factor analysis, presented data which, they claimed, supported the idea of a schizophrenic cluster in an unselected sample of psychiatric patients while Everitt *et al.* (1971) made a similar claim for 'paranoid schizophrenia' and 'chronic schizophrenia' using cluster analysis.

One major problem with these techniques is that at all stages they are dependent on subjective judgements, from judgements about the selection of phenomena to be rated to judgements about which of the many possible groupings which the analyses might reveal should be chosen as best reflecting the data. As Kendell (1975b) has pointed out, there are no clear rules for making these decisions nor for making decisions about the validity of clusters. Maxwell (1971) and Kendell have also pointed out that some of the groupings supposedly revealed may be a consequence not of the data but of the method: factor analysis produces factors while some cluster-analysis programmes will produce clusters from data known not to contain any. There is, thus, the danger, highlighted by Mischel (1968) in relation to 'personality' assessment, that the results reveal more about the researchers' beliefs than about the data.

There is one aspect of these beliefs which is of particular interest here. There is considerable evidence, some of which will be reviewed in the next chapter, that beliefs about the co-occurrence of particular phenomena can strongly influence reports of their co-occurrence. There is no reason to believe that psychiatrists' and psychologists' ratings of the presence or absence of 'symptoms' are not influenced by their beliefs about whether particular 'symptoms' 'go together'. Thus, even if there existed a statistical analysis which *did* reflect 'real' clusters in rating data, it would be difficult to know, without independent evidence of the clusters' validity, whether they had not, so to speak, been put there by the researchers in the process of data collection.

Slade and Cooper (1979) have highlighted a different, but equally serious, problem of this kind of research. They point out that the samples used, far from being unselected, are highly selected in that they have been brought to the attention of psychiatrists. Because people with few disturbing behaviours are less likely to be noticed than people with many, the inter-correlations amongst 'symptoms' observed in a psychiatric population might be artificially inflated. Slade and Cooper therefore suggested that statistically significant inter-correlations amongst a group of 'schizophrenic' symptoms might be the result of selection factors and have little to do with the actual relationships amongst these phenomena in a truly unselected population. As one way of evaluating this hypothesis, Slade and Cooper used certain of the data reported by Trouton and Maxwell in their factor-analytic study of psychiatric 'symptoms'. They constructed three hypothetical groups, each containing fifty cases displaying 'schizophrenic' behaviour and 139 who did not (these proportions were the same as in the original study). But in Slade and Cooper's study, the presence or absence of particular 'schizophrenic symptoms' in each case (mood disturbance, delusions, motor disturbance, hallucinations, thought-disorder) was determined randomly, using a set of bingo numbers, with the limitations that the frequency of each 'symptom' in the sample was proportional to that in the original study and that 'schizophrenic symptoms' did not occur in the hypothetical 'non-schizophrenic' cases. Slade and Cooper's analysis revealed average inter-correlations of 'schizophrenic symptoms' for each of their hypothetical groups of +0.70; +0.71; +0.66 – virtually identical to Trouton and Maxwell's +0.67.

Although these criticisms make it very difficult to see what role multivariate analysis could have in supporting the concept of schizophrenia, it is worth noting, as Bentall (1986) has pointed out, that even without these criticisms, the data from multivariate studies provide little support for the idea of a 'schizophrenic' cluster and that in general, patients diagnosed as schizophrenic are distributed across clusters containing patients given quite other diagnoses.

Chapter eight

Why has 'schizophrenia' survived?

It could be argued that any discussion of why 'schizophrenia' has been retained, in spite of lack of supporting empirical evidence, is inseparable from
discussion of why the psychiatric profession has come to play such a major role
in dealing with many kinds of unwanted behaviour. Such a coverage, however,
is beyond the scope of this chapter and the discussion here will be limited to
possible reasons why 'schizophrenia' and the assumptions and practices surrounding it have been retained. But it must be said that the concepts of
schizophrenia and mental illness are so closely related that it is virtually impossible to discuss the retention of 'schizophrenia' without asking why we
should wish to call unwanted behaviour 'illness'. Inevitably, the discussion will
not only be limited but also speculative as there is no obvious way of knowing
whether the factors which will be suggested actually do operate to retain the
concept; they are put forward merely as more or less probable. Three major
sets of reasons will be discussed. The first concerns the functions which may
be served by 'schizophrenia', both for those who apply it and for the general
public. The second set considers 'schizophrenia' as an exemplar or a result of
particular ways of thinking and reasoning which are common amongst lay
people; while the third set is concerned with the ways in which the presentation of the literature on 'schizophrenia', both to professionals and to the
public, might function to maintain belief in its validity.

The functions of 'schizophrenia' – for psychiatry

It has been emphasised already that the concept of 'schizophrenia' and the
activities of classification, diagnosis and physical intervention function to support psychiatrists' claim to be medical professionals. Just as it is difficult to
imagine a branch of the legal profession whose activities have nothing whatsoever in common with solicitors or barristers or judges, it is difficult to
imagine a branch of the medical profession whose activities bear no relationship to the practice of medicine. That this is indeed the case is emphasised by
the remarks of an American Professor of Psychiatry:

Now, it is in the tradition of such experts [medical specialists] that they are masters of knowledge about an organ system. What is the organ system of psychiatrists? If the domain of the cardiologist is the heart and circulatory system, then surely the domain of the psychiatrist is the brain and its system therein. To qualify and *survive* as physician specialists, we must become better brain specialists.

(Hanley, 1985, cited in Szasz,1987: 69; emphasis added)

Psychiatrists, however, are in the potentially embarrassing position of being brain specialists who for the most part rely on judgements about behaviour, and not brain functioning, to make their diagnoses and who have failed to demonstrate clear links between these behaviours and brain functioning. Both opponents and proponents of 'schizophrenia' have emphasised the centrality of this concept to psychiatrists' claim to be functioning in a manner similar to their medical colleagues and, therefore, to psychiatry's credibility as a medical profession. It might therefore reasonably be argued that the *language,* or the *idea,* of behaviour as illness and of 'schizophrenia' as a particular and serious form of illness is important in maintaining the impression of similarity between psychiatry and the various medical specialties, in the absence of some important actual similarities in their activities. The crucial differences between medicine and psychiatry can perhaps best be summarised by saying that whereas medical scientists study bodily functioning and describe patterns in it, psychiatrists behave *as if* they were studying bodily functioning and *as if* they had described patterns there, when in fact they are studying behaviour and have assumed – but not demonstrated – that certain types of pattern *will be* found there. It can be argued that it is this 'as if' or metaphorical quality of psychiatry which makes the concept of disease so important to it as a discipline. And if the concept of mental disease is indispensable to psychiatry, then it is equally important to identify mental diseases, otherwise we might begin to suspect that they did not exist. Given the central role attributed to 'schizophrenia', the vast literature surrounding it and the research effort to validate claims made about it, it seems reasonable to suggest that it functions as the prototypical psychiatric disease.

The problem remains as to why disciplines and professional groups which have no obvious vested interest in maintaining concepts of illness and schizophrenia should still do so. It may be that the use of the concept of schizophrenia in the face of incomprehensible behaviour gives the impression of knowledge so important in maintaining the credibility of any group which claims expertise. This is not to suggest that professionals who use 'schizophrenia' are deliberately pretending knowledge; an understandable reliance on secondary sources may have convinced them that the concept does have predictive power. This, together with the operation of some of the factors which will be discussed in the next sections, may at least partly account for the retention of 'schizophrenia' by many non-psychiatric disciplines and professional groups.

The functions of 'schizophrenia' – for the public

Although psychiatrists clearly have much to gain by retaining the concept of schizophrenia, they are apparently strongly supported in their views by the general public. A series of articles in *The Times* (February/March 1986), for example, did not once question the idea that there exists an illness called schizophrenia whose sufferers require treatment from doctors; it resulted in many supporting letters. Similarly, the considerable power which psychiatrists are able to exert by using the term schizophrenia was granted by Parliament, albeit after submissions by a medical lobby. But there is little indication (see, for example, Bean, 1980) that these submissions did not meet with wide agreement. The question then arises as to why the public should wish to believe in 'schizophrenia' and what functions the concept might serve for them. One possible function has been clearly suggested by Jablensky, interviewed about research which supposedly showed 'schizophrenia' to have a biological basis: "Those who take comfort from the evidence that schizophrenia has a biological basis should be further reassured" (*The Times*, 3 March 1986). Cumming (1970) has made a similar suggestion: "the discovery of a virus or a replaceable biochemical link would be a double deliverance, for epidemiologists as well as from a truly awful illness" (122).

It is not immediately obvious why we should regard the fact that at least one in every hundred people in the population is suffering from an incurable brain disease, as distinct, say, from the fact that they have learned to behave in particular ways, as a deliverance or be comforted by the idea. There has certainly never been the slightest suggestion in any neurology text that people should be comforted by the idea that their relatives have a brain disease; on the contrary, this news is usually seen as meriting sympathy and pity. The answer is, apparently, that the idea of brain disease somehow absolves the 'victim', relatives or society in general from responsibility for having caused the person's disturbing behaviour:

> Even though [the genetic evidence] exonerates parents from having caused their child's schizophrenia by their methods of rearing...
> (Gottesman and Shields, 1982: 200)

> The study should relieve any feelings of guilt. Families cannot be blamed...
> (Jablensky, *The Times*, 3 March 1986)

> We, as a parent support group (People Acting Together in Hope) are extremely grateful for your series on schizophrenia....Recognition has long been overdue that this terrible brain disease is the fault of neither the vic-

tim nor their families, but is of neurobiological or genetic origin....We need the understanding and help of all society to see this disease as it truly is – a disabling brain disease.

(Rose, 1986; cited in Szasz, 1987: 76)

How could anybody do such a horrible thing? The answer is schizophrenia, an overpowering mental illness that robbed John of his ability to control his thoughts and actions.... John is *desperately* ill.... [T]he disease is the culprit, not the person.

(parents of John Hinkley, 1983, quoted in Szasz, 1987: 255; emphasis in original)

It appears, then, that if the concept of schizophrenia as brain disease were to be abandoned, then the blame for disturbing behaviour might be placed squarely on either the actor or his or her family. (The difficulties we seem to have in interpreting bizarre behaviour other than in these ways will be discussed later.) Given the potency of the ideas of guilt and blame in our society, it is hardly surprising that people should wish to evade them. But the idea of people being comforted by particular ideas recalls not scientific but lay ideas (that there is life after death; that education will harm women's brains; that black people are inferior to white people); ideas which, it is reasonable to suggest, are expressly designed to comfort particular groups and may be used to justify actions which might otherwise be called into question.

To claim that we should not be concerned with how comforting our theories of disturbing behaviour might be, and, indeed, that we should be suspicious of theories with no direct support but which are said to comfort or exonerate, is not to downgrade the plight of those diagnosed schizophrenic or their relatives. It is, however, to emphasise that when people are faced with incomprehensible, disturbing and aversive phenomena for which they might be blamed, then they are likely to grasp at explanations which not only appear to exonerate them but which also remove the disturbance. In the case of behaviours which lead to a diagnosis of schizophrenia, the disease or illness idea is used to justify removing persons to 'a place of safety' and 'treating' them without their consent. The concept and the assumptions which surround it thus have the threefold advantage of exonerating disturbing people and their relatives, of removing and apparently helping 'the sufferer' and of apparently achieving this not only with humanity but also with the support of science.

The idea of schizophrenia as a disease might not only serve to justify intervention without consent, but also to distance us from disturbing people. It may do this by placing them in a separate category and by postulating uncommon processes to account for their behaviour, processes which by definition do not operate for ordinary people. Lerner (1980) has emphasised our apparent need to believe in a stable and orderly world and our tendency to use 'internal' and pejorative labels to characterise those who in some way challenge this belief. We thus not only achieve distance between them and us but also foster the belief that we can avoid a similar fate.

'Schizophrenia' as an exemplar of fallacies in reasoning and judgement

The problem of pattern recognition

The question of the validity of 'schizophrenia' centres on the demonstration that it is derived from a reliably observed pattern, an above-chance co-occurrence of phenomena. As has been emphasised here, any claims to predictive power are dependent on this demonstration's having been made. It is clear that many of those who use the concept believe that it is derived from a pattern. It is equally clear, from the literature reviewed in earlier chapters, that this is not and never has been the case. The question arises, then, of why this belief should persist. It may, of course, be reinforced by the processes discussed in the first two sections, but that cannot be the whole story. There is, in fact, now a considerable literature which suggests a powerful tendency to 'see' patterns which are not there and which clarifies some of the processes which may foster this habit.

It is well demonstrated that we tend to assume that unusual or distinctive stimuli which arise from the same person or group are related (Hamilton, 1981). The behaviours from which schizophrenia is inferred are both unusual and distinctive. This process may operate to encourage the belief not only that, for example, delusions and hallucinations are related, but that both are related to other unusual and distinctive acts such as murder or arson. This process is not dissimilar to that suggested by Slade and Cooper (1979), whose work was discussed in Chapter 7. They suggested that a spurious impression of co-occurrence of 'schizophrenic symptoms' might be fostered simply by the fact that several odd behaviours, even if they co-occur by chance, are more noticeable than only one. Thus, the psychiatric population, which comprises, after all, those who have been noticed and brought to psychiatric attention, will by definition contain more cases of co-occurrence than of single disturbing behaviours. Although this process is likely to create a strong subjective impression of a pattern of co-occurrence where none exists it might also, as Slade and Cooper (1979) have suggested, be responsible for the creation of apparently significant statistical patterns. If those who are brought to psychiatric attention already contain an excess of 'co-occurrences', then this impression is likely to be further strengthened by diagnostic practices. As was pointed out in Chapter 5, the development of DSM-III marked the first serious attempt to impose a national and international operational definition of schizophrenia. If psychiatrists regularly apply this definition then inevitably a population of 'schizophrenics', all of whom show a similar cluster of behaviours, will be created. Given that the arbitrariness of the DSM-III criteria appears to have been lost sight of, then their application may strengthen still further the idea that 'schizophrenia' refers to a distinct pattern.

These processes may operate amongst both psychiatrists and lay people. There is, however, another important factor which may influence the perception of patterns but which is more likely to operate amongst professionals and that is previously held beliefs about co-occurrences. Lay people presumably know that 'schizophrenia' is supposed to have a number of symptoms but they are unlikely to know what particular phenomena are used as diagnostic criteria. Psychiatrists and other professionals, however, have access to textbooks or colleagues who tell them what the supposed cluster is and, it can be argued, give them the expectation that they will find it.

Chapman and Chapman (1967, 1982) and Shweder (1977) have provided striking demonstrations of the way in which previously held beliefs can induce us to 'see' patterns which do not exist. Using random pairings of symptom statements and test results, Chapman and Chapman showed that lay people 'found' relationships between the two which apparently reflected cultural beliefs about how people with various characteristics would respond to projective tests. Chapman and Chapman were also able to show that the effect, which they called the 'illusory correlation', was remarkably resistant to their attempts to abolish it. Shweder, in an ingenious re-analysis of Newcomb's 1929 study of co-operation and competition in a boys' camp, showed that camp staff reported, via rating forms, highly significant co-occurrences between various behaviours which observation of the boys had shown not to co-occur at all. Shweder was able to demonstrate that the *reported*, i.e. false, co-occurrences reflected commonly held beliefs that certain behaviours 'were like each other'. Although this research has used lay people as subjects and demonstrated the effects of cultural beliefs, there is no reason to suppose that the same effect does not hold for 'specialist' beliefs. Bennett (1983); for example, presented psychiatrists and lay people with 'cases' showing psychiatric symptoms. Half the subjects were also presented with a diagnosis of schizophrenia or manic-depressive psychosis, possibly consistent with the symptoms (WHO, 1973). In a recall task one week later, psychiatrists, but not lay people, erroneously recalled the presence of symptoms which, according to WHO, 'made up' the schizophrenia cluster. The effect, however, was limited to those psychiatrists whose 'cases' had received a diagnosis of schizophrenia. (An identical effect was found for 'manic depressive psychosis'.)

Given results such as these, it is not surprising that a number of writers have commented on – and provided strong evidence for – the considerable difficulties we seem to have in making accurate judgements of correlations or co-variation (Shweder, 1977; Nisbett and Ross, 1980; Crocker, 1981; Kahneman *et al.*, 1982). Indeed, it can be argued that the whole scientific enterprise is one which seeks to reduce these biases as much as possible. This is reflected in part in the demand that constructs inferred from putative patterns should have predictive power and, similarly, in medicine's demand that the criteria for inferring diagnostic concepts should include reliably observable 'signs'. It is therefore very disturbing to find an apparently total lack of awareness of these effects in the 'schizophrenia' literature; on the contrary, there is open acceptance of processes which give considerable scope for the operation of biases – Kraepelin's and Bleuler's method of introducing constructs on the basis of personal beliefs completely unsupported by data; the defence of 'schizophrenia' merely by offering shared beliefs; the practice of allowing committee judgement to determine diagnostic criteria; the failure to appreciate the profound effects on data collection of using strongly pre-selected 'psychiatric' samples, and so on. But before psychiatry is castigated for failing to put its house in order, it must be emphasised that there seems to be a general problem here. Shweder (1977), for example, implies that western anthropologists' are inclined to discuss 'magical thinking' in so-called primitive peoples as if it were part of being primitive rather than a characteristic of all cultures, including advanced western societies. Similarly, Mischel (1968) has demonstrated the power of *beliefs* about co-occurrences of behaviour on academic personality theory, while Sarbin (1968) has pointed to the confusion of lay and scientific constructs in psychological theory. It is difficult to avoid the conclusion that when the subject-matter is ourselves, we are inclined to overestimate the veracity of our beliefs.

The problems of question-begging and reification

It was pointed out in the last chapter that 'schizophrenia' is supported by various non-empirical arguments and it was demonstrated that many of them are fallacious. The question arises as to why this has not been widely realised. One important reason may be that the arguments are based on what Thouless (1974) has called "dishonest tricks commonly used in arguments". In other words, no special form of argument is used to support 'schizophrenia'; rather the arguments are in a form all of us use some of the time in good faith that we have a strong case, and are thus less likely to be detected as false.

Perhaps the most frequently used 'dishonest trick' in the 'schizophrenia' literature is that of begging the question, of taking for granted what is in dispute or of assuming in a definition what has to be proved. What is remarkable is the extent to which this device is used. It was pointed out earlier that the whole of Kraepelin's, Bleuler's and Schneider's writings, for example, are based on it, as is virtually the whole of the literature on the search for an operational definition of schizophrenia and the development of classification systems. As Thouless has pointed out, it is easier to use this device, or indeed any false device, successfully when the argument is stated in such a way that it is not apparent that it is being used. It seems reasonable to suggest that one set of circumstances in which it would be relatively easy to obscure the fact that important questions were being begged is those in which what is taken for granted is strongly and widely believed; some examples of the strength of belief in the existence of an illness called schizophrenia have already been given.

A second notable feature of the 'schizophrenia' literature is the habit of reification, of talking about ideas or concepts as if they were things. The habit has been well described (see, for example, Ryle, 1949; Young, 1951) and Szasz's (1987) observation that the *Dictionary of the History of Ideas* has no entry for 'mental illness' is a good example of it. Crookshank (1956), in a sharply critical paper condemning the widespread use of reification in medicine (actually written in 1923), talked of the "tyranny of names" and claimed that "few now comprehend the distinctions between Words, Thoughts and Things, or the relations engaged between them when statements are communicated" (340). Emmet (1968) expressed the hope that this way of thinking was now less prevalent in medicine but this seems not to be so. As was pointed out in Chapter 4, the modern ICD still talks of constructs as being 'the names of diseases'; DSM-III talks of psychiatrists diagnosing disorders which people have while DSM-IIIR claims that it is using the "more accurate" expression (than that of 'a schizophrenic'), of "a person with schizophrenia" (xxiii).

It is not difficult to see why we might reify ideas. It is, after all, much more difficult to juggle with abstract concepts and symbols than with material entities; indeed it is this very skill which is assumed to discriminate between people with high and low IQs. Ogden and Richards (1956) have suggested another reason: that "if we are ever to finish making any general remark, [we must] contract and condense our language" (133). It is, however, as Ogden and Richards were well aware, precisely these contractions which allow reification, *if they are used without acknowledgement of what is being done.* Examples of this kind of contraction are easy to find in medicine: 'You have diabetes' (or multiple sclerosis, rheumatoid arthritis, and so on) instead of 'Your body shows a cluster of phenomena which previous research suggests is a pattern which justifies inferring a hypothetical construct which in this case we call diabetes.' 'Doctors find new treatment for multiple sclerosis' instead of 'Doctors have identified a biochemical agent which changes (or abolishes) some parts of the pattern from which they infer the construct of multiple sclerosis.' 'Your prognosis is very good' instead of 'Observation of people who show a pattern of phenomena similar to yours suggests that the pattern tends to disappear in a relatively short time.' The problem is that these devices are often used without acknowledgement that the contractions do not mean what they seem to mean, that is, acknowledgement that they are, to use Ogden and Richards' terms, conveniences in description and not necessities in the structure of things. This means that when psychiatrists, who use the language of medicine, employ the same devices, it is not at all obvious that the expansion statement has a quite different meaning from that which it would have in medicine. Thus, when a psychiatrist says 'You have schizophrenia', the medical expansion is false, because no pattern which would justify inferring the construct has ever been observed. Also, because the true expansion is rarely made, the concept is protected.

It was pointed out in the previous chapter that some of the arguments used to support 'schizophrenia' are based on a confusion of observation and inference. The habit of reification encourages this confusion, by failing to make clear this crucial distinction, by, in effect, treating inferences as if they were observations. It may be, also, that reification encourages question-begging. It is, after all, easier to take for granted the existence of a thing than of an idea; and, conversely, it is much more difficult for critics to convince an audience that a thing does not exist than that an idea might be wrong or a concept invalid.

It is perhaps easier to understand why the search for an operational definition of schizophrenia should have proceeded back to front, if it is seen as exemplifying both reification and question-begging. Instead of treating 'schizophrenia' as a construct whose lack of an original empirical base meant that it could not constructively be used, those seeking an operational definition treated the term as if it referred, say, to a car which did not work very well, which had to have some bits removed and new bits added and which might very well improve even more in the future, but which was always indisputably a car.

The use of emotional language

As Radcliffe-Richards (1982) has pointed out, there are certain words in our language whose emotional connotations are so strong, they encourage us to take leave of our critical senses. The effect is well recognised. Crookshank (1956) talks of "The emotive use of language [which] so sways the intellect" (345) while Stevenson (1944) commented on the fact that our language abounds with persuasive words with vague and ever-changing descriptive meanings and strong emotional connotations. The literature on 'schizophrenia' also abounds with such words: help; treatment; victim; sick; patient; rehabilitation; care, and so on. One effect of these is to make it extremely difficult for critics to make negative comments about the concept of schizophrenia or about what is done in the name of the concept, lest they be accused of 'not caring about what happens to these sick people' or of 'trying to deprive these people of the help they need'. Kety (1974), for example, talks about someone who had done so much to help the mentally ill but did not find it necessary to criticise the concept, while Sedgwick accuses those who claim that mental illnesses do not exist of depriving the mentally ill of the services they need.

It has already been pointed out that these arguments are examples of question-begging in that they assume that there are mental illnesses which require help of a certain kind. But because the persuasive power of words like these is such as to obscure the assumptions and actions which they involve, it is difficult to put forward convincing arguments about the need to examine and question them, without calling forth another of Thouless' 'dishonest tricks' – that of blackening the uncaring critics, while avoiding answering the argument.

The search for explanations

Our tendency to construct explanations of events has often been remarked upon (for example, Scheibe and Sarbin, 1965; Peckham, 1979; Witelson, 1986). Indeed, Peckham has emphasised that we cannot manage ourselves or others without manufacturing explanations. Although, as Peckham says, we are constantly explaining events, there are circumstances under which we might be inclined to put more effort into the process, and regard it as more important to come up with a satisfactory explanation. We would probably, for example, make more effort when the events were apparently incomprehensible, that is, they defied easy analysis with the usual cultural explanations. We would also make more effort when the events were disturbing, upsetting or frightening, particularly if they directly impinged on us. The behaviours which lead to a diagnosis of schizophrenia fulfil both these criteria. Invoking 'schizophrenia', of course, is no explanation at all. The important point, however, is that 'schizophrenia' seems to explain the inexplicable and thus, presumably, to make it less threatening. What is of interest here, however, is not that we try to explain the inexplicable and disturbing so much as the type of explanation which is suggested.

Ross (1977) has highlighted our propensity to explain others' behaviour in terms of internal, stable dispositions (and, he might well have added, in terms of stable biological factors). So strong is this tendency to ignore the context in which behaviour occurs that Ross has dubbed it the 'fundamental attribution error'. (See also Jones, 1979; Nisbett and Ross, 1980.) He has suggested that we are more likely to construct 'internal' explanations when the behaviour in question is distinctive (or more distinctive than its context) and when it is perceived as uncommon. 'Schizophrenic' behaviour is both. But 'schizophrenia' is not only an internal or dispositional explanation; it is a biological one. Some reasons for preferring biological explanations of very bizarre behaviour have already been mentioned – they function to support the psychiatric profession, they apparently absolve from blame and thus seem humane and they may distance us from disturbing people. Two more reasons for preferring biological explanations can be suggested. First, biological factors are apparently seen as more fundamental, more important than any others in accounting for behaviour. Hemmings and Hemmings (1978), for example, claimed that: "For years lip service has been paid to a belief in a biological basis for schizophrenia, but nevertheless psychosocial and psychodynamic 'theories' of schizophrenia have been promulgated and these have detracted from the all important biological work" (xi).

This naive but highly prevalent view of behaviour, which not only suggests that biology is fundamental but that its contribution can be separately quantified, has been severely criticised (see, for example, Sahlins, 1977; Rose, 1984; Rose *et al.*, 1984). It has been aptly dubbed the 'wedding cake view' by Hallam (1985b) for its presentation of culture or environment as something that is perched on top of the more basic structures below. When behaviour is presented like this, however, then it appears that, as Rose (1984) has depicted it, in order to deal properly with disordered behaviour, we must find and deal with disordered molecules. This view, of course, is supported by the idea that doctors cure people by altering their biology, not their environment. A second reason for this preference for biological explanations is that they may be seen as more scientific. It was pointed out in Chapter 2 that the change to a medical perspective of disturbing behaviour was presented then, and is presented now, as a scientific alternative to explanations which depicted the mad as possessed or subhuman. And because these latter explanations had been associated with cruelty, it was easy, in the later confusion of medical and moral approaches to lunacy, to miss the fact that the medical approach was neither scientific nor particularly humane. The problem today is that biological explanations are still presented as the scientific alternative as if the systematic study of behaviour did not exist. We are thus presented with various dichotomies which do not allow the non-evaluative description of relationships between behaviour and its context. A recent television documentary, for example ('Out of Court', BBC2, February 1987), publicised, without critical comment, the suggestion that 50 per cent of prisoners have committed offences not because they are evil but because they are sick. Similar dichotomies have been put forward by others:

> [Schizophrenia] is not mystical; it has physical causes.
>
> (*New Scientist* Editorial, 1970)

> [Schizophrenia] is not caused by devils or difficult mothers or tyrannical fathers or latent homosexuality or stress.... Schizophrenia is a physical *disease*.
>
> (Hoffer and Osmond, 1965; cited in Szasz, 1976: 113; emphasis in original)

> Schizophrenia is not a punishment from God. It is not a product of faulty upbringing. It is a disease of the brain and mind.
>
> (Blakemore, 1988)

This kind of comment is consistent with the idea, discussed earlier, that biological explanations absolve both the 'victim' and the family from blame.

Part of the difficulty of constructing environmental or contextual accounts of bizarre behaviour would seem to be that these are not only seen as less scientific but also as placing blame. It seems to be extraordinarily difficult for us simply to describe the functional relationships between, say, the behaviour of mother and son without it being suggested that we are either praising or blaming, according to how we evaluate the outcome. It is interesting to note, however, that it is apparently acceptable to suggest that environmental factors may *contribute* to schizophrenia, may make it better or worse while maintaining that families need not feel guilty (see, for example, Gottesman and Shields, 1982; Jablensky, 1986). This view has been to some extent forced from researchers by the results of genetic and outcome research but it may be made socially acceptable by the fact that it retains the idea of a fundamental biological weakness which makes the person vulnerable to ordinary events.

But it is not difficult to see how the idea that 'biological explanation' and 'scientific explanation' are synonymous could have gained credence. Our image of the scientist as someone who works in a laboratory, who uses chemicals and test-tubes and complicated measuring equipment is well established. And it is undoubtedly true that much of what we now know of our biology and biochemistry was observed in that kind of setting. Similarly, the kind of variables which are postulated in biological theories of schizophrenia – neurotransmitters, for example – do 'exist'. By contrast, psychological or contextual accounts can seem either like common sense or to be full of abstract jargon. Thus, the fact that explanations of someone's 'schizophrenic' behaviour based on chemical imbalances and explanations based on possession or witchcraft both owe more to belief than evidence is hidden because, in the twentieth century, one *sounds* more scientific.

The presentation of 'schizophrenia'

There is good reason to suppose that the way in which 'schizophrenia' is presented, both in the academic and lay literature, might help to account for its persistence. Two aspects of this presentation will be briefly considered. First, the flexibility of the concept in the face of non-supporting evidence and second, the gap between the data and methods described in original research papers and their presentation in secondary sources.

The adaptability of 'schizophrenia'

It has been emphasised here that in medical research, people who share some characteristics are grouped together for research purposes in the hope of observing further shared attributes which, without this grouping, might go unobserved. It has also been emphasised that this grouping process is fraught with difficulty because it can be carried out in so many different ways; the dif-

ficulty is in knowing whether any shared characteristics are actually important, whether any proposed cluster of shared characteristics co-occurs above
chance level. The success of a grouping in leading to new observations is, of
course, the major way of finding out. Because it has never been demonstrated
that 'schizophrenia' is derived from such a pattern, it follows that the group
called schizophrenic cannot be assumed to share important characteristics. If
this is the case, then, if 'schizophrenia' is used as an independent variable, and
a search made for as yet unobserved shared characteristics, the result would
be equivocal and unreplicated data. This is, in fact, one of the main characteristics of the literature. In a considerable understatement, Neale and
Oltmanns (1980) say that "The literature we have reviewed here does not all
fit together into a tidy theory" (453); the discussant of a series of symposium
papers (Spaulding and Cole, 1984) points out that some of the theoretical
models described had been developed only by ignoring the large amount of
noise in a diverse literature; Buchsbaum (1977) notes that "a biologically
homogeneous sub-group has been elusive" (12) while Sarbin and Mancuso
(1980) more directly call the literature on cognitive functioning chaotic. It is
exceptionally rare to find that this disarray results in suggestions that the concept of schizophrenia be abandoned. Instead, two major procedures have been
suggested or used to try to achieve some sort of order (apart, of course, from
simply ignoring the 'noise'). The first, and older, has been to divide the population of 'schizophrenics' into sub-groups, in the hope that the smaller groups
would prove homogeneous where the larger had not. And, by definition, they
are more so, if only because they are defined by the fact that their members
share one or more obvious features, in addition to the features which characterise the larger group. Unfortunately, as was pointed out in Chapter 5, no
good evidence has been provided that the similarity is more than superficial.

But although there is little evidence that this procedure has been successful
in producing order, it might seem plausible (and thus protect the concept) for
two reasons. First, as was mentioned earlier, it does create groups which are
superficially more homogeneous. Second, the procedure is valid in principle,
and has been used to some effect in medicine as, for example, in creating sub-
groups for the 'rheumatic diseases'. Thus, it might reasonably be supposed,
particularly if belief in the parent concept is strong, that if one set of sub-
groupings does not work, then another might. A related suggestion to that of
creating sub-groups is the idea that 'schizophrenia' probably has many causes
(see, for example, Buchsbaum, 1977; Lander, 1988; Wing, 1988) and therefore
the failure reliably to find some event in association with the diagnosis is to
be expected. Again, this plausible suggestion can protect the concept by dis-
tracting attention from the more likely possibility that the failure is the result
of searching for antecedents of non-existent patterns.

A second major attempt to create order amongst the group of 'schizophrenics' has been made more recently and has been described as 'multi-axial' or
'multi-variable' diagnosis (see, for example, Strauss, 1975; APA, 1987). The

procedure has already been mentioned, in Chapter 5, but, briefly, involves characterising people along a number of axes which always include 'syndrome' or 'primary diagnosis' and may include judgements about, for example, duration of 'symptoms', work performance, personal relationships, supposed antecedents, and so on. Because this type of system has not yet been widely adopted, it is too early to say what its effects will be. But problems can be anticipated because the system remains based on the inference to 'schizophrenia', and simply adds the suggestion that diagnosticians should make additional judgements about supposed antecedents, relationships, and so on. Like the practice of creating sub-groups, however, the procedure could seem plausible. It might, for example, apparently achieve its goal of enhancing the predictive power of a diagnosis of schizophrenia if accurate observations are made of factors, such as work status and relationships, which might influence, say, response to intervention. But the fact that the concept of schizophrenia might well be irrelevant – in other words, that the relationship between predictor and outcome variables might hold with or without the concept – is unlikely to be seriously considered, so that again the concept is protected. Multi-axial evaluation might seem plausible also because, like the practice of creating sub-groups, it has been suggested as a way of increasing the value of some medical diagnoses (for example, Engel, 1977, 1980).

Although these practices represent explicit attempts to adapt the construct in the face of dismayingly diverse data, it is worth noting that concepts whose referents are uncertain and often changing and whose theoretical networks are unclear are almost by definition adaptable because it is never quite clear what predictions should be made and whether data do or do not support them. A number of examples of this situation were presented in Chapter 6, where it was shown that, in the face of data which did not support an initial prediction, some researchers changed their definitions of dependent and independent variables and still concluded that their predictions had been supported.

The gap between data and conclusions

It was suggested earlier that many of those who read about 'schizophrenia' will do so in secondary sources. McCulloch (1983) has suggested that reliance on secondary sources is likely to be one major reason for the creation of what might be called myths, if the sources do not properly represent what was actually done and described in primary sources. The extent to which secondary sources have misrepresented the genetic research has already been described. It is probably true to say that it is this area which has suffered most from misrepresentation, although, as has been seen, Kraepelin's and Bleuler's work has also been misrepresented. One factor which might allow this misrepresentation is that claims made for Kraepelin's and Bleuler's work and for genetic research, while necessary to establish the concept and its major assumptions, need have no immediate practical consequences, apart, of course, from supporting the use of medical theories and practices. If, however, it were to be claimed that some biochemical feature had been reliably associated with a diagnosis of schizophrenia, then it might reasonably be asked why this was not now used as a diagnostic criterion. But though it is readily noted that no such feature has been observed, descriptions of this research, whether in academic, semi-academic or obviously lay texts, still present it in a simplified and optimistic way which suggests that the problem lies in the complexity of the brain and not in the deficiencies of 'schizophrenia'. Thus, it is supposed that the problem will be solved given increasingly sophisticated research methods. Wing (1988), for example, suggests that the lack of non-invasive methods of studying brain functioning may have been chiefly responsible for the lack of progress in schizophrenia research. In the mean time, the lack of clear data may be obscured by the use of optimistic language which tells us more about researchers' feelings and opinions than about the quality of the data. Certain theories, for example, are said to be front runners; researchers are excited or hopeful; new findings in the neurosciences may provide the answer; new leads are being followed, and so on (see, for example, Clare, 1976; Wing, 1978b; Neale and Oltmanns, 1980; Strauss and Carpenter, 1981; Seeman *et al.*, 1982; Cutting, 1985). And Karson *et al.*'s (1986) comment that "the biochemical basis of the schizophrenic syndrome remains elusive" (495) begs more questions and conjures up a quite different picture from the more direct statement that 'researchers have failed to find ...'.

Finally, it might reasonably be suggested that the concept of schizophrenia survives because there is no strong alternative. Certainly, it has been argued (for example, Lakatos, 1978) that it is the presence of a plausible alternative, rather than a weight of negative evidence, which mainly determines whether a concept or theory will persist. But if the arguments presented here are valid, then it is impossible to have a useful alternative 'theory of schizophrenia', so that it is hardly surprising that a strong theory should not have emerged. What is possible, however, are alternatives to the concept of schizophrenia. As will be seen in the next chapter, plausible alternatives to the concept (to describing and interpreting 'schizophrenic' behaviour) do exist and the question of interest is why they have not been widely adopted. At least one answer may be found in the professional and social functions served by the present concept and theory and which are unlikely to be duplicated by alternative interpretations.

Chapter nine

Living without 'schizophrenia' – issues and some alternatives

The major argument which has been presented here is that the concept of schizophrenia was introduced and has been developed and used in a way which bears little resemblance to the methods of construct formation used in medical and other empirical sciences. It has also been argued that any attempt to transform the concept to a scientific one is futile and is based on a serious misunderstanding of the methods used to develop concepts whose claim to scientific status is less equivocal. Before the implications of these arguments are discussed, it is as well to repeat what has not been argued. It is not claimed that some people do not behave in strange and disturbing ways or have disturbing experiences. Nor is it claimed that these behaviours and experiences may not cause considerable distress, that they may not be preceded by changes in brain chemistry or that they may not be altered by certain drugs. What is challenged is the current interpretation of these phenomena; the usefulness of 'schizophrenia' or any of its sub-types as an inference from them. The implication is obvious: any attempt at the systematic investigation of these phenomena, the search for patterns, for antecedents and maintaining factors should proceed without any inference to schizophrenia. This chapter will consider some of the ways in which this search has, and might in the future, proceed. Before this is done, however, it is worth noting that the issue is rather more complicated than this. 'Schizophrenia' is not simply used as a research tool, but is an integral part of the legal system in that it informs decisions about the disposal of those to whom the term is applied, whether or not they have broken criminal or civil law. Although a detailed discussion of the legal implications of 'schizophrenia' is beyond the scope of this chapter, three important issues will be considered very briefly.

The first is that of invoking 'schizophrenia' as an explanation of criminal behaviour. To do so is to claim to have demonstrated a clear connection between the brain state said to underlie the symptoms of schizophrenia, and, say, the act of murder. No such demonstration has ever been attempted, far less made. It could, of course, be made in principle if the status of the concept were more secure. As it is, the claim that people commit criminal acts because they are suffering from schizophrenia is simply nonsensical. None of this, of course, precludes the search for relationships between, say, auditory halluci-nations and violent behaviour, but without invoking 'schizophrenia' (see Blackman, 1981; Judkins and Slade, 1981; and Launay and Slade, 1981). The second issue is the use of 'schizophrenia' apparently to absolve people of re-sponsibility for their behaviour. As Toon (1982) has pointed out, however, this involves an attempt to make scientific – or supposedly scientific – con-cepts do the work of philosophical and moral ones and inevitably ends in confusion. The third, and related, issue concerns the use of 'schizophrenia' to justify involuntary detention and intervention by medical authorities. Like the ascription of blame, this has nothing to do with science but involves a *prescrip-tive* judgement about what ought to happen to certain people. Taken together, these issues emphasise the fact that legal use of 'schizophrenia' is problematic regardless of the scientific status of the concept. Acceptance of its non-scien-tific status, however, might at least help to make clear the need to articulate and radically rethink the assumptions and practices surrounding the law as it relates to bizarre behaviour.

Issues and alternatives – research and intervention

The two major assumptions which guide research using the concept of schizo-phrenia are that certain behaviours cluster together and that this cluster has biological (and genetic) antecedents. Research groups are therefore defined by diagnosis and a search made for common antecedents of their 'schizophre-nia'. Research which did not use 'schizophrenia' would obviously proceed in a quite different way. It would, first, make no assumptions – in the absence of evidence – that certain behaviours co-occurred meaningfully or had a certain type of antecedent. Second, it would study populations who had not been brought to the attention of psychiatrists. The importance of this point can hardly be over-emphasised and it will be returned to in later sections. The study of 'normal' groups who display bizarre behaviour would also highlight the central and neglected question of the conditions under which certain be-haviour comes to be labelled pathological; the existence of 'schizophrenia' encourages us to believe that it is so labelled because it *is* pathological.

But given that no research programme is assumption free, what assump-tions might guide 'schizophrenia'-free research? It can reasonably be suggested that, in the absence of evidence that certain odd behaviours require a different type of explanation, then methods and concepts found useful in the study of behaviour in general should be used in the study of bizarre behaviour. It will be suggested here that methods derived from the experimental analysis of behaviour might prove particularly useful – that is, analyses which clearly specify the behaviour in question (or verbal or other report of the experience in question), and which relate variation in behaviour to variation in setting conditions and consequences. Although it obviously follows from the arguments presented here, it is perhaps worth emphasising that retaining the concept of schizophrenia will prove equally obstructive to attempts to clarify brain–behaviour links and environment–behaviour links. Biological state may be one kind of setting condition for or, indeed, consequence of the behaviour which will be discussed here. And it has already been suggested that the origins of the concept of schizophrenia make plausible the idea that certain instances of bizarre behaviour may have an as-yet undiscovered infection as one antecedent. This chapter, however, will concentrate on social and psychological analyses of bizarre behaviour. It must be emphasised that the analyses are not intended to provide a full account and are in any case based on relatively few data. They may, however, help to redress the unfortunate balance of power in a literature which has given such prominence to biological factors. The analyses may also help to emphasise the fact that we cannot assume *a priori* that biological factors are more basic or fundamental as explanations of bizarre behaviour than are social and psychological factors, or that biological factors must come first, and that culture and learning somehow act 'on top of' a vulnerable constitution. The belief in a genetic cause of 'schizophrenia' does, of course, strongly reinforce this kind of one-way temporal and conceptual analysis.

But if the concept of schizophrenia, and the idea of prior diagnosis are to be abandoned, there remains the important problem of how to define groups for research. The issue will be discussed later; for the moment, the discussion will be based on those groupings made by the researchers. The first part of the discussion will concentrate on what are said to be the most typical symptoms of schizophrenia – reports of hearing voices in the absence of external source and 'delusional' beliefs. The first of these will be discussed in some detail in order to demonstrate how an analysis of a putative symptom can proceed with reference neither to the idea of symptom nor to that of schizophrenia. The second part of the discussion will examine two approaches to the study of bizarre behaviour which actually retain the concept of schizophrenia. They are included partly because of their potential usefulness but also to illustrate the problems of attempting to face in two directions at once – to apply an analysis of behaviour and the environmental conditions which support it but at the same time to claim that the behaviour is a function of an illness. It must be emphasised that it is not the aim of the discussion to provide an alternative theory of bizarre behaviour; to do so would be to indulge in the kind of premature theory construction which has been so criticised here. Rather, the aim is to explore what may be promising approaches to the analysis of certain behaviours, and societal reactions to them, and to highlight some important research principles. It is perhaps worth repeating that the term bizarre behaviour is used here simply to mean behaviour which is incomprehensible to an observer.

Hallucinations

Reports of hearing voices in the absence of external stimuli are said to be one of the most common or typical symptoms of schizophrenia (WHO, 1973; Falloon *et al.*, 1984). Partly for this reason, the phenomenon will be considered in some detail. Its study, however, also illustrates well the problems of viewing certain behaviours as symptoms of schizophrenia and offers a useful framework for the development of alternative theories.

As Sarbin and Juhasz (1978) have pointed out, medical definitions of the term hallucination are problematic. The American Psychiatric Association's 1964 Glossary, for example, calls it "A false sensory perception in the absence of an actual external stimulus." Sarbin and Juhasz rightly comments that sensation can hardly be true or false. A similar problem is evident in the definition offered in a standard medical encyclopaedia: "Sensation without physical origin" (Wingate, 1976). Nor is the problem solved by Wallace's (1959) suggestion of hallucination as "pseudoperception, without relevant stimulation of external or internal sensory receptors" (59), because, while we can be reasonably sure whether someone is talking to the person who reports hearing voices, there is no easy way of knowing what internal stimulation accompanies the report. Sarbin (1967) has suggested that the common referent for the term 'hallucination' is reported imaginings or, more specifically, reporting imaginings as real. As will be made clear, however, not all instances of these reports earn the title 'hallucination' and certainly not all of them lead to the inference 'schizophrenia'. For ease of expression, however, the term will be used here to mean reporting imaginings as real. It should be noted also that, because the systematic study of this phenomenon is in its infancy, it is not yet clear what is the appropriate language to describe such reports or the parameters along which they can usefully be measured. This problem will be circumvented here by describing, wherever relevant, how individual researchers have measured hallucinatory experiences.

With this in mind, two major questions will be considered. First, under what conditions are imaginings reported as real and, second, under what conditions are some of these reports called pathological?

Reporting imaginings as real

Reported imaginings cannot be considered independently of their social context and, in particular, of societal reactions to them. It is generally agreed (see, for example, Wallace, 1959; Holt, 1964; Al-Issa, 1977) that, while reactions differ across social groups, modern western societies are particularly hostile to such reports:

> In a factually oriented, skepical, anti-intraceptive, brass-tacks culture
> like ours, where the para-normal is scoffed at and myth and religion are
> in decline, the capacity for vivid imagery has little survival value and even

less social acceptability. We live in an age of literalism, an era that distrusts the imagination, while at the same time it develops its beat fringe of avid seekers after drugs that may artificially restore the capacity for poetic vision. It is little wonder that adults are made uneasy by the admission that they can experience things that are not factually present.

(Holt: 262)

Rational cultures that make a rigid distinction between reality and fantasy tend to consider hallucinations negatively, as they are expected to interfere with daily activities and interaction with the physical environment. Individuals are thus actively discouraged from assigning credibility to certain imaginings. They even learn to ignore these experiences and to remain unaware of their existence. These cultures would generally be conducive to a high threshold in the observation of hallucinations and to a negative attitude towards these experiences.

(Al-Issa: 576)

Staff members frequently take a negative view of hallucinations and hallucinating patients are subject to measures which, from the patient's standpoint, may be punishments (delay in discharge, restriction of privileges, questioning on sensitive issues, subtle contempt, even ridicule, from both staff and other patients).

(Wallace: 59)

Both Al-Issa and Wallace have emphasised the frequent co-occurrence of reports of hallucinations and of anxiety in western groups. By contrast, in some non-western groups, the experience may not only be accepted but actively sought (under certain socially approved conditions) using, for example, sleep deprivation, fasting, intense pain or social isolation. Al-Issa has linked the strict social control over the initiation, content and duration of such hallucinatory experiences with the fact that they are generally short-lived and distress-free.

Jaynes (1976) has developed a rather more elaborate theory of the suppression of hallucinatory experiences which, he suggests, paralleled the development of what we think of as consciousness and the ability to reflect on our own behaviour and mental processes. Jaynes' thesis (which even he admits sounds preposterous) is that this habit of self-reflection, the awareness of an 'I', is relatively recent – Jaynes dates it at after 2000–1000 BC. Before this, Jaynes suggests, the place of 'consciousness' was taken by auditory hallucinations which were reported as the voices of gods. These were heard when plans had to be made, or decisions taken, whenever behaviour might depart from clear, habitual (and unconscious) paths. Jaynes suggests that the hallucinated voices reflected right-hemispheric activity channelled via cerebral commissures to the left or speech hemisphere and interpreted as linguistic utterances. One of Jaynes' major sources of support is the *Iliad*, the early part of which (in so far as it can be accurately dated) apparently contains no reference to consciousness, to mental acts, to free will or to self-reflection. Instead, action was apparently to a large extent initiated by the hallucinated voices (of gods), which directed, commented and advised. Jaynes implicates increases in population and social complexity, and the development of writing, in the 'breakdown' of what he calls the bicameral mind. Direct communication with the gods, via their hallucinated voices, was, he claims, replaced by indirect communications, via prophets, oracles and divination. It is interesting to note Jones' suggestion (1974, cited in Witelson, 1986) that the Greek word *phronsis*, representing inwardly conscious awareness or introspection, was introduced by the philosopher Heraclitus during the 6th century BC. He was, Jones suggests, seeking a new word which would denote a mental process that he, but not many of his contemporaries, believed was going on in the mind.

It must be said that it is exceptionally difficult to offer direct support for Jaynes' theory, based as it is on a particular interpretation of generally accepted events. Certainly critics (see, for example, Miller, 1986) are able to offer only alternative interpretations with no obvious criteria for choosing amongst them. Nevertheless, a number of suggestions may be derived from Jaynes' ideas and from other anthropological research. First, hallucinatory experiences are apparently ubiquitous; indeed, Wallace (1959) has called them "one of the most ancient and most widely distributed of the modes of human experience" (58). Second, the thresholds both for experiencing and publicly reporting imaginings as real have in general become higher in the last, say, 2,000 years but have reached different levels in different social groups. Third, the study of hallucinations will present particular problems in western cultures because of the negative value placed on them and their strong association with diagnoses of mental illness.

Reports of hallucinations by western subjects

Studies of the 'normal' population (for example, McKellar, 1968; Posey and Losch, 1983; Bentall and Slade, 1985b) suggest that between 10 and 50 per cent of people have experienced auditory or visual hallucinations. Even higher rates may be obtained in experimental situations designed to foster the experience. Almost a century ago, Seashore (1895), writing of his experiments on "measurements of illusions and hallucinations in normal life", concluded that hallucinations of touch, taste, smell and electric shocks could be produced by:

1. Leading the observer to expect the respective sensations at a certain time and in a definite manner; 2. by associating the desired sensations with a warning; and 3. by associating them with simultaneous and continuous stimulation of other senses.

(cited in Sarbin and Juhasz, 1967: 352)

The role of suggestion, emphasised by Seashore, has been supported by subsequent research. Barber and Calverley (1964), for example, asked subjects to 'hear' a record playing 'White Christmas' or to 'see' a cat on their lap. Subjects were later divided into hypnotic induction (i.e. asked to re-perform under hypnosis); task motivation (suggested to them that they could do better); and control. Forty-two per cent of the hypnotised subjects and 27 per cent of the task-motivation subjects reported that they heard the record and believed that it was really playing, as compared with 15 per cent of control subjects who made this report. In the visual condition, the figures were 27, 15 and 0 per cent. Sarbin *et al.* (1971) induced at least one gustatory hallucination (reporting a non-existent stimulus as present) in 93 per cent of a 'normal' group and at least one experience of auditory hallucination in 59 per cent. Slade (1976a, 1976b) has also suggested a number of factors which may contribute to hallucinatory experiences, including 'stress' events and prevailing level of external stimulation.

Slade (1976a) uses the term stress to refer to aversive events associated with reports of negative mood states. He was able to show (1972) an apparently systematic relationship between reports of anxiety and reports of auditory hallucinations, such that the negative mood state appeared to precede, rather than accompany, the hearing of voices. More important, Slade was able to demonstrate that training in relaxation and imaginal desensitisation resulted in a significant decrease in reports of both anxiety and auditory hallucinations. This suggestion of a relationship between reported anxiety and hearing voices is interesting given Jaynes' suggestion that, in ancient times, the only 'stress' necessary to induce auditory hallucinations was the requirement to make a decision: "any choice between whom to obey, or what to do, anything that required any decision at all was sufficient to cause an auditory hallucination" (93). Nydegger (1972) has provided what sounds like a modern example of this phenomenon, although he makes no mention of Jaynes' work. Nydegger described a man, diagnosed as paranoid schizophrenic, who, it was claimed,

> often felt trapped at the choice point where a decision was necessary. When this decision had implications for other people, he was often unable to respond in any way, and the conflict and subsequent confusion generated the "symptoms" – withdrawal, hallucinations or rigid adherence to his delusions. The situations which were decided by the voices were always those about which he had conflicts.

(226)

Following a short period of coaching in making decisions and reinforcement for talk of 'thoughts' or 'decisions', reports of auditory hallucinations and accompanying behaviours were reduced to zero.

A relationship between 'stressful' situations and hallucinations has also been suggested by Brown *et al.* (1972); Leff and Vaughn (1981) and Falloon *et al.* (1984) but this work will be described in more detail later. In the absence of considerably more data it is clearly difficult to draw strong conclusions about the relationship between aversive events and reports of hallucinations, although it is interesting to note that, in a questionnaire study (Alpert and Silvers, 1970), only 50 per cent of subjects claimed a relationship between hearing voices and stressful events. At least four questions are of particular interest for future research. First is that of the relationship between aversive events and hallucinations in the psychiatric and non-psychiatric populations (which is not to commend psychiatric diagnoses as independent variables but to ask whether the hallucinations of those who report themselves, or are reported to authority, are under the control of similar variables to those of people who remain beyond psychiatric attention); second is that of the relationship between the content of hallucinatory experiences and the aversive situation and third the question of the mechanisms by which hallucinations might reduce reported anxiety and change the situation (for example, by shifting responsibility, by advising on action, and so on). The fourth question concerns the extent to which teaching alternative responses to aversive situations might reduce reports of hallucinations.

A number of writers have noted the possible contribution of structured external stimulation, and the extent to which it engages the attention of the subject, to reports of auditory and visual hallucinations (Schultz, 1965; Slade, 1974; Margo *et al.*, 1981). It is suggested that reports of hallucinations are more probable in the absence of meaningful auditory stimulation or in the absence of a requirement to respond. Slade (1974), for example, manipulated the reported frequency of auditory hallucinations by requiring subjects to process auditory information. Margo *et al.* (1981) found that ratings of intensity and duration of auditory hallucinations were lowest in an experimental condition which required subjects to read aloud and later to describe the content of a prose passage, and highest in a white-noise condition. Interestingly, although ratings of intensity and duration were (non-significantly) lower during 2 mins of sensory restriction than during white noise, ratings of clarity were highest during sensory restriction. The role of meaningful auditory stimulation in hallucinations is also suggested by the apparent relationship between acquired deafness and auditory hallucinations (Hammeke *et al.*, 1983).

Imagery strength and reality testing

It has been suggested (Mintz and Alpert, 1972; Slade, 1976b) that the occurrence of hallucinations may be related to reported vividness of imagery in the appropriate mode, and evidence has been offered in support. Bentall and Slade (1985a), however, have concluded that the hypothesis has, in general, not been strongly supported. They suggest that an additional hypothesis put forward by Mintz and Alpert and by Slade (1976b), that hallucinators are deficient in reality testing, has more to recommend it.

Mintz and Alpert asked 'normals', non-hallucinating and hallucinating 'schizophrenics' to listen to recorded phrases against a background of noise. Subjects were asked to report what was said or, if they were unsure, to guess. They also reported, on a six-point scale, how confident they were that they had heard the phrase correctly. Correlations were then computed between accuracy and confidence scores so that the more these matched, the higher the correlations. The mean correlation achieved by the 'normal' group was significantly higher than that of the non-hallucinating 'schizophrenics', which in turn was significantly higher than that of the hallucinating 'schizophrenics'. Mintz and Alpert interpreted these results as indicating that defective reality testing may be a prerequisite to reports of auditory hallucinations.

Slade (1976b) used a quite different task, derived from observation of the 'verbal transformation effect' described by Warren and Gregory (1958). Subjects (sixteen 'normals'; eight hallucinating and eight non-hallucinating 'schizophrenics') were asked to listen to a tape on which the word 'tress' was repeated 342 times in a 10-minute period. Warren and Gregory's observations suggested that subjects would eventually 'hear' words which had not been spoken. Contrary to prediction, the three groups did not differ significantly in any of the main measures: latency to first reported word change; number of word changes and number of different words. An analysis of the phonetic relationship between 'tress' and the new words 'heard' did, however, reveal that, compared with the two control groups, the hallucinating 'schizophrenics' 'heard' fewer words with a strong phonetic relationship to the original and more words with a weak phonetic relationship. From these data, Slade concluded that poor reality testing in the auditory modality provided one aspect of a predisposition for the experience of auditory hallucinations.

A major problem of these studies is that they did not include a group of 'normal' subjects who had reported hallucinations. Bentall and Slade (1985a) rectified this by presenting their task to four groups: male students with high and low scores on the Launay–Slade Hallucination Scale and hallucinating and non-hallucinating 'schizophrenics'. Subjects were presented with fifty 15-second noise trials and fifty 15-second signal and noise trials in a random order. Each trial was made up of a 1-second warning tone; 1-second silence; 5-seconds white noise (or noise plus signal at 3 seconds) and 8-seconds silence, during which subjects recorded, on a five-point scale, how sure they were that they had heard, or not heard, a voice. The signal chosen was the word 'who' and the signal-to-noise ratio was set such that accurate detection was extremely difficult. There were no significant differences amongst the groups on a measure of 'perceptual sensitivity' but, in both 'normal' and 'schizophrenic' groups, there were significant differences in bias, i.e. reporting the signal present when absent. High scorers on the Hallucination Scale were more 'biased' than low in the two 'normal' groups while hallucinating 'schizophrenics' were more 'biased' than the non-hallucinators. What is particularly interesting about these results is that the pattern of differences was virtually identical in the 'normal' and in the 'schizophrenic' groups.

Although these studies present extremely interesting ideas about the processes associated with auditory hallucinations and some ingenious ways of exploring them, it would be well to be cautious about the interpretation of their data. It is unfortunate that the term defective reality testing (or similar) has been used, for several reasons. First, although the authors might not intend it, it gives the impression that there exists a 'reality' which some people are 'in touch with' and others are not. Second, the use of terms such as defect, defective or deficient involves evaluation and not description. Third, to talk of defective reality-testing implies the possession of a trait: it is something which those who report hallucinations 'have' and which partly causes them to hallucinate. This problem is particularly serious when it is considered that the studies described here have used quite different tasks to infer deficient reality-testing and that no data are available on the relationships amongst them. In addition, group statistics all too readily become statements about individuals. Thus, group differences in specific performance measures, combined with assumptions about what the performance means, can become statements about traits or characteristics supposedly possessed by each member of the group.

To their credit, Bentall and Slade (1985a) provide scores for each subject so that the reader can see the extent of overlap amongst group scores. They also caution against simplistic assumptions about the relationship between 'perceptual bias', scores on a Hallucination Scale and independent reports of hallucinations by pointing out that the correlation between the first two of these, though significant, was a modest 0.56. But secondary reporting of such research remains a problem. It is all too likely that it will be routinely reported that 'hallucinating schizophrenics are deficient in reality testing' and yet another 'cognitive deficit' will be added to the considerable list already said to afflict 'schizophrenics'. Interpretation of hallucinations in terms of a supposed cognitive defect would also tend to obscure cultural and motivational aspects of reported imaginings, to distract attention from potentially important environmental variables. More recently, however, Johnson (1988) and Bentall (1990) have provided accounts which move away from the idea of deficits in reality-testing and towards analyses of the conditions under which errors are made in discriminating the origins of information. This framework fits well with Gould's (1950) and McGuigan's (1966) conclusion that auditory hallucinations could represent a mislabelling of sub-vocal speech, and Bentall and Slade (1986) had already suggested that the labelling of inner speech as unintended might be a major antecedent of the inference that its source was external. This latter idea might relate to Antrobus et al.'s (1966) study of stimulus-independent thoughts which are reported to increase when attention is not engaged by external stimuli.

Finally, Sarbin (1970) has suggested that people may resort to imaginings (and report some as real) when conventional linguistic thinking or interaction with the outside world provides minimal utility for them. While it is unclear under what conditions this might happen, it is interesting to note that Posey and Losch (1983) found that subjects with high scores on a scale of self-reported interest and skill in music, art, poetry and mathematics obtained significantly higher scores on their hallucination scale.

Labelling imaginings as pathological

Before this issue is discussed, it is important to clarify the possible implications of data which suggest that hallucinations are relatively common in the general population. By themselves, these data cannot be used to criticise the concept of schizophrenia. It was pointed out in Chapter 1 that symptoms or complaints which form part of the clusters from which medical constructs are inferred may be widely distributed in the general population. We should not consider the frequent reporting of nausea or fatigue as evidence against the scientific status of concepts such as cancer or diabetes. And, certainly, users of 'schizophrenia' have never suggested that 'hearing voices' is always a symptom of schizophrenia. The reason why the general-population data are problematic for the concept of schizophrenia and why they suggest that subject-selection procedures must be modified is that unlike constructs such as cancer, schizophrenia has no independent criteria, apart from its widely distributed and supposed symptoms, for inferring it; nor is there evidence that when reported imaginings co-occur with other putative symptoms the cluster has different antecedents from the 'single' phenomenon reported in the general population. Thus, there is no evidence that hallucinations called symptoms of schizophrenia are different in some important way from those not so called or that forming two groups – hallucinating schizophrenics and hallucinating non-schizophrenics – is a useful way to proceed. This does not, of course, imply that the two groups may not differ – perhaps in the frequency, intensity or perceived aversiveness of their experiences – but it does imply that 'schizophrenia' cannot be implicated.

The fact that there is no apparent justification for calling some reported imaginings symptoms of schizophrenia suggests that the process whereby this labelling happens must be quite different from that implied by the medical framework which users of 'schizophrenia' claim to adopt. Certainly, as Sarbin and Juhasz (1967) have pointed out, it seems to be taken for granted that the implied medical framework is used. Thus, it is assumed that there are normal illusions and pathological hallucinations: what are called false alarms in psychophysics are called symptoms of schizophrenia in psychiatric hospitals. Sarbin and Juhasz have pointed to the role of chapter organisation in perpetuating this view:

In a widely used [psychology] introductory text, Kimble and Garmezy state: "Hallucinations are false sensory impressions. The schizophrenic may see things that aren't there or voices that don't exist, except for him." This is in the chapter on "behaviour pathology". In the chapter on "detection and interpretation of stimulation" illusions are defined as "false perceptions that produce various sorts of distortions of the world." The practitioner who uses [this] text ... is required to differentiate between *false perceptions* and *false sensory impressions*: in the one case he is dealing with a normal human, and in the other with a possible madman!

(353; emphasis in original)

A similar confusion is evident in the posing of some questions about hallucinatory experiences. Hoffman (1986), for example, asks "How is it that some schizophrenics identify some instances of verbal imagery as hallucinatory?" (503) while Al-Issa (1977) suggests that "A basic problem in the definition of hallucinations is to establish a criterion to differentiate psychotic or schizophrenic from other hallucinatory experiences and normal imagery" (571). It will be assumed here, instead, that the important question is not some variant of 'Why do some schizophrenics hallucinate?' but 'When do observers decide that some reported imaginings are symptoms of schizophrenia?' (There remains, of course, the question of the circumstances under which some *people* identify some instances of verbal imagery as real, and not, as Hoffman would have it, hallucinatory.)

Users of 'schizophrenia' are aware that not all instances of reported imaginings are labelled pathological. They have therefore sought to justify so labelling some of these reports by suggesting differences between 'schizophrenic' and other hallucinations. Al-Issa (1977) has suggested that, in psychiatric practice, hallucinations are considered to be an indication of functional psychosis when the precipitating conditions in which, or the processes by which, someone comes to experience hallucinations are not detectable. This may well be the case, but psychiatrists' failure intuitively to understand the occurrence of any behaviour can hardly be used to justify inferring brain disorder. And the claim that 'schizophrenic' hallucinations are characterised by unknown setting conditions gives the quite erroneous impressions first, that psychiatrists routinely conduct comprehensive analyses, involving systematic and reliable observation of the behaviour and the conditions under which it occurs, and, second, that the processes and conditions involved in the reported imaginings of those not labelled schizophrenic would be easily detectable by psychiatrists. There is no evidence that either of these is true. Hare (1973) suggests that a belief in the reality of the hallucinatory experience is considered as one criterion for the determination of abnormality. Again, this is questionable in practice. The general population surveys (and in particular that of Posey and Losch) suggest that belief in the reality of the experience and attribution of the voices to other people is not uncommon. Further, although emphasis has also been placed on the spontaneous and unintended nature of hallucinations in those diagnosed schizophrenic (Slade, 1972), there is no evidence that the hallucinatory experiences of 'normal' people appear to them any less spontaneous or more under their control.

Although they are of dubious validity, attempts may be made to apply these criteria in psychiatric practice, i.e. psychiatrists, in an unsystematic and intuitive way, may try to determine the source of the experience or whether the person believes it to be real or to be spontaneous, and so on. But in the absence of evidence that this process is other than intuitive and that 'normal' hallucinations do not show these characteristics, it is reasonable to suggest that the assignment of a pathological label to reported imaginings is influenced by a quite different set of considerations. Three possible factors – social performance, language use and context – will be considered here, although it must be emphasised that their contribution is as yet speculative.

Hallucinations and social performance

Sarbin and Juhasz (1967, 1978) have described the complexity of the process of labelling some reported imaginings as abnormal. They have emphasised that the concern to distinguish 'good' and 'bad' hallucinations – or those calling for action from authority and those not – is not new, but can, in the west, be traced (at least) to the preoccupations of medieval theologians (Sarbin and Juhasz correctly point out that it is not so much a decision to label some 'hallucinations' as good or desirable and others bad or undesirable, but a decision to apply the usually pejorative term hallucinations to certain imaginings. But the term will continue to be used here in a neutral sense).

It is suggested that observers, in this case psychiatrists, are more likely to judge reported imaginings as pathological when the report is made by someone who has already been devalued in some way – who is of low social status, poor education, who is less powerful, who has 'failed' in the performance of certain social roles, and so on. Sarbin and Juhasz suggest, with Szasz and Goffman, that diagnostic labelling, or the claim that certain behaviours are symptoms, occurs *after* the person has violated other social norms. Although these writers have not presented direct evidence for their conclusions, two sources of indirect support, which at least suggest that the hypothesis is worthy of further consideration, can be suggested.

The first is the relationship of diagnoses to judgements of 'social competence'. In a study of over 500 psychiatric patients, Phillips *et al.* (1966) divided 'symptoms' (defined as descriptions of a patient's behaviour by a psychiatrist at the time of initial institutional contact) into 'Thought', 'Affect' and 'Actions'. 'Hallucinations' was classified as a thought symptom. Subjects were rated, from high to low, on occupation, IQ and education, and a global 'social maturity' scale was then computed. That group of subjects said to have hallucinations showed the second lowest mean social maturity score. Unfortunately, Phillips *et al.* did not analyse these data nor provide sufficient raw data for analysis. But using them, the authors grouped 'symptoms' according to their 'social-maturity level' and showed that diagnoses of schizophrenia were in general associated with lower level (in terms of their scale) symptoms than were diagnoses of, for example, manic depressive psychosis or character disorder. Phillips *et al.* concluded that "a patient's level of social maturity finds expression in his symptomatology and that this combination of maturity and symptom expression is an important factor in the diagnosis he receives" (213). The hypothesis might have been better put that when someone judged to be of low social maturity also reports imaginings as real, then he or she is more likely to be said to be hallucinating and more likely to be called schizophrenic. The data presented by Phillips *et al.* do not permit that conclusion, but do suggest the hypothesis. The study also illustrates well the problems of attempting to construct theories about a phenomenon without observing a representative sample of its occurrences. Phillips *et al.* studied only people who had come to the attention of psychiatrists. We have no way of knowing how these psychiatrists would have reacted to the imaginings of those who reported hallucinations in general population surveys, although Posey and Losch did ask clinicians to examine psychiatric questionnaires completed by their hallucinating students – all were pronounced 'completely normal'.

Support for the idea that these terms are more likely to be applied to those whose social functioning has already been devalued comes, second, from DSM-III itself. It was pointed out in Chapter 5 that one of the criteria for inferring schizophrenia is 'deterioration from a previous level of functioning in such areas as work, social relations and self-care'. Spitzer *et al.* (1978a) have stated that:

> Central to our concept of schizophrenia is the notion that the disorder interferes with normal social functioning. Yet occasionally one encounters individuals with one or more of the characteristic schizophrenic symptoms, such as bizarre delusions of longstanding, without any apparent disruption of their functioning. We believe that in such problematic cases the diagnosis of Atypical Psychosis is preferable.
>
> (493)

Spitzer *et al.* provide no data to support their idea that these people occur only occasionally. They may meet them occasionally, but that is another matter. And as 'schizophrenia' cannot in any meaningful sense be said to interfere with anything, it is not surprising that Spitzer *et al.* provide no evidence for this assertion. Again, the more reasonable conclusion may be that offered earlier: that reports of bizarre behaviour or experience are more likely to be labelled pathological when they are made by or about people whose social functioning is otherwise deemed inadequate.

Further, albeit very indirect, support for the importance of social behaviour is provided by Falloon *et al.* (1984). They point out that, when relatives are asked to comment on the behaviour of the 'schizophrenic' in the family, then the most frequent cause for complaint is not the so-called symptoms, but failure to perform valued social behaviours – to talk to family members or visitors; get up in the morning; make friends; obtain employment; take up hobbies, and so on. Although Falloon *et al.*'s data do not allow this conclusion, it seems reasonable to suggest that relatives are more likely originally to complain to the psychiatric services when bizarre behaviour is accompanied by 'social failure'.

The role of language

In the psychiatric literature, people's reporting of their imaginings, and the labelling of these as hallucinations, is presented as a relatively straightforward matter. But Al-Issa (1977) has argued that:

> the linguistic sophistication of the suspected hallucinator seems to play a dominant part in influencing the decision of the diagnostician. His public report is, for example, unlikely to be declared false or considered hallucinatory if he includes in his statements such qualifiers as "it is *as if* I hear ..., I *thought* I saw..."
>
> (574; emphasis in original)

Sarbin (1970) has made a similar point:

> In reporting his construction [that he saw the Virgin Mary] *literally* the speaker might show ignorance of current norms regarding language constraints to be used when talking about [the world of imaginings]; in interpreting such a report *literally* the hearer might mistake the metaphoric intent of the speaker. These confusions, which may lead to tragic or comic outcomes, are not just signs of ignorance or lack of knowledge but a predictable result of the metaphorical language when employed to communicate about imaginings.
>
> (Sarbin, 1970: 66–7; emphasis in original)

Although there are virtually no data available which would clarify this suggested role of language in determining responses to reported imaginings, it is interesting to note that Miller *et al.* (1965), using a descriptive language task, found that the performance of hallucinating 'schizophrenics' was inferior to that of non-hallucinating 'schizophrenics'. Their vocabulary was also described as more restricted (using a different test). In addition, their performance on a 'metaphor selection test' deviated more from normative standards than did that of the non-hallucinating 'schizophrenics'. Miller *et al.* concluded that "The deviant language observed in hallucinating schizophrenics may not only reflect an attempt to describe inner experiences which are vague, strange and frightening, but may also reflect a lack of sufficient language skills to formulate metaphors which meaningfully convey these inner experiences" (51). Unfortunately, Miller *et al.* did not study hallucinating subjects who had not been diagnosed as schizophrenic. Obviously, no strong conclusions can be drawn from so few data, but they do suggest that the issue is worth pursuing. Language skills may, of course, interact with the kind of variable used by Phillips *et al.* to rate 'social maturity'.

The social context of reported imaginings

Al-Issa (1977) and Wallace (1959) have emphasised the role of social factors in determining the occurrence, content and duration of hallucinatory experiences in non-western societies. Littlewood and Lipsedge (1982), discussing a wider range of behaviours, have suggested that it is not necessarily the performance of certain behaviours *per se* which invite pathological labels, but their performance outside a prescribed social context. Although the frequent use of terms like mental illness in western society gives the impression that pathological labels are attached to pathological people, there is little reason not to suppose that here, too, it is performance outside accepted social contexts which attracts 'illness' or 'symptom' labels.

It was pointed out earlier that, in general, reporting imaginings as real is negatively valued in modern western societies, so that there are few contexts where such behaviour would be acceptable. But there are exceptions. One is when reported imaginings have a religious content. It may be, however, that this behaviour is more acceptable in European countries with a strong Catholic tradition than in northern European Protestant culture. It is also increasingly being suggested (see Littlewood and Lipsedge, 1982) that reported imaginings should not be called symptoms if they are made by certain immigrant groups. Reporting hallucinations and, in particular, hearing voices is, apparently, also acceptable in the context of the Spiritualist Church when the claim is made by a recognised or aspiring medium. Indeed, the extent to which this is the case can perhaps be gauged by the fact that the late Doris Stokes was able to publish books with titles like 'Voices in my Ear'; 'Whispering Voices' and 'A Host of Voices' without coming to psychiatric attention, and that she merited obituaries in the 'quality' press, where she was lauded for her great gift. While it is difficult on superficial examination to see much difference between Doris Stokes' hallucinatory experiences and those of 'schizophrenics' – she claimed to listen intently to her voices; they were apparently unwilled; she held conversations with them – there are potentially important other differences. First, Doris Stokes, as far as can be seen, was judged to be performing adequately in other social roles. Second, she performed one of the few valued social roles available to those who claim to hear voices in western countries – that of communicator with the dead. Third, and perhaps most important, she clearly gave people something they badly wanted; she fulfilled an apparently important social function and thus became a powerful figure. Judging from the number of people who attended her sessions, it is not difficult to imagine the outcry which would have followed any attempt to declare her to be psychiatrically disturbed and in need of treatment.

The content and function of hallucinations

The content of hallucinations, i.e. what is claimed to be said by voices or the nature of visions, has been relatively ignored in the psychiatric and psychological literature, although the topic has received more attention from anthropologists. Two possible reasons can be suggested for this. First, that emphasis on the form, rather than the content, of putative symptoms can be used to deflect criticism that psychiatrists selectively suppress, for example, certain beliefs, rather than attending neutrally to the form or structure of the 'symptom'. This aspect has apparently become more salient with increasing criticism of Soviet psychiatry (see, for example, Lader, 1977; Wing, 1978b; Clare, 1980). A second, and related, reason is that a content-free analysis is apparently seen as more scientific. Lindsley (1963), for example, sought to provide a description of 'psychotic symptoms' by examining the frequency and intensity of certain behaviours under free-operant conditioning. He suggested that:

> Such a definition permits automatic laboratory measurement and definitions of symptoms and frees the investigator from concern with
> hallucinatory content and bizarreness. It brings the hallucinatory symptom into the body of natural science in terms of the functional properties
> which differentiate it from other forms of skeletal behaviour.
>
> (296)

It may be that this view is taken because the content of hallucinations is seen as idiosyncratic, while the structure may be shared by all. But it is difficult to see how the idea of the study of the content of hallucinations can be rejected on principle or why systematic study should not be possible, in spite of difficulties in constructing a useful language to describe it and to relate it to other variables. Indeed, it might be argued that if we are usefully to describe the variables which control these experiences, to design effective intervention for those who request it and understand social reactions to them, then an acknowledgement of content may be extremely important. Slade (1976a) has suggested that the content of hallucinatory experiences may be directly related to the 'stressful' events which precede them while Littlewood and Lipsedge (1982) have provided a study of the relationship between content and personal and cultural background which offers suggestions for future research. Schaefer and Martin (1969) were able to show that the reported content of the hallucinated voices of a 'schizophrenic' woman varied systematically with the status of the listener. These ideas echo anthropological accounts where the content of hallucinatory experiences may be directly 'given' under certain conditions and where it may vary across tribes but be similar within them.

An additional reason for attending to the content of hallucinations is that it may provide clues to the functions they serve; but, like content, this aspect of hallucinations has been generally disregarded in both psychological and psychiatric literature. The emphasis placed on the functions served by any behaviour is largely a consequence of the theoretical model adopted. And while this aspect has been strongly emphasised by learning or social-learning-theory accounts of behaviour, it has been largely neglected by the individualistic, biological models apparently favoured by users of 'schizophrenia'. When environmental variables have been investigated it has usually been in the most general way (for example, what influences 'outcome' or 'relapse'?) rather than involving rigorous functional analyses. And where more detailed and systematic analyses have been attempted, it has usually been in an institutional rather than a wider social framework (for example, Ayllon and Azrin, 1968; Schaefer and Martin, 1969; Rutner and Bugle, 1969; Nydegger, 1972; Anderson and Alpert, 1974). But they have at least demonstrated the important point that the experience and reporting of hallucinations, at least in institutional samples, is to some extent under social control.

In the absence of more comprehensive data, it is possible only to speculate about the possible functions of experiencing and reporting hallucinations. One function particularly emphasised by anthropologists (see, for example, Wallace, 1959; Murphy, 1978) is that of fostering the belief that it is possible to communicate with the dead and with spirits, to control them and to convey messages from them. This 'power' may allow the occupation of a valued social role, as prophet, shaman or medium. And it is not difficult to see how such an experience may be reinforcing for an individual who 'hears' the voice of a dead relative, or of an unattainable object of admiration. Mednick (1958) and Sarbin and Juhasz (1978) have emphasised the role of fantasy, and possibly hallucinations, as escape or avoidance responses in the face of aversive situations and as responses which may allow control, in fantasy, over otherwise uncontrollable situations. Slade (1976a) has also emphasised that the response of hallucinating may reduce aversive mood states and thus be reinforced, while Posey and Losch (1983) commented that many of their sample claimed to find their hallucinations comforting or said that they provided guidance. This, of course, is reminiscent of Jaynes' theory that the original function of hallucinated voices was to guide action. But it would be naive to ignore the fact that in our society reporting hallucinations can have drastic social consequences, such as freedom from performing certain social roles or obligations, and not to consider the extent to which these may be rather welcome to some of those who report their imaginings. It is interesting to note here an observation made in passing by Brown *et al.* (1972), and which apparently puzzled them: that those people who resisted admission to psychiatric hospital showed fewer 'symptoms' on follow-up than did those who did not resist.

Some individual examples of the possible functions served by hallucinations may be of interest. Fonagy and Slade (1982) reported an attempt to reduce the frequency of auditory hallucinations during sessions in which white noise was made contingent or non-contingent on reports of hallucinations. One of their subjects – whose hallucinations were apparently becoming less frequent – stopped reporting 'romantic voices' (of her boss, declaring his love) and reported only voices which ordered her to steal. In other words, as Fonagy and Slade point out, she was apparently, and unsurprisingly, arranging only for those voices she disliked to be subject to therapeutic consideration. Falloon *et al.* (1984) described an adolescent who, each time her parents tried to take a short holiday, reported hearing threatening voices. Nydegger (1972) reported on a hospitalised man who claimed to be less anxious there than at home. Whenever his parents tried to arrange a weekend at home, he reported visions and his leave was cancelled. Finally, it is not difficult to guess at the possible functions of imaginings reported in a study of the female fans of pop stars (BBC2, 28 May 1987). One fan said that she often held conversations with her idol in which he "really answered" while another reported feeling that her idol was always with her and that she received guidance from him. What was notable about the fans was their apparent lack of interest in what seemed to them to be dull or aversive ordinary lives, in contrast with their fantasy life.

Research directions

Sarbin (1970) has made a plea for the integration of research on supposedly abnormal hallucinations and research on imaginative behaviour and 'normal' perceptual processes. In the absence of evidence of the validity of 'schizophrenia' or that different theories are necessary to account for the reported imaginings of 'schizophrenics' and the rest of us, then there seems no reason why the integration should not proceed. With this in mind, it is difficult to do better than to repeat the general, but central, research questions posed by Sarbin (1967):

(1) What biographical and stimulus conditions lead to covert imaginative behaviour?
(2) What biographical and stimulus conditions lead to public reporting of imaginings? (i.e. reports to authority).
(3) What are the psychological and social criteria that lead a professional to declare that certain reported imaginings are hallucinations and others are not?

To these could be added many subsidiary and more specific questions, particularly concerning the attribution of sources to stimuli, but the major themes should remain: that imaginative behaviours and public reporting of them cannot adequately be described without reference to the environmental conditions in which they occur, and that we should ask not 'How can we define schizophrenic hallucinations?' but 'Under what social conditions are some reported imaginings called symptoms of schizophrenia?'

False beliefs or delusions

Although the term belief has acquired surplus meanings implied by the ideas that beliefs cause behaviour and that they are attributes of people, it will be used here simply to mean 'a persistent claim that such-and-such is the case'.

Clare (1980) has suggested that "In so far as there is a single mark of madness popularly conceived, such a mark is surely the *delusion*" (94; emphasis in original). He goes on to claim that there are several characteristics, in addition to falsity, the presence of which determines the delusional status of the belief in question. These are that it is held with absolute conviction; that it is incorrigible (not amenable to reason, persuasion, and so on); that it is often preoccupying; that it is usually absurd or impossible and that it is not culturally shared. Such beliefs, when not explicable by organic factors, are said to be (at least in this country) important indicators of mental disorder, including schizophrenia. In other words, it is suggested that theories which deal with 'ordinary' false beliefs will not do for these.

It is not difficult to show that this attempt to distinguish 'normal' and 'abnormal' false beliefs is based, to say the least, on weak foundations. No evidence has been presented that the beliefs of 'schizophrenics' are held with any greater conviction or are more preoccupying (whatever that might mean) than are beliefs which would not be labelled as symptoms. At least on superficial examination, it is difficult to see how the beliefs of someone who attends church daily, who prays frequently and who believes that people are re-united with loved ones after death, are any different, on these two criteria, from those of the 'schizophrenic' man who believes that his neighbours control his thoughts. Nor has evidence been presented that 'schizophrenic' beliefs are never amenable to reason or persuasion. There is, on the contrary, evidence that this is not the case. Watts *et al.* (1973) and Milton *et al.* (1978) demonstrated significant decreases in the stated conviction with which 'delusional' beliefs were reported by 'schizophrenics', using systematic interventions derived from the literature on attitude change, while Johnson *et al.* (1977) reported on the apparently successful modification of claims made by a 'paranoid schizophrenic' using what they called a re-attribution framework. But even if these modifications had not been achieved, or even if we took seriously Heinrichs' (1988) untestable comment that this latter patient may not have been schizophrenic, the distinction remains false, because it is based on the highly questionable assumption that 'ordinary' beliefs *are* routinely changed by rational means (see, for example, Kuhn, 1970 and C.A. Anderson *et al.*, 1980). The criterion of improbability or impossibility is equally problematic, and Clare does acknowledge the difficulties with this criterion (and see Heise, 1988). To someone from outside the culture, it would surely be difficult to choose, on that criterion, between the ideas that an invisible being can 'hear' and respond to certain thought patterns and that the BBC send coded personal messages through radios.

This leaves the final criterion – that the belief is idiosyncratic and not culturally shared, in other words, it supposedly cannot be explained by cultural learning. It is this criterion which is being increasingly emphasised in the face of criticism of Soviet psychiatric practice (for example, Lader, 1977) and of western psychiatrists' dealings with ethnic minorities (for example, Littlewood and Lipsedge, 1982; Mercer, 1986). Spitzer and Endicott (1978), attempting to justify the inclusion of certain phenomena in a medical rather than a social or psychological framework, have declared what appears to be a commonly held view that: "Certainly the incomprehensibility of these conditions to the untrained observer is further support for viewing these conditions as evidence of an organismic dysfunction" (34). There are two major problems with these ideas. The first is that they are apparently based on the assumption that the number of people who make certain claims should influence the judgement as to whether the claim is a symptom of a medical disorder. (And see the discussion of Littlewood and Lipsedge's (1982) work later in this chapter.) This implies that it is *a priori* impossible for someone to construct a radically different belief system, seen by the majority culture as highly improbable, except under the influence of mental disorder. And if we accept this criterion, then we must also accept that, for example, devout Christians (judged by psychiatrists not to be ill) are in fact victims of a *folie à millions* because they subscribe to the (now) culturally acceptable but, some would say, highly improbable, claim (that he was the Son of God) put forward with great conviction by one apparently preoccupied man, against what was culturally acceptable at the time. Littlewood and Lipsedge (1982) have provided a tautological escape route from this paradox by claiming that psychotics are rarely able to convince others of the validity of their beliefs.

The second, and much more serious problem with these ideas is that they imply that an observer's ability to understand how a belief system could have come about, in terms of the person's cultural background, should serve as one criterion of whether the belief is a symptom of a medical disorder. The absurdity and the dangers of applying such a criterion can hardly be overstated. It implies, first, that psychiatrists (and, in this context, it is they who are usually the observers) are – or could become – omniscient, that they could know everything that could ever be known about how environmental and personal factors interact to produce certain claims; second, that they systematically and comprehensively assess the presence or absence of each of these factors in every case; and third, that having concluded that none is present, they are entitled to infer brain disorder or, at least, mental illness. None of these, of course, is true. It implies no disrespect to psychiatrists to say that their intuitive understanding of people's belief systems is quite irrelevant to attempts to construct scientific theories of the antecedents of the phenomenon. Psychiatrists, of course, like anyone else, might make reliable observations which could form the basis of these theories, but that is not what Clare is talking about. Wings' (1978b) comment that a psychiatric examination must be grounded in a thorough familiarity with the subjective experience of human beings (intended to offer reassurance about how some beliefs are labelled symptoms of illness) shows a dismaying lack of appreciation of this point. And it cannot be argued that psychiatrists' understanding is more than intuitive by virtue of their training or that they can call on the services of members or students of particular cultures. The fact is that we are as yet profoundly ignorant about how belief systems now labelled 'schizophrenic' might develop.

Clare's attempt to separate 'ordinary' and 'delusional' beliefs is, of course, not the only one (see Oltmanns, 1988 for a brief review and also APA, 1987). The criteria suggested are similar, and emphasise the personal quality of supposedly delusional beliefs, their improbability and the conviction with which they are held. A major problem with all the attempts is that, like attempts to define 'schizophrenia', they work backwards, from the lay concept of delusion to a set of referents which reflect not a previously observed pattern, but an authority's stereotype of a deluded person. Because 'being deluded' or 'suffering from delusions' is then taken to be a pathological attribute of the individual, the criteria, not surprisingly, take little account of the social context in which the judgement that someone is deluded is made. As Heise (1988) has pointed out, however, the judgement is intrinsically social, "involving a comparison of minds, in which one is treated as authoritative and the other as deficient....A belief becomes a delusion when the psychiatrist judges that no-one wants to hear it and that the patient does not care to adjust the belief in the direction of social value" (267, 270). Clearly, the extent to which someone can convince others of the value of their beliefs will vary with time and place as well as with other attributes of the 'believer'.

The development and maintenance of 'delusions'

Perhaps because it has been assumed that certain belief systems are a symptom of schizophrenia, the literature on their development and maintenance is very sparse. And because at the moment there is a serious lack of reliable description of the claims said to be symptoms of schizophrenia (although see Brett-Jones *et al.*, 1987 for one possible method of measurement), the conditions under which they occur and their consequences, all that can be suggested here are possibly useful frameworks which might guide data collection and theory development.

Scheibe and Sarbin (1965) have drawn on anthropological descriptions, the observations of Skinner (1948) on 'superstitious' behaviour in animals and the theory of Rotter (1954) about 'generalised expectancy' to suggest that individual and social belief systems, whether bizarre or not, develop in response to gaps about cause–effect relationships in important areas of knowledge and as part of a general human habit of constructing explanations – with little regard for their validity – which can be used to support behaviour. Thus, one setting condition for the development of personal and cultural belief systems is uncertainty regarding a valued outcome. Although, again, we lack data on this point, it is difficult to see how an adequate account of the development of individual belief systems can be offered without reference to their content: people, will, presumably, construct explanations or infer meanings about events which are of concern to them. Brennan and Hemsley (1984), for example, showed that the illusory correlation effect, that is the perception of relationships between unrelated stimuli, was heightened for subjects diagnosed as paranoid schizophrenic, when the stimuli were of persecutory content.

W.G. Johnson *et al.* (1977) have also suggested that the study of 'delusions' should be integrated into the study of 'normal' belief systems and that what appear to be bizarre beliefs may be amenable to analysis by the methods and theories used to investigate day-to-day inferences about relations between behaviour and its causes. They provide an example, of a man originally called paranoid schizophrenic, which might illustrate one function of 'delusional' beliefs: to offer an acceptable explanation of otherwise unacceptable events. The subject reported that he was having (unsolicited) intercourse with a warm form. The man denied ever having masturbated and considered it inappropriate. Observation, however, indicated that his claim was associated with penile stimulation with his legs, and he was, apparently successfully, encouraged to accept this alternative explanation of his experience. Kaney and Bentall (1989) have also presented data within an attribution framework. These authors found that patients diagnosed as suffering from persecutory delusions were more likely to make external attributions for negative events and internal attributions for positive events than were depressed or 'normal' groups. We cannot, of course, assume that any apparent 'style' *predisposes* people to develop bizarre belief systems. Generalised styles of interpretation may develop at the same time as, or even after, idiosyncratic beliefs about particular events.

Maher and Ross (1984) and Maher (1988) have put forward a framework rather similar to that of Scheibe and Sarbin and Johnson *et al.* in its emphasis on our constant search for explanations and on the continuity between ordinary and 'delusional' beliefs. Their model, however, gives prominence to the role of anomalous personal experiences in the development of 'delusional' beliefs. Maher (1988) reviews some of the research which emphasises the apparent ease with which 'irrational' beliefs can be provoked in ordinary people under anomalous environmental conditions. He also discusses the work of Southward, early in this century, in which post-mortem findings for patients said to have been deluded suggested that many of their beliefs served an explanatory function for symptoms of pathology undiagnosed in life but obvious at post-mortem. It is interesting to recall here the plight of Kraepelin's and Bleuler's patients, many of whom experienced anomalous physical and cognitive changes which were as bewildering to their doctors as to themselves. Not surprisingly, some of their beliefs appear to be attempts to explain the inexplicable: their inability to carry out 'willed' acts; impulsive acts they had not 'willed'; chronic constipation, and so on. Maher's emphasis on anomalous experiences could, however, be rather problematic for the model if only because there may be no clear means of determining in advance what constitutes such an experience; rather, it is defined by the person themselves. Maher talks also of "puzzles", of "discrepancies between what we expect to observe and what we do observe", but, as Maher is well aware, this still leaves us with the problem of knowing why people react to the same "puzzle" in such different ways or why what is self-evident or trivial to one person should be puzzling or significant to another. It is difficult to see how this can be understood without reference to other aspects of people's belief systems and lifestyles.

One set of circumstances which might favour the development of idiosyncratic beliefs in the face of unexplained events is social isolation (Maher and Ross, 1984; Johnson, 1988). An interesting observation made by Milton *et al.* (1978) may be relevant here. As part of their attempts to modify the claims made by patients said to be persistently deluded, the authors administered a Social Anxiety Questionniare, although the content of their subjects' claims did not obviously suggest that the results would be of interest. Nevertheless, subjects' mean scores were very much higher than that of the standardisation group (82.8 versus 28). Unfortunately, individual scores were not given, nor do we know whether these subjects actually were socially isolated. It could be speculated, however, that in the past these subjects had either excluded themselves or been excluded from social interaction, and had thus been deprived of valuable sources of feedback on their claims; that, for want of shared social concerns, they became concerned about matters irrelevant to most of us or that they constructed belief systems which conferred a social status they lacked. Johnson (1988) has also suggested that, the less time is spent with social stimulation, the more is spent with self-generated processes, perhaps with 'rehearsing' or thinking repeatedly about certain events. Johnson suggests several reasons why this might be conducive to the development of bizarre belief systems. First, the frequency of occurrence of the event, and therefore its significance, might be overestimated. Second, the event will be readily available for recall and may therefore exert special influence over the interpretation of future events. Third, the event, or its interpretation, may seem more true, the more often it is rehearsed.

The conclusions which can be drawn from this type of analysis are similar to those drawn here from the analysis of hallucinations. First, it is very difficult indeed to justify separating, for research purposes, the belief systems of 'schizophrenics' from those of the rest of us or to justify the *a priori* claim that special theories are needed to account for them. Second, if a separation is made, it should perhaps be in the interests of studying social reactions to certain claims and the processes whereby some bizarre beliefs come to be labelled pathological.

An anthropological approach

Although Lipsedge and Littlewood (1979), Littlewood (1980) and Littlewood and Lipsedge (1982, 1989) have recently developed this approach in detail, the ideas it embodies are not new (see, for example, Kiev, 1963). It is discussed here for two reasons. First, because it may prove fruitful as a source of research hypotheses and theories about bizarre behaviour and, second, because it illustrates well the problems of attempting to develop alternative theories of bizarre behaviour but at the same time to retain the concept of schizophrenia.

The starting-point of Littlewood and Lipsedge's (1982) discussion is their "realization" that diagnoses of schizophrenia, when made about immigrant groups, "often conveyed the doctor's lack of understanding rather than the presence of the 'key symptoms' by which this reaction is conventionally recognised by British psychiatrists. Patients appeared to be regarded as unintelligible because of their cultural background" (7). Littlewood and Lipsedge are emphasising here the important role of the perception of irrationality in judgements of insanity, an idea explored in detail by Szasz (1987). With this in mind, Littlewood and Lipsedge have developed two major themes: first, that "With a sympathetic knowledge of another's culture and of their personal experience it is possible to understand much of what otherwise appears as inexplicable irrationality"; and second, that "there is always an interrelation between personal experience and cultural preoccupations which is not haphazard, which is related to the interests of the group as a whole (or certain dominant sections of it) and which can be understood historically" (1989: 216–17). In order to illustrate how these ideas might operate in practice, Littlewood and Lipsedge describe the behaviour and backgrounds of a number of immigrant people – of West Indian, Cypriot, Jewish and Irish extraction – referred to them. They attempt to show how apparently incomprehensible behaviour, which might earn the label schizophrenia, can be rendered comprehensible by close examination of cultural beliefs and practices (for example, about the behaviour of spirits, ways of warding off threat, and so on) and of personal experiences (racial discrimination, family disputes, conflict between the values of the old and new cultures, and so on).

While the major strength of Littlewood and Lipsedge's analysis is their attempt to describe relationships between behaviour and its context, its major weakness is similar to that discussed earlier for 'delusions': the assumption that an observer's understanding of another's behaviour can serve as one criterion for inferring schizophrenia and its attendant assumptions. It is clear that Littlewood and Lipsedge wish to retain the diagnosis of schizophrenia for those people who, even after all their efforts, they still cannot understand. In other words, they assume that they are discussing *misdiagnosis*, and that it is possible 'properly' to diagnose schizophrenia:

> Nor is the diagnosis of schizophrenia merely futile labelling....If we say that patients like CJ or MO are schizophrenic when they are not, we are subjecting them to unnecessary long-term medication, the stigma of mental illness and a self-perception as an invalid. If, on the other hand, we fail to recognize schizophrenia, we have again misinterpreted our patient's experience and possibly condemned him to a gradual process of emotional deterioration, with its harmful effect on his personality, family and livelihood....It is essential for the psychiatrist to be able to distinguish between serious mental illnesses which, although they may have social precipitants, are not self-limiting and situational reactions which can be explained best in social and political terms.

(111)

Littlewood and Lipsedge provide no evidence for the validity of this distinction nor of the concept of schizophrenia. Rather, and as with decisions about 'delusions', it is apparently assumed that schizophrenics can be distinguished from pseudo-schizophrenics by the idiosyncrasy of their belief systems and their behaviour. Indeed, Littlewood and Lipsedge provide a chart which purports to illustrate the relationship between the number of people who adhere to a belief system and its status as 'delusional':

individual psychotic delusions	*folie à deux*	transient and obscure sects	psychic epidemics	widely held religious beliefs

Thus, 'schizophrenics' are said to be recognisable by the fact that they adopt highly idiosyncratic symbols or belief systems: "EW uses acceptable symbols in her own rather unusual way, but EA, who is schizophrenic, employs a much more personal and less accessible type of symbol" (1989: 220). Again, no evidence is provided for the validity of the diagnosic term; instead, it is implied that the symbols are unacceptable and that "To symbolize is a cognitive process and schizophrenic patients have been found to have unusual cognitive patterns" (1989: 220).

By retaining the concept of schizophrenia for apparently idosyncratic behaviour and by implying that intuitive understanding of behaviour is important in diagnosing schizophrenia, Littlewood and Lipsedge are led to the conclusion that we need different explanations for similar phenomena, when displayed by, say, a native Londoner or a West Indian immigrant:

> We felt that the causes of mental illness in ethnic minorities were the same as for members of the majority culture and the problem was simply one of understanding the background so as to make a conventional diagnosis....We began increasingly to question this assumption. The experiences of migration and of discrimination in housing, employment and everyday life were frequently expressed by patients, not as conscious complaints but symbolically in the actual structure of their illness.
>
> (1982: 7)

Although Littlewood and Lipsedge do not make the idea explicit, the inference could be drawn that the indigenous population do *not* express their experiences symbolically "in the actual structure of their illness". Yet there is no reason to suppose that indigenous groups will not also express *their* experiences of isolation, rejection, discrimination, uncertainty or conflict in just this way. It would be unfortunate if a potentially useful approach, which emphasises the social control of bizarre behaviour and the fact that people construct possibly self-serving explanations in the face of uncertainty or distress, were to come to be seen as applying only to minority cultures. It must be emphasised that none of the arguments presented here is changed by recent claims that, using strict and carefully applied diagnostic criteria, the rates of schizophrenia diagnoses amongst people of Afro-Caribbean ethnic origin living in England are higher than expected (see, for example, Harrison *et al.*, 1988). Even if, incautiously, we were to take these figures at face value, the fact that certain behaviour occurs more frequently in one group does not tell us how we should interpret such behaviour and cannot in itself be used to justify the application of a particular theoretical model. And, as was pointed out earlier, the status of the concept of schizophrenia makes the idea of 'careful diagnosis' meaningless.

The analysis of family interaction

While Littlewood and Lipsedge are concerned to relate bizarre behaviour to cultural beliefs and practices, a number of researchers (for example, Leff *et al.*, 1982; Falloon *et al.*, 1982; Falloon *et al.*, 1984) have been concerned with the relationship between such behaviour and more specific processes of family interaction and with the effects on odd behaviour of manipulating family interaction (see Falloon, 1988, for a review). Their work, like Littlewood and Lipsedge's, may prove a fruitful source of research hypotheses about the development and maintenance of deviant behaviour. It also provides yet another illustration of the problems of attempting to retain the concept of schizophrenia within a theoretical framework which makes quite different assumptions about behaviour. Because it is representative of the approach and because it provides so much detail, only the work of Falloon *et al.* (1984) will be described here.

The major assumption made by Falloon *et al.* is that stress, defined as a perceived discrepancy between environmental or personal resources and environmental demands, plays a major part in exacerbating the symptoms of schizophrenia and in determining its course. The emphasis on family interaction comes from two sources. One is the reasonable assumption that a major source of 'stress' may be the family itself, either in terms of the demands members make on each other or in the way the family attempts to solve problems. The second and more specific source is a series of studies which examined the relationship between particular kinds of family interaction and 'relapse' in 'schizophrenics'. This work (see, for example, Brown *et al.*, 1972; Vaughn and Leff, 1976; Leff and Vaughn, 1981) suggested that particular behaviours on the part of relatives were likely to result in the 'schizophrenic's' re-admission to hospital and in an increase in frequency or intensity of bizarre behaviour. The relatives' behaviours (all of which were rated from interviews) included critical comments, or statements indicating dissatisfaction or dislike, expressions of worrying, disregard for privacy, interrupting, and so on. High ratings on these resulted in an overall rating of high 'expressed emotion'.

Falloon *et al.* designed a major and innovative programme of intervention, to be carried out in the homes of people diagnosed as schizophrenic and their families. The programme had two major aims. The first was to teach a positive style of communication, the second to teach problem-solving skills. Thus, families were taught, amongst other skills, to listen to each other, to express criticism constructively, to make clear positive requests for behavioural change, to reinforce desired behaviour, to set realistic goals, to volunteer and evaluate a number of solutions and to plan, step-by-step, their implementation. This kind of intervention has much in common with those designed for marital problems (see, for example, Jacobsen and Margolin, 1979; Bornstein and Bornstein, 1986) and for more general use (for example, Spivak *et al.*, 1976). Falloon *et al.* describe the content of the intervention: "problem issues may range from housing and finances to paranoid beliefs, or from hallucinations to the taking of street drugs or plasma levels of prescribed drugs" (162). It is clear also from their account that considerable efforts were directed towards developing the 'schizophrenic's' social behaviour – obtaining employment, making friends, having an independent social life, and so on.

It would be easy to criticise the methodology of Falloon *et al.*'s programme and its assessment and to overlook the immense practical problems involved in carrying out and evaluating this kind of large-scale and time-consuming intervention – at times in the face of considerable consumer resistance. Criticism here will therefore be restricted to the assumptions made by Falloon *et al.* and the ways in which they influenced the design of the intervention. The major and most problematic assumption was that subjects were suffering from an illness of unknown cause but with a strong genetic component and which "appears to produce an imbalance of the brain chemistry" (180). Thus, the programme was seen as an attempt to reduce the vulnerability of someone with a disordered brain and to prevent a "recrudescence of schizophrenia". This assumption created a number of problems. Relatives – and supposed sufferers – were 'educated', prior to the beginning of the programme, with what were described as some basic facts about the illness. These included the idea of genetic and biochemical involvement, lists of symptoms and the necessity to take major tranquillisers. Much of this clearly functioned to absolve parents of responsibility for their child's behaviour as well as, presumably, to justify the medical setting:

> Some families worry that they might be to blame for schizophrenia in one of the members. We often hear the notion that schizophrenia is caused by an unhappy childhood. A lot of publicity has been given to various theories that families that raised their children in certain ways could cause them to develop schizophrenia later. However, there is no conclusive scientific evidence that families in any way cause schizophrenia.
>
> (191)

In order to justify the programme, however, families were told that there is abundant evidence that families may be able to help improve the outcome of the illness. Families were not told that there is no strong evidence to support the idea of schizophrenia or the assumptions which surround it. Instead, families were informed of the beliefs of 'experts' about the involvement of genes and biochemistry. Quite apart from the ethical issues of misrepresenting evidence, this framework presents families with the problem of distinguishing the results of undemonstrated biochemical disturbances from the results of family interaction. It is apparently important that the distinction is made, because the two phenomena must be accounted for and dealt with in different ways:

> there is the danger that family members may consider all inappropriate behaviours to be "symptoms". One father considered the "irrational" temper tantrums of his 25-year-old son a symptom of schizophrenia and was unwilling to adopt a firm, no-nonsense approach to dealing with this inappropriate behaviour.
>
> (187)

By contrast, behaviours such as staying in bed all morning, failing to carry out agreed plans, and so on are seen as part of the illness which families are urged to treat with tolerance and understanding and to "allow time for recovery" (189). It is not clear how the distinction between symptoms and inappropriate behaviour is to be made: Falloon *et al.* rely on textbook rules but also suggest that families should remember that the index patient is the "expert" on the experiences of schizophrenia in the family. As the supposed cause of 'symptoms' has never been observed, far less demonstrated and measured in any individual, then it is difficult to see how 'sufferers' can possibly know when their behaviour is a symptom of schizophrenia. In any case, Falloon *et al.* appear later to contradict themselves by asserting that:

> We [supported] the notion that antisocial behaviour is never acceptable in the community regardless of the mental status of the patient, and that the same social sanctions should be imposed on the mentally ill offender as on any other member of the community. In other words, punishment should fit the crime. Dramatic improvements in destructive behaviour followed arrests, court appearances, and jail sentences in those few instances of police intervention. One patient summarised our posture when he said, "It doesn't matter how far gone you get, you always know what is right and wrong."

(409)

This theoretical confusion could be avoided by abandoning premature assumptions about the antecedents of behaviour. Shorn of these assumptions, the work of Falloon *et al.* and that on 'expressed emotion' suggests a number of potentially fruitful research areas. The first concerns the relationship between aversive situations and, for example, reports of hearing voices or the expression of 'strange' beliefs. It may be that concepts developed in the study of animal behaviour such as conflict and uncontrollability would be useful in describing aversive situations within the family; and abandoning the idea of these behaviours as manifestations of illness means that we are free to study their relationship to the situation, what functions they serve, in what way they alter it, and so on. A second area of interest concerns the role of reinforcement patterns in the shaping and maintenance of bizarre behaviour; for while Falloon *et al.* are prepared to allow reinforcement a role in maintaining bizarre behaviour, they are reluctant to consider the idea that it may be involved in shaping it. A third area of interest is one discussed earlier: that of the relationship between bizarre behaviour and social performance. Given what was suggested earlier about the importance of social performance in determining responses to bizarre behaviour, it is interesting to note the very strong emphasis given by Falloon *et al.* to their clients' social behaviour, and the importance they attach to changing it.

It has been emphasised here that 'schizophrenia'-free research must be concerned with the general population and not only with those who have come to the attention of psychiatrists. It is of considerable interest to know in what way the reporting of bizarre behaviour within the family, family reactions to it and accompanying social behaviours interact in both the development of the behaviour and the labelling of it as problematic. This kind of research also demands changes in the collection and reporting of data. If it is assumed that 'symptoms' can easily be inferred from reports of behaviour and that these are manifestations of an illness, then little attempt may be made to describe behaviour precisely or to specify its relationship to environmental events, except in rather general terms. Thus, a good deal of potentially useful information may be lost.

The problem of classification

It was pointed out in Chapter 7 that one argument put forward in defence of 'schizophrenia' is that it is necessary to group, to classify, phenomena in order to study them scientifically. This argument implies that abandoning 'schizophrenia' might lead to conceptual chaos. This is, of course, not the case. To abandon 'schizophrenia', and the type of classification system in which it is embedded, is not to abandon the search for order or patterns. It does, however, demand that we rethink how the phenomena of interest might be grouped or conceptualised.

The major purpose of classification is to group like with like in order to predict new observations and to enable statements to be made which will generalise to new exemplars of a phenomenon. The requirement that scientific classification systems predict new observations is essential, given the almost infinite number of ways in which various phenomena could be said to resemble each other. Classification systems in the natural and biological sciences are based on groupings in terms of stable 'attributes', and from which concepts such as mammal and fruit are inferred. It is not difficult to see how problematic it would be for researchers working within those systems if, say, the same cow sometimes reproduced by giving birth and suckling and sometimes by laying eggs; if the seeds which define a tomato as a fruit were there on Monday, had disappeared on Tuesday, but returned on Wednesday or Thursday, and so on. But it can be argued that this is exactly the situation faced by psychologists and psychiatrists with respect to behaviour and one which has been widely ignored: rather than confronting the fact that the same person may behave in very different and quite opposing ways, and attempting to account for this variability, a search has been made for underlying stable attributes, whether they be 'mental illnesses' or 'personality traits', in terms of which, it is supposed, people may be grouped.

The problems of this approach have been well described (see, for example, Mischel, 1968; Ullman and Krasner, 1969; Skinner, 1974; Jones, 1979) and will not be repeated in detail here, but three major criticisms should be briefly noted. The first is that such systems have proved remarkably unsuccessful at predicting new observations. The attributes posited by them have an unfortunate tendency to persist in spite of contrary data and their proponents to introduce *post hoc* explanations which preserve the attribute, rather than facing the variability in the data. The second criticism, and one particularly developed by Mischel (1968) and Hampson (1988) in relation to personality theory, is that the posited attributes, rather than being possessed by subjects, exist, so to speak, in the heads of researchers. In other words, they represent cultural beliefs about the organisation of behaviour and its causes rather than reliable statements about observations. A third criticism, more rarely stated, concerns the belief that psychiatric classification systems are concerned with a definable subset of behaviour, called abnormal or disturbed or disordered, and that their subject-matter is stable illnesses, disorders or conditions which people have and which may be inferred from abnormal behaviour. The problems of this assumption about subject-matter have already been discussed but it is worth quoting Begelman (1976) as a summary:

> Clinicians have for many years now been led to pose the question "What is problem behaviour?" with that kind of innocence born of the conviction that the answer is just round the corner, and not the anguished product of enquiries forever plagued by false starts....Regardless of the focus involved, all such definitions will be found to be wanting because they are predicated on the root assumption of a behaviour disturbance being a *psychological*, not a *moral* concept.
>
> (36, 38; emphasis in original)

With these issues in mind, two major requirements for an alternative conceptualisation can be suggested. The first is that it confronts the variability of behaviour and recognises that behaviour cannot be discussed independently of the context in which it occurs. The second is that the subject-matter must be descriptions of *behaviour* in its widest sense, and including verbal reports of experiences. Of course, behaviour is the starting-point of all classification systems in psychology and psychiatry, but this is obscured by assumptions about the nature of the subject-matter and by premature inferences to underlying attributes. By 'behaviour' here is also meant that there should be no division between supposedly normal and abnormal behaviour. It is exceptionally difficult to justify this division on scientific grounds in the absence of evidence that we need different theories to account for these two sorts of behaviour. It is not the intention here to describe a new classification system. All such systems must be developed empirically and it is certainly not yet clear what might be useful ways of grouping behaviour. At this stage in the development of alternatives to psychiatric classification, a variety of methods needs to be explored.

Salzinger (1986) has suggested that behaviours should be grouped according to their functional properties: that behaviours elicited by the same class of discriminative stimuli and/or which have the same consequences should be grouped together or considered part of the same response class. This approach is similar to that adopted by Ullman and Krasner (1969) and is derived from the experimental analysis of behaviour (Skinner, 1953). It is clear that the same 'type' of behaviour, for example, smoking, may simultaneously be a member of different response classes for any individual. Hallam (1985a), although not discussing this point, has provided a good example of the way in which this kind of analysis would result in a quite different grouping of behaviours than is traditionally seen in psychiatric texts. He points out that 'agora-phobia' would be better described as 'staying-at-home behaviour' to emphasise the fact that staying at home is an avoidance response to aversive somatic events. Hallam notes that these same somatic events (often described as panic) are often reported by those who drink heavily and that drinking, like staying at home, may be an avoidance response to somatic stimuli. The 'choice' of avoidance behaviour may be partly dependent on cultural factors, with women more likely to stay at home and men more likely to drink heavily. This analysis suggests that drinking and staying at home may usefully be seen as members of the same response class, with implications for the design of interventions. This is, of course, not to say that these behaviours should always be grouped together for research purposes; clearly they will not always be members of the same response class.

A more one-sided approach would involve the analysis of stimulus settings and their relationship to patterns of response. This approach has long been used in animal research and in particular in the study of so-called experimen-tal neurosis in which specified patterns of aversive stimuli are applied and responses monitored. Mineka and Kihlstrom (1978) have suggested a number of similarities amongst these patterns and ways in which they might serve as a model for the analysis of human behaviour. It is interesting to note that re-sponding to apparently non-existent stimuli (hallucinating) is one noted response to some of these settings. The advantages of this approach are that it emphasises the wide variety of behaviour which may result from exposure to a particular setting, both between and within subjects, and that it may pre-vent us from assuming that different behaviours must have different antecedents. It is notable that 'schizophrenics' make a number of complaints (of, for example, anxiety or depression), apart from displaying bizarre beha-viour (Falloon *et al.*, 1984) but that little theoretical attention is paid to these because they are not seen as important symptoms of schizophrenia. Thus the fact that these and the bizarre behaviour may have common antecedents is overlooked. Behaviour might, on the other hand, be grouped according to consequences. It remains unclear how consequences might best be described. A division into responses which are positively and negatively reinforced or which are punished is likely to be too broad. Divisions might be made into responses which result in social or sexual contact or withdrawal from these situations; in eating or the avoidance of food, and so on.

These approaches emphasise the functional rather than the topographical properties of behaviour and ensure that behaviour is not considered separate-ly from its context. It would, however, be possible to begin by grouping behaviour topographically (for example, all claims to hear voices in the ab-sence of obvious external stimuli) and then to investigate the variables which influence it. This is, of course, the approach taken in individual functional analyses and earlier in this chapter. This approach has the advantage of ad-dressing directly the obvious point of concern – behaviour; it is also likely that similar behaviour (for example, smiling, hitting people) elicits similar 'natural' consequences, although these will obviously depend on the context. But the approach is potentially problematic when it is applied to *groups* said to display similar behaviour. It is easy to assume that people who display apparently similar behaviour must have attributes in common and that they must be different from people who show dissimilar behaviour. It is these assumptions which underlie psychiatric classification. It is thus easy to fall back on to internal explanations, to lose sight of the possible heterogeneity of such groupings and of the relationship between behaviour and its context. In other words, if, in attempts to construct alternatives to 'schizophrenia', behaviours are grouped topographically, we must beware of ending up back where we started.

The emphasis in this chapter has been on the importance of considering behaviour in its social context. The emphasis throughout has been on the relationship between the concept of schizophrenia and the context in which it was introduced and developed. It has been suggested that this context includes the habits of seeking internal – and especially biological – explanations of behaviour; of assuming patterns rather than demonstrating them; of filling gaps in knowledge with questionable explanations; of inferring before describing; of mistaking evaluation for description; of begging important questions; of using language to obscure rather than to clarify; and of expecting scientific (or supposedly scientific) concepts to solve complex moral and political problems. It is unlikely that constructive alternatives to 'schizophrenia' (as distinct from its replacement with equally problematic concepts) will be developed unless we face not only the deficiencies of the concept but also the social and intellectual habits which have allowed it to flourish.

Bibliography

Abrams, R. and Taylor, M.A. (1977) Catatonia: prediction of response to somatic treatments. *American Journal of Psychiatry* 134: 78–80.

Al-Issa, I. (1977) Social and cultural aspects of hallucinations. *Psychological Bulletin* 84: 570–87.

Allen, G., Harvald, B. and Shields, J. (1967) Measurement of twin concordance. *Acta Genetica* (Basel) 17: 475–81.

Allen, M.G., Cohen, S. and Pollin, W. (1972) Schizophrenia in veteran twins: a diagnostic review. *American Journal of Psychiatry* 128: 939–45.

Alpert, M. (1985) The signs and symptoms of schizophrenia. *Comprehensive Psychiatry* 26: 103–12.

Alpert, M. and Silvers, K.N. (1970) Perceptual characteristics distinguishing auditory hallucinations in schizophrenics and acute alcoholic psychosis. *American Journal of Psychiatry* 127: 298–302.

American Psychiatric Association (1952) *Diagnostic and Statistical Manual of Mental Disorders*, 1st edn. Washington: APA.

American Psychiatric Association (1968) *Diagnostic and Statistical Manual of Mental Disorders*, 2nd edn. Washington: APA.

American Psychiatric Association (1980) *Diagnostic and Statistical Manual of Mental Disorders*, 3rd edn. Washington: APA.

American Psychiatric Association (1987) *Diagnostic and Statistical Manual of Mental Disorders*, 3rd edn (Revised). Washington: APA.

Anderson, C.A., Lepper, M.A. and Ross, L. (1980) Perseverance of social theories: the role of explanation in the persistence of discredited information. *Journal of Personality and Social Psychology* 39: 1037–49.

Anderson, L.T. and Alpert, M. (1974) Operant analysis of hallucination frequency in a hospitalised schizophrenic. *Journal of Behaviour Therapy and Experimental Psychiatry* 5: 13–18.

Antrobus, J.S., Singer, J.L. and Greenberg, S. (1966) Studies in the stream of consciousness: experimental enhancement and suppression of spontaneous cognitive processes. *Perceptual and Motor Skills* 23: 399–417.

Arieti, S. (1979) *Understanding and Helping the Schizophrenic: A Guide for Family and Friends*. New York: Simon & Schuster.

Astrachan, B.M., Harrow, M., Adler, D., Brauer, L., Schwartz, A., Schwartz, C. and Tucker, G.A. (1972) A checklist for the diagnosis of schizophrenia. *British Journal of Psychiatry* 121: 529–39.

Astrup, C. and Noreik, K. (1966) *Functional Psychosis: Diagnostic and Prognostic Models*. Springfield, Illinois: Charles C. Thomas.

Ayllon, T. and Azrin, N. (1968) *The Token Economy: A Motivational System for Therapy and Rehabilitation*. New York: Appleton-Century-Crofts.

Barber, T.X. and Calverley, D.S. (1964) An experimental study of "hypnotic" (auditory and visual) hallucinations. *Journal of Abnormal and Social Psychology* 68: 13–20.

Bean, P. (1980) *Compulsory Admissions to Mental Hospitals*. Chichester: Wiley.

Beck, A.T. (1962) Reliability of psychiatric diagnoses: a critique of systematic studies. *American Journal of Psychiatry* 119: 210–16.

Beck, A.T., Ward, C., Mendelson, M., Mock, J. and Erbaugh, J. (1962) Reliability of psychiatric diagnoses: 2. A study of consistency of clinical judgements and ratings. *American Journal of Psychiatry* 119: 351–7.

Beck, L.W. (1953) Constructions and inferred entities. In H. Feigl and M. Brodbeck (eds) *Readings in the Philosophy of Science*. New York: Appleton-Century-Crofts.

Beckman, H. and Haas, S. (1980) High dosage diazepam in schizophrenia. *Psychopharmacology* 71: 79–82.

Begelman, D.A. (1976) Behavioral classification. In M. Hersen and A.S. Bellack (eds) *Behavioral Assessment: A Practical Handbook*. New York: Pergamon.

Benjamin, A.C. (1937) *An Introduction to the Philosophy of Science*. New York: Macmillan.

Benjamin, L.S. (1976) A reconsideration of the Kety and associates' study of genetic factors in the transmission of schizophrenia. *American Journal of Psychiatry* 113: 1129–33.

Bennett, E. (1983) The Biasing Effect of Possession of Information on Clinicians' Subsequent Recognition of Client Information. Unpublished Master's Thesis, North East London Polytechnic.

Bentall, R.P. (1986) The scientific status of schizophrenia: a critical evaluation. In N. Eisenberg and D. Glasgow (eds) *Current Issues in Clinical Psychology*, Vol. 5. Aldershot: Gower.

Bentall, R.P. (1990) The illusion of reality: a review and integration of psychological research on hallucinations. *Psychological Bulletin* 107: 82–95.

Bentall, R.P. and Slade, P.D. (1985a) Reality testing and auditory hallucinations: a signal-detection analysis. *British Journal of Clinical Psychology* 24: 159–69.

Bentall, R.P. and Slade, P.D. (1985b) Reliability of a scale measuring disposition towards hallucination: a brief report. *Personality and Individual Differences* 6: 527–9.

Bentall, R.P. and Slade, P.D. (1986) Verbal hallucinations, unintendedness and the validity of the schizophrenia diagnosis. *The Behavioural and Brain Sciences* 9: 519–520.

Bentall, R.P., Jackson, H.F. and Pilgrim, D. (1988) Abandoning the concept of 'schizophrenia': some implications of validity arguments for psychological research into psychotic phenomena. *British Journal of Clinical Psychology* 27: 303–24.

Berscheid, E. and Walster, E.H. (1978) *Interpersonal Attraction*, 2nd edn. Reading, Mass.: Addison-Wesley.

Blackman, D.E. (1981) On the mental element in crime and behaviourism. In S. Lloyd-Bostock (ed.) *Law and Psychology*. Oxford: SSRC Centre for Socio-Legal Studies.

Blakemore, C. (1988) The Mind Machine, BBC2 Television, 18 October.

Blashfield, R.K. and Draguns, J.G. (1976) Evaluative criteria for psychiatric classification. *Journal of Abnormal Psychology* 85: 140–50.

Bleuler, E. (1950) *Dementia Praecox or the Group of Schizophrenias*, trans. J. Zitkin. New York: International Universities Press (originally published in 1911).

Bockoven, J.S. (1956a) Moral treatment in American psychiatry. *Journal of Nervous and Mental Diseases* 124: 167–94.

Bockoven, J.S. (1956b) Moral treatment in American psychiatry. *Journal of Nervous and Mental Diseases* 124: 292–321.

Bornstein, P.H. and Bornstein, M.T. (1986) *Marital Therapy: a Behavioral Communications Approach*. New York: Pergamon.

Brennan, J.H. and Hemsley, D.R. (1984) Illusory correlations in paranoid and non-paranoid schizophrenia. *British Journal of Clinical Psychology* 23: 225–6.

Brett-Jones, J., Garety, P and Hemsley, D. (1987) Measuring delusional experiences: a method and its application. *British Journal of Clinical Psychology* 26: 257–66.

Bridgman, P.W. (1927) *The Logic of Modern Physics*. New York: Macmillan.

Brill, H. (1974) Classification and nomenclature of psychiatric conditions. In S. Arieti (ed.) *American Handbook of Psychiatry*, 2nd edn, Vol. 1. New York: Basic Books.

Brockington, I.F., Kendell, R.E. and Leff, J.P. (1978) Definitions of schizophrenia: concordance and prediction of outcome. *Psychological Medicine* 8: 387–98.

Brown, G.W., Birley, J.L.T. and Wing, J.K. (1972) Influence of family life on the course of schizophrenic disorders: a replication. *British Journal of Psychiatry* 121: 241–58.

Buchsbaum, M.S. (1977) Psychophysiology and schizophrenia. *Schizophrenia Bulletin* 3: 7–14.

Bynum, W.F. (1964) Rationales for therapy in British psychiatry: 1780–1835. *Medical History* 18: 317–35.

Cancro, R. (1976) Some diagnostic and therapeutic considerations of the schizophrenic syndrome. In R. Cancro (ed.) *Annual Review of the Schizophrenic Syndrome*, Vol. 5. New York: Bruner Mazel.

Cantor, N. and Mischel, W. (1977) Traits as prototypes: effects on recognition memory. *Journal of Personality and Social Psychology* 35: 38–48.

Cantor, N., Smith, E.E., de Sales French, R. and Mezzich, J. (1980) Psychiatric diagnosis as prototype categorization. *Journal of Abnormal Psychology* 89: 181–93.

Carnap, R. (1937) Testability and Meaning. Part IV. *Philosophy of Science* 4: 1–40.

Carnap, R. (1974) *An Introduction to the Philosophy of Science*, ed. M. Gardner. New York: Basic Books.

Carpenter, W., Bartko, J. and Strauss, J.T.S. (1978) Signs and symptoms as predictors of outcome: a report from the International Pilot Study of Schizophrenia. *American Journal of Psychiatry* 135: 940–5.

Carpenter, W.T., Strauss, J.S. and Bartko, J. (1973a) Flexible system for the diagnosis of schizophrenia: report from the International Pilot Study of Schizophrenia. *Science* 182: 1275–8.

Carpenter, W.T., Strauss, J.S. and Salvatore, M. (1973b) Are there pathognomic symptoms in schizophrenia?: an empiric investigation of Schneider's first-rank symptoms. *Archives of General Psychiatry* 28: 847–52.

Castel, R., Castel, F. and Lovell, A. (1982) *The Psychiatric Society*. New York: Columbia University Press.

Cerasi, E. and Luft, R. (1967) Insulin response to glucose infusion in diabetic and non-diabetic monozygotic twin pairs. Genetic control of insulin response? *Acta Endocrinologica* 55: 330–45.

Chapman, L.J. and Chapman, J.P. (1967) The genesis of popular but erroneous psychodiagnostic observations. *Journal of Abnormal Psychology* 72: 193–204.

Chapman, L.J. and Chapman, J.P. (1982) Test results are what you think they are. In D. Kahneman, P. Slovic and A. Tversky (eds) *Judgement Under Uncertainty: Heuristics and Biases*. Cambridge: Cambridge University Press.

Clare, A. (1980) *Psychiatry in Dissent: Controversial Issues in Thought and Practice*, 2nd edn 1980. London: Tavistock.

Cole, J.O. (1964) Phenothiazine treatment in acute schizophrenia. *Archives of General Psychiatry* 10: 246–61.

Cooper, J.E., Kendell, R.E., Gurland, B.J., Sharpe, L., Copeland, J.R.M. and Simon, R. (1972) *Psychiatric Diagnosis in New York and London. A Comparative Study of Mental Hospital Admissions*. Institute of Psychiatry and Maudsley Monographs No. 20. London: Oxford University Press.

Crocker, J. (1981) Judgement of covariation by social perceivers. *Psychological Bulletin* 90: 272–92.

Cronbach, L.J. and Meehl, P.E. (1955) Construct validity in psychological tests. *Psychological Bulletin* 52: 281–302.

Crookshank, F.G. (1956) The importance of a theory of signs and a critique of language in the study of medicine. A supplement to C.K. Ogden and I.A. Richards (eds) *The Meaning of Meaning*, 10th edn. London: Routledge and Kegan Paul.

Crow, T.J. (1984) A re-evaluation of the viral hypothesis: is psychosis the result of retroviral integration at a site close to the cerebral dominance gene? *British Journal of Psychiatry* 145: 243–53.

Crow, T.J., Macmillan, J.F., Johnson, A.L. and Johnson, E.C. (1986) The Northwick Park study of first episodes of schizophrenia – 2: a controlled trial of neuroleptic treatment. *British Journal of Psychiatry* 148: 120–7.

Cumming, E. (1970) Epidemiology: some unresolved problems. *American Journal of Psychiatry* 126: 121–2.

Cutting, J. (1985) *The Psychology of Schizophrenia*. Edinburgh: Churchill Livingstone.

Delva, N.J. and Letemendia, F.J.J. (1982) Lithium treatment in schizophrenia and schizoaffective disorders. *British Journal of Psychiatry* 141: 387–400.

Dunton, W.R. (1944) The American Journal of Psychiatry 1844–1944. *American Journal of Psychiatry* 100: 45–60.

Editorial (1970) Two minds on schizophrenia. *New Scientist* 48: 424.

Emmet, E.R. (1968) *Learning to Philosophise*, 2nd edn. Harmondsworth: Penguin Books.

Engel, G.L. (1977) The need for a new medical model: a challenge for biomedicine. *Science* 196: 129–36.

Engel, G.L. (1980) Clinical applications of the biosocial model. *American Journal of Psychiatry* 137: 535–44.

Engle, R.L. (1963) Medical diagnosis: past, present and future. II. Philosophical foundations and historical development of our concepts of health, disease and diagnosis. *Archives of Internal Medicine* 112: 520–9.

Engle, R.L. and Davis, B.J. (1963) Medical diagnosis: past, present and future. I. Present concepts of the meaning and limitations of medical diagnosis. *Archives of Internal Medicine* 112: 512–19.

Essen-Möller, E. (1941) Psychiatrishe Untersuchungen an einer Serie von Zwillingen. *Acta Psychiatrica et Neurologica Scandinavica* Suppl. 23.

Everitt, B.S., Gourlay, A.J. and Kendell, R.E. (1971) An attempt at validation of traditional psychiatric syndromes by cluster analysis. *British Journal of Psychiatry* 119: 399–412.

Falloon, I.R.H. (1988) Expressed emotion: current status. *Psychological Medicine* 18: 269–74.

Falloon, I.R.H., Boyd, J.L. and McGill, C.W. (1984) *Family Care of Schizophrenia*. New York: The Guilford Press.

Falloon, I.R.H., Boyd, J.L., McGill, C.W., Razani, J., Moss, H.B. and Gilderman,

A.M. (1982) Family management in the prevention of exacerbations of schizophrenia: a controlled study. *New England Journal of Medicine* 306: 1437–40.

Farran-Ridge, C. (1926) Some symptoms referable to the basal ganglia and occurring in dementia praecox and epidemic encephalitis. *Journal of Mental Science* 72: 513–23.

Feighner, J.P., Robins, E., Guze, S.B., Woodruff, R.A., Winokur, G. and Munoz, R. (1972) Diagnostic criteria for use in psychiatric research. *Archives of General Psychiatry* 26: 57–63.

Feldman, M.P. (ed.) (1983) *Developments in the Study of Criminal Behaviour. Vol. 2: Violence.* Chichester: Wiley.

Fenton, W.S., Mosher, L.R. and Matthews, S.M. (1981) Diagnosis of schizophrenia: a critical review of current diagnostic systems. *Schizophrenia Bulletin* 7: 452–76.

Fischer, M. (1973) Genetic and environmental factors in schizophrenia. *Acta Psychiatrica Scandinavica* Suppl. 238.

Fonagy, P. and Slade, P.D. (1982) Punishment versus negative reinforcement in the aversive conditioning of auditory hallucinations. *Behaviour Research and Therapy* 20: 483–92.

General Register Office (1949) *Manual of the International Statistical Classification of Diseases, Injuries and Causes of Death*, Vol. 1. London: HMSO.

General Register Office (1968) *A Glossary of Mental Disorders*. Studies on Medical and Population Subjects No. 22. London: HMSO.

Gift, T.E., Strauss, J.S., Kokes, R.F., Harder, D.W. and Ritzler, B.A. (1980) Schizophrenia: affect and outcome. *American Journal of Psychiatry* 137: 580–85.

Gottesman, I.I. and Shields, J. (1972) *Schizophrenia and Genetics: A Twin Study Vantage Point.* London: Academic Press.

Gottesman, I.I. and Shields, J. (1976) A critical review of recent adoption, twin and family studies of schizophrenia: behavioural genetics perspectives. *Schizophrenia Bulletin* 2: 360–98.

Gottesman, I.I. and Shields, J. (1982) *Schizophrenia: The Epigenetic Puzzle.* Cambridge: Cambridge University Press.

Gould, L.N. (1950) Verbal hallucinations as automatic speech: the reactivation of a dormant speech habit. *American Journal of Psychiatry* 107: 110–19.

Gould, S.J. (1981) *The Mismeasure of Man.* New York: W.W. Norton.

Grange, K. (1962) The ship symbol as a key to former theories of the emotions. *Bulletin of the History of Medicine* 36: 512–23.

Gurling, H. (1989) Letter. *Lancet* 14 Feb.: 277.

Haier, R.J., Rosenthal, D. and Wender, P.H. (1978) MMPI assessment of psychopathology in the adopted-away offspring of schizophrenics. *Archives of General Psychiatry* 35: 171–5.

Hallam, R.S. (1985a) *Anxiety: A Psychological Approach to Panic and Agoraphobia.* New York: Academic Press.

Hallam, R.S. (1985b) Letter. *Bulletin of the British Psychological Society* 38: 341.

Haller, M.M. (1963) *Eugenics.* Rutgers: The State University.

Hamilton, D.L. (ed.) (1981) *Cognitive Processes in Stereotyping and Intergroup Behavior.* Hillsdale, NJ: Lawrence Erlbaum Associates.

Hammeke, T.A., McQuillen, M.P. and Cohen, B.A. (1983) Musical hallucinations associated with acquired deafness. *Journal of Neurology, Neurosurgery and Psychiatry* 46: 570–2.

Hampson, S.E. (1988) *The Construction of Personality*, 2nd edn. London: Routledge.

Hare, E.H. (1959) The origin and spread of dementia paralytica. *Journal of Mental Science* 105: 594–626.

Hare, E.H. (1973) A short note on pseudo-hallucinations. *British Journal of Psychiatry* 122: 469–76.

Hare, E.H. (1983) Was insanity on the increase? *British Journal of Psychiatry* 142: 439–55.

Hare, E.H. (1986) Schizophrenia as an infectious disease. In A. Kerr and P. Snaith (eds) *Contemporary Issues in Schizophrenia*. London: Royal College of Psychiatrists/Gaskell.

Harrison, G., Owens, D., Holton, A., Neilson, D. and Boot, D. (1988) A prospective study of severe mental disorder in Afro-Caribbean patients. *Psychological Medicine* 18: 643–57.

Hawk, A.B., Carpenter, T. and Strauss, J.S. (1975) Diagnostic criteria and 5-year outcome in schizophrenia. *Archives of General Psychiatry* 32: 343–7.

Heinrichs, D.W. (1988) The treatment of delusions in schizophrenic patients. In J.F. Oltmanns and B.A. Maher (eds) *Delusional Beliefs*. New York: Wiley.

Heise, D.R. (1988) Delusions and the construction of reality. In J.F. Oltmanns and B.A. Maher (eds) *Delusional Beliefs*. New York: Wiley.

Hemmings, G. (ed.) (1982) *Biological Aspects of Schizophrenia and Addiction*. Chichester: Wiley.

Hemmings, G. and Hemmings, W.A. (eds) (1978) *The Biological Basis of Schizophrenia*. Lancaster: MTP Press.

Hempel, C.G. (1961) Introduction to the problems of taxonomy. In J. Zubin (ed.) *Field Studies in the Mental Disorders*. New York: Grune and Stratton.

Hendrick, I. (1928) Encephalitis lethargica and the interpretation of mental disease. *American Journal of Psychiatry* 7: 989–1014.

Hoffer, A. and Pollin, W. (1970) Schizophrenia in the NAS-NRC panel of 15,909 veteran twin pairs. *Archives of General Psychiatry* 23: 469–77.

Hoffman, R.E. (1986) Verbal hallucinations and language production processes in schizophrenia. *The Behavioral and Brain Sciences* 9: 503–17.

Holt, R.R. (1964) Imagery: the return of the ostracized. *American Psychologist* 19: 254–64.

Hoskins, R.G. (1933) Schizophrenia from the physiological point of view. *Annals of Internal Medicine* 7: 445–56.

Hoskins, R.G. and Sleeper, F.H. (1933) Organic factors in schizophrenia. *Archives of Neurology and Psychiatry* 30: 123–32.

Iversen, S.D. and Iversen, L.L. (1975) *Behavioural Pharmacology*. New York: Oxford University Press.

Jablensky, A. (1986) An Interview. *The Times* 3 March.

Jacobsen, N. and Margolin, G. (1979) *Marital Therapy: Strategies Based on Social Learning and Behavior Exchange Principles*. New York: Brunner Mazel.

Jaspers, K. (1963) *General Psychopathology*. Chicago: University of Chicago Press.

Jaynes, J. (1976) *The Origins of Consciousness in the Breakdown of the Bicameral Mind*. London: Allen Lane.

Jelliffe, S.E. (1927) The mental pictures in schizophrenia in epidemic encephalitis. Their alliances, differences and a point of view. *American Journal of Psychiatry* 6: 413–65.

Johnson, M.K. (1988) Discriminating the origin of information. In J.F. Oltmanns and B.A. Maher (eds) *Delusional Beliefs*. New York: Wiley.

Johnson, W.G., Ross, J.M. and Mastia, M.A. (1977) Delusional behaviour: an attributional analysis of development and modification. *Journal of Abnormal Psychology* 86: 421–6.

Jones, E.E. (1979) The rocky road from acts to dispositions. *American Psychologist* 34: 107–17.

Jones, E. E., Farina, A., Hastorf, A.H., Markus, H., Miller, D.T. and Scott, R.A. (1984) *Social Stigma: The Psychology of Marked Relationships*. New York: Freeman.

Jones, K. (1972) *A History of the Mental Health Services*. London: Routledge and Kegan Paul.

Judkins, M. and Slade, P.D. (1981) A questionnaire study of hostility in persistent auditory hallucinations. *British Journal of Medical Psychology* 54: 243–50.

Kahneman, D., Slovic, P. and Tversky, A. (eds) (1982) *Judgement under Uncertainty: Heuristics and Biases*. New York: Cambridge University Press.

Kallmann, F.J. (1938) *The Genetics of Schizophrenia*. Locust Valley, New York: J.J. Augustin.

Kallmann, F.J. (1946) The genetic theory of schizophrenia: an analysis of 691 schizophrenic twin index families. *American Journal of Psychiatry* 103: 309–22.

Kallmann, F.J. (1950) The Genetics of Psychosis: an Analysis of 1232 Twin Index Families. Actualités Scientifiquies et Industrielles 1101, Congrès International de Psychiatrie, Paris, VI Psychiatrie Sociale. Herman et Cie, Paris.

Kaney, S. and Bentall, R.P. (1989) Persecutory delusions and attributional style. *British Journal of Medical Psychology* 62: 191–8.

Karson, C.N., Kleinman, J.E. and Wyatt, R.J. (1986) Biochemical concepts of schizophrenia. In T. Millon and G.L. Klerman (eds) *Contemporary Directions in Psychopathology. Towards the DSM-IV*. New York: The Guilford Press.

Kendell, R.E. (1972) Schizophrenia: the remedy for diagnostic confusion. *British Journal of Hospital Medicine* 8: 383–90.

Kendell, R.E. (1975a) The concept of disease and its implications for psychiatry. *British Journal of Psychiatry* 127: 305–15.

Kendell, R.E. (1975b) *The Role of Diagnosis in Psychiatry*. Oxford: Blackwell Scientific Publications.

Kendell, R.E., Brockington, I.F. and Leff, J.P. (1979) Prognostic implications of six alternative definitions of schizophrenia. *Archives of General Psychiatry* 36: 25–31.

Kendell, R.E., Everitt, B., Cooper, J.E., Sartorius, N. and David, M.E. (1968) The reliability of the 'Present State Examination'. *Social Psychiatry* 3: 123–9.

Kennedy, J.L., Giuffra, L.A., Moises, H.W., Cavalli-Sforza, L.L., Pakstis, A.J., Kidd, J.R., Castiglione, C.M., Sjogren, B., Wetterberg, L. and Kidd, K.K. (1988) Evidence against linkage of schizophrenia to markers on chromosome 5 in a northern Swedish pedigree. *Nature* 10 November, 336: 167–9.

Kety, S.S. (1974) From rationalization to reason. *American Journal of Psychiatry* 131: 957–63.

Kety, S.S. (1978) Heredity and environment. In J.D. Shershaw (ed.) *Schizophrenia: Science and Practice*. Cambridge, Mass.: Harvard University Press.

Kety, S.S., Rosenthal, D. and Wender, P.H. (1978) Genetic relationships within the schizophrenia spectrum: evidence from adoption studies. In R.L. Spitzer and D.F. Klein (eds) *Critical Issues in Psychiatric Diagnosis*. New York: Raven Press.

Kety, S.S., Rosenthal, D., Wender, P. and Schulsinger, F. (1968) The types and prevalence of mental illness in the biological and adoptive families of adopted schizophrenics. In D. Rosenthal and S.S. Kety (eds) *The Transmission of Schizophrenia*. Oxford: Pergamon.

Kety, S.S., Rosenthal, D., Wender, P. and Schulsinger, F. (1971) Mental illness in the biological and adoptive families of adopted schizophrenics. *American Journal of Psychiatry* 128: 302–6.

Kety, S.S., Rosenthal, D., Wender, P. and Schulsinger, F. (1976) Studies based on a total sample of adopted individuals and their relatives: why they were necessary, what they demonstrated and failed to demonstrate. *Schizophrenia Bulletin* 2: 413–28.

Kety, S.S., Rosenthal, D., Wender, P.H., Schulsinger, F. and Jacobsen, B. (1975) Mental illness in the biological and adoptive families of adopted individuals who have become schizophrenic. A preliminary report based on psychiatric interviews. In R. Fieve, D. Rosenthal and H. Brill (eds) *Genetic Research in Psychiatry*. London: Johns Hopkins University Press.

Kety, S.S., Rosenthal, D., Wender, P.H., Schulsinger, F. and Jacobsen, B. (1978) The biologic and adoptive families of adopted individuals who became schizophrenic: prevalence of mental illness and other characteristics. In L.C. Wynne, R.L. Cromwell and S. Matthysse (eds) *The Nature of Schizophrenia: New Approaches to Research and Treatment*. New York: Wiley.

Kiev, A. (1963) Beliefs and delusions of West Indian immigrants. *British Journal of Psychiatry* 109: 356–63.

King, D.J. and Cooper, S.J. (1989) Viruses, immunity and mental disorder. *British Journal of Psychiatry* 154: 1–7.

Klein, D.F. (1978) A proposed definition of mental illness. In R.L. Spitzer and D.F. Klein (eds) *Critical Issues in Psychiatric Diagnosis*. New York: Raven Press.

Kraepelin, E. (1896) *Psychiatrie*, 5th edn. Leipzig: Barth.

Kraepelin, E. (1899) *Psychiatrie*, 6th edn. Leipzig: Barth.

Kraepelin, E. (1905) *Lectures on Clinical Psychiatry*. London: Baillière Tindall.

Kraepelin, E. (1919) *Dementia Praecox and Paraphrenia*, trans. R.M. Barclay. Edinburgh: Livingstone (originally published in *Psychiatrie*, 8th edn., 1913).

Kramer, M., Sartorius, N., Jablensky, A. and Gulbinat, W. (1979) The ICD-9 classification of mental disorders: a review of its development and contents. *Acta Psychiatrica Scandinavica* 59: 241–62.

Kräupl-Taylor, F. (1971) A logical analysis of the medico-psychological concept of disease. *Psychological Medicine* 1: 356–64.

Kräupl-Taylor, F. (1976) The medical model of the disease concept. *British Journal of Psychiatry* 129: 588–94.

Kräupl-Taylor, F. (1979) *The Concepts of Illness, Disease and Morbus*. Cambridge: Cambridge University Press.

Kräupl-Taylor, F. (1982) Sydenham's disease entities. *Psychological Medicine* 12: 243–50.

Kringlen, E. (1964) Schizophrenia in male monozygotic twins. *Acta Psychiatrica Scandinavica* Suppl. 178.

Kringlen, E. (1966) Schizophrenia in twins: an epidemiological-clinical study. *Psychiatry* 29: 173–84.

Kringlen, E. (1968) An epidemiological-clinical twin study on schizophrenia. In D. Rosenthal and S.S. Kety (eds) *The Transmission of Schizophrenia*. Oxford: Pergamon.

Kringlen, E. (1976) Twins – still our best method. *Schizophrenia Bulletin* 2: 429–39.

Kuhn, T.S. (1970) *The Structure of Scientific Revolutions*. International Encyclopaedia of Unified Science, Vol. 2, No. 2, 2nd edn. Chicago: Chicago University Press.

Lader, M. (1977) *Psychiatry on Trial*. Harmondsworth: Penguin.

Lakatos, I. (1978) History of science and its rational reconstruction. In J. Worrall and G. Currie (eds) *Imre Lakatos: Philosophical Papers Vol. 1. The Methodology of Scientific Research Programmes*. Cambridge: Cambridge University Press.

Lander, E.S. (1988) Splitting schizophrenia. *Nature* 10 November, 336: 105–6.

Langfeldt, G. (1960) Diagnosis and prognosis of schizophrenia. *Proceedings of the Royal Society of Medicine* 53: 1047–52.

Launay, G. and Slade, P.D. (1981) The measurement of hallucinatory predisposition in male and female prisoners. *Personality and Individual Differences* 2: 221–34.

Leff, J. and Vaughn, C. (1981) The role of maintenance therapy and relatives' expressed emotion in relapse of schizophrenia: a two-year follow-up. *British Journal of Psychiatry* 139: 102–4.

Leff, J., Kuipers, L., Berkowitz, R., Eberlein Vries, R. and Sturgeon, D. (1982) A controlled trial of social intervention in the families of schizophrenic patients. *British Journal of Psychiatry* 141: 121–34.

Leigh, D. (1961) *The Historical Development of British Psychiatry. Vol. 1. 18th and 19th Centuries*. Oxford: Pergamon.

Leonhard, K. (1980) Contradictory issues in the origin of schizophrenia. *British Journal of Psychiatry* 136: 437–44.

Lerner, M.J. (1980) *The Belief in a Just World: A Fundamental Delusion*. New York: Plenum.

Lewis, N.D.C. (1966) History of the nosology and the evolution of the concept of schizophrenia. In P.H. Hoch and J. Zubin (eds) *Pathology of Schizophrenia*. New York: Grune and Stratton.

Lidz, T. and Blatt, S. (1983) Critique of the Danish–American studies of the biological and adoptive relatives of adoptees who became schizophrenic. *American Journal of Psychiatry* 140: 426–34.

Lidz, T., Blatt, S. and Cook, B. (1981) Critique of the Danish–American studies of the adopted away offspring of schizophrenic parents. *American Journal of Psychiatry* 138: 1063–8.

Lindsley, O. (1963) Direct measurement and functional definition of vocal hallucinatory symptoms. *Journal of Nervous and Mental Diseases* 136: 293–7.

Lipsedge, M. and Littlewood, R. (1979) Transcultural psychiatry. In K. Granville-Grossman (ed.) *Recent Advances in Psychiatry*, 3rd edn. Edinburgh: Churchill Livingstone

Littlewood, R. (1980) Anthropology and psychiatry: an alternative approach. *British Journal of Medical Psychology* 53: 213–25.

Littlewood, R. and Lipsedge, M. (1982) *Aliens and Alienists: Ethnic Minorities and Psychiatry*. Harmondsworth: Penguin. 2nd edn (1989) London: Unwin Hyman.

Luchins, D. (1975) The dopamine hypothesis of schizophrenia: a critical analysis. *Neuropsychobiology* 1: 365–78.

Luxenburger, H. (1928) Vorläufiger Bericht über psychiatrische Serienuntersuchungen an Zwilligen. *Zeitschrift für die gesamte Neurologie und Psychiatrie* 116: 297–326.

McCabe, M.S., Fowler, R.C., Cadoret, R.J. and Winokur, G. (1971) Familial differences in schizophrenia with good and poor prognosis. *Psychological Medicine* 1: 326–32.

MacCorquodale, K. and Meehl, P.E. (1948) On a distinction between hypothetical constructs and intervening variables. *Psychological Review* 55: 95–107.

McCulloch, M.L. (1983) A testing time for the test of time. *Bulletin of the British Psychological Society* 36: 1–5.

McGuffin, P., Festenstein, H. and Murray, R. (1983) A family study of HLA antigens and other genetic markers in schizophrenia. *Psychological Medicine* 13: 31–43.

McGuigan, F.J. (1966) Covert oral behaviour and auditory hallucinations. *Psychophysiology* 3: 73–80.

McKellar, P. (1968) *Experience and Behaviour*. Harmondsworth: Penguin.

Maher, B.A. (1988) Anomalous experience and delusional thinking: the logic of explanations. In J.F. Oltmanns and B.A. Maher (eds) *Delusional Beliefs*. New York: Wiley.

Maher, B.A. and Ross, J.S. (1984) Delusions. In H.E. Adams and P.B. Sutker (eds) *Comprehensive Handbook of Psychopathology*. New York: Plenum Press.

Margo, A., Hemsley, D. and Slade, P.D. (1981) The effects of varying auditory input on schizophrenic hallucinations. *British Journal of Psychiatry* 139: 122–7.

Marshall, J.R. (1984) The genetics of schizophrenia re-visited. *Bulletin of the British Psychological Society* 37: 177–81.

Marshall, J.R. (1985) Schizophrenia and the need for a critical analysis of information. In J.M. Brittain (ed.) *Consensus and Penalties for Ignorance in the Medical Sciences*. London: Taylor Graham.

Marshall, J.R. and Pettitt, A.N. (1985) Discordant concordant rates. *Bulletin of the British Psychological Society* 38: 6–9.

Maudsley, H. (1873) *Body and Mind*. London: Macmillan.

Maxwell, A.E. (1961) *Analysing Qualitative Data*. London: Methuen.

Maxwell, A.E. (1971) Multivariate statistical methods and classification problems. *British Journal of Psychiatry* 119: 121–7.

Medawar, P. (1984) *Plato's Republic*. Oxford: Oxford University Press.

Mednick, S.A. (1958) A learning theory approach to research in schizophrenia. *Psychological Bulletin* 55: 316–27.

Meehl, P.E. (1972) A critical afterword. In I.I. Gottesman and J. Shields (eds) *Schizophrenia and Genetics: A Twin Study Vantage Point*. New York: Academic Press.

Mercer, K. (1986) Racism and transcultural psychiatry. In P. Miller and N. Rose (eds) *The Power of Psychiatry*. Cambridge: Polity Press.

Miller, J. (1986) Primitive thoughts. *Canadian Psychologist* 127: 155–7.

Miller, M.D., Johnson, R.L. and Richmond, L.H. (1965) Auditory hallucinations and descriptive language skills. *Journal of Psychiatric Research* 3: 43–56.

Milton, F., Patwa, V.K. and Hafner, R.J. (1978) Confrontation versus belief modification in persistently deluded patients. *British Journal of Medical Psychology* 51: 127–30.

Mineka, S. and Kihlstrom, J.F. (1978) Unpredictable and uncontrollable events: a new perspective on experimental neurosis. *Journal of Abnormal Psychology* 87: 256–71.

Mintz, S. and Alpert, M. (1972) Imagery vividness, reality testing and schizophrenic hallucinations. *Journal of Abnormal Psychology* 79: 310–16.

Mischel, W. (1968) *Personality and Assessment*. New York: Wiley.

Morris, J.N. (1978) *The Uses of Epidemiology*, 3rd edn. Edinburgh: Churchill Livingstone.

Murphy, J.M. (1978) The recognition of psychoses in non-western societies. In R.L. Spitzer and D.F. Klein (eds) *Critical Issues in Psychiatric Diagnosis*. New York: Raven Press.

Nair, N.P. (1977) Drug therapy of schizophrenia in the community. *Journal of Orthomolecular Psychiatry* 6: 348–53.

Naylor, G.T. and Scott, C.R. (1980) Depot injections for affective disorders. *British Journal of Psychiatry* 136: 105.

Neale, J.M. and Oltmanns, T.F. (1980) *Schizophrenia*. New York: Wiley.

Nisbett, R.E. and Ross, L.D. (1980) *Human Inference: Strategies and Shortcomings of Social Judgement*. Englewood Cliffs, New Jersey: Prentice-Hall.

Nydegger, R.V. (1972) The elimination of hallucinatory and delusional behavior by verbal conditioning and assertive training: a case study. *Journal of Behaviour Therapy and Experimental Psychiatry* 3: 225–7.

Ogden, C.K. and Richards, I.A. (eds) (1956) *The Meaning of Meaning: A Study of the Influence of Language on Thought and of the Science of Symbolism*, 10th edn. London: Routledge and Kegan Paul.

Oltmanns, T.F. (1988) Approaches to the definition and study of delusions. In J.F. Oltmanns and B.A. Maher (eds) *Delusional Beliefs*. New York: Wiley.

Paikin, H., Jacobsen, B., Schulsinger, F., Godtfredsen, K., Rosenthal, D., Wender, P. and Kety, S.S. (1974) Characteristics of people who refused to participate in a social and psychological study. In S.A. Mednick, F. Schulsinger, J. Higgins and B.Bell (eds) *Genetics, Environment and Psychopathology*. Amsterdam: North Holland Publishing Co.

Paton-Saltzberg, R. (1982) Letter. *Bulletin of the British Psychological Society* 35: 397–8.

Paul, G.L., Tobias, L.L. and Holly, B.L. (1972) Maintenance psychotropic drugs in the presence of active treatment programs. A triple blind withdrawal study with long-term mental patients. *Archives of General Psychiatry* 27: 106–15.

Peckham, M. (1979) *Explanation and Power: The Control of Human Behavior*. New York: Seabury Press.

Phillips, L., Broverman, I.K. and Zigler, E. (1966) Social competence and psychiatric diagnosis. *Journal of Abnormal Psychology* 71: 209–14.

Posey, T.B. and Losch, M. (1983) Auditory hallucinations of hearing voices in 375 normal subjects. *Imagery, Cognition and Personality* 3: 99–113.

Price, B. (1950) Primary biases in twin studies: a review of prenatal and natal difference-producing factors in monozygotic pairs. *American Journal of Human Genetics* 2: 293–352.

Pyke, D.A., Cassar, J., Todd, J. and Taylor, K.W. (1970) Glucose tolerance and serum insulin in identical twins of diabetics. *British Medical Journal* 4: 649–51.

Radcliffe-Richards, J. (1982) *The Sceptical Feminist*. Harmondsworth: Penguin.

Revely, A. and Murray, R.M. (1980) The genetic contribution to the functional psychoses. *British Journal of Hospital Medicine* 24: 166–71.

Robins, E. and Guze, S.B. (1970) Establishment of diagnostic validity in psychiatric illness: its application to schizophrenia. *American Journal of Psychiatry* 126: 983–7.

Rosanoff, A.J., Handy, L.M., Plesset, I.R. and Brush, S. (1934) The etiology of so-called schizophrenic psychoses with special reference to their occurrence in twins. *American Journal of Psychiatry* 91: 247–86.

Rose, S. (1984) Disordered molecules and diseased minds. *Journal of Psychiatric Research* 18: 351–60.

Rose, S., Kamin, L.J. and Lewontin, R.C. (1984) *Not in Our Genes*. Harmondsworth: Penguin.

Rosenhan, D.I. (1973) On being sane in insane places. *Science* 179: 250–58.

Rosenthal, D. (1962a) Problems of sampling and diagnosis in the major twin studies of schizophrenia. *Psychiatric Research* 1: 116–34.

Rosenthal, D. (1962b) Familial concordance by sex with respect to schizophrenia. *Psychological Bulletin* 59: 401–21.

Rosenthal, D. (1970) *Genetic Theory and Abnormal Behavior*. New York: McGraw-Hill.

Rosenthal, D., Wender, P.H., Kety, S.S., Schulsinger, F., Welner, J. and Østergaard, L. (1968) Schizophrenics' offspring reared in adoptive homes. In D. Rosenthal and S.S. Kety (eds) *The Transmission of Schizophrenia*. Oxford: Pergamon.

Rosenthal, D., Wender, P.H., Kety, S.S., Welner, J. and Schulsinger, F. (1974) The adopted away offspring of schizophrenics. In S.A. Mednick, F. Schulsinger, J. Higgins and B. Bell (eds) *Genetics, Environment and Psychopathology*. Amsterdam: North Holland Publishing Co.

Ross, L. (1977) The intuitive psychologist and his shortcomings: distortions in the attribution process. In L. Berkowitz (ed.) *Advances in Experimental Social Psychology*, Vol. 10. New York: Academic Press.

Roth, M. and Kroll, J. (1986) *The Reality of Mental Illness*. Cambridge: Cambridge University Press.

Rotter, J.B. (1954) *Social Learning and Clinical Psychology*. New York: Prentice-Hall.

Rowe, J.T.W. (1906) Is dementia praecox the "new peril" in psychiatry? *American Journal of Insanity* 63: 385–93.

Rutner, R.I. and Bugle, C. (1969) An experimental procedure for the modification of psychotic behavior. *Journal of Consulting and Clinical Psychology* 33: 651–3.

Ryle, G. (1949) *The Concept of Mind*. New York: Harper and Row.

Sacks, O. (1971) Parkinsonism: a so-called new disease. *British Medical Journal* 3: 111.

Sacks, O. (1982) *Awakenings*. London: Pan Books.

Sahlins, M. (1977) *The Use and Abuse of Biology: An Anthropological Critique of Sociobiology*. London: Tavistock.

St Clair, D., Blackwood, D., Muir, W., Baillie, D., Hubbard, A., Wright, A. and Evans, H.J. (1989) No linkage of chromosome 5q11–q13 markers to schizophrenia in Scottish families. *Nature* 25 May, 339: 305–9.

Salzinger, K. (1986) Diagnosis: distinguishing among behaviors. In T. Millon and G.L. Klerman (eds) *Contemporary Directions in Psychopathology: Towards the DSM-IV*. New York: The Guilford Press.

Sandler, M. (1978) The dopamine hypothesis revisited. In G. Hemmings and W.A. Hemmings (eds) *The Biological Basis of Schizophrenia*. Lancaster: MTP Press.

Sarbin, T.R. (1967) The concept of hallucination. *Journal of Personality* 35: 359–80.

Sarbin, T.R. (1968) Ontology recapitulates philology: the mythic nature of anxiety. *American Psychologist* 23: 411–18.

Sarbin, T.R. (1970) Towards a theory of imagination. *Journal of Personality* 38: 52–76.

Sarbin, T.R. and Juhasz, J.B. (1967) The historical background of the concept of hallucination. *Journal of the History of the Behavioral Sciences* 3: 339–58.

Sarbin, T.R. and Juhasz, J.B. (1978) The social psychology of hallucinations. *Journal of Mental Imagery* 2: 117–44.

Sarbin, T.R. and Mancuso, J.C. (1980) *Schizophrenia: Medical Diagnosis or Moral Verdict?* New York: Pergamon.

Sarbin, T.R., Juhasz, J.B. and Todd, P. (1971) The social psychology of "hallucinations". *Psychological Record* 21: 87–93.

Sartorius, N., Jablensky, A. and Shapiro, R. (1978) Cross-cultural differences in the short-term prognosis of schizophrenic psychoses. *Schizophrenia Bulletin* 4: 102–12.

Schaefer, H.H. and Martin, P.L. (1969) *Behavioral Therapy*. New York: McGraw-Hill.

Scheibe, K.E. and Sarbin, T.R. (1965) Towards a theoretical conceptualization of superstition. *British Journal for the Philosophy of Science* 62: 143–58.

Schneider, K. (1959) *Clinical Psychopathology*, 5th edn. New York: Grune and Stratton.

Schneider, K. (1974) Primary and secondary symptoms in schizophrenia. In S.R. Hirsch and M. Shepherd (eds) *Themes and Variations in European Psychiatry*. Bristol: John Wright.

Schultz, D.P. (1965) *Sensory Restrictions: Effects on Behavior*. New York: Academic Press.

Scull, A.T. (1975) From madness to mental illness: medical men as moral entrepreneurs. *Archives of European Sociology* 16: 218–51.

Scull, A.T. (1979) *Museums of Madness: The Social Organisation of Insanity in Nineteenth Century England*. London: Allen Lane.

Sedgwick, P. (1982) *Psychopolitics*. London: Pluto Press.

Seeman, M.V., Littmann, S.K., Plummer, E., Thornton, J.F. and Jeffries, J.J. (1982) *Living and Working with Schizophrenia*. Milton Keynes: The Open University Press.

Serban, G. (1980) *The Adjustment of Schizophrenics in the Community*. Lancaster: MTP Press.

Shepherd, M. (1976) Definition, classification and nomenclature: a clinical overview. In D. Kemali, G. Bartholini and D. Richer (eds) *Schizophrenia Today*. Oxford: Pergamon.

Sherrington, R., Brynjolfsson, J., Petursson, H., Potter, M., Dudleston, K., Barraclough, B., Wasmuth, J., Dobbs, M. and Gurling, H. (1988) Localization of a susceptibility locus for schizophrenia on chromosome 5. *Nature* 10 November, 336: 164–7.

Shields, J., Gottesman, I.I. and Slater, E. (1967) Kallmann's 1946 schizophrenic twin study in the light of new information. *Acta Psychiatrica Scandinavica* 43: 385–96.

Shweder, R.A. (1977) Likeness and likelihood in everyday thought: magical thinking in judgements about personality. *Current Anthropology* 18: 637–58.

Silberman, R.M. (1971) *CHAM: A Classification of Psychiatric States*. Amsterdam: Excerpta Medica.

Skinner, B.F. (1948) Superstition in the pigeon. *Journal of Experimental Psychology* 38: 168–72.

Skinner, B.F. (1953) *Science and Human Behavior*. New York: Macmillan.

Skinner, B.F. (1974) *About Behaviorism*. New York: Knopf.

Skultans, V. (1975) *Madness and Morals: Ideas on Insanity in the Nineteenth Century*. London: Routledge and Kegan Paul.

Skultans, V. (1979) *English Madness: Ideas on Insanity 1580–1890*. London: Routledge and Kegan Paul.

Slade, P.D. (1972) The effects of systematic desensitisation on auditory hallucinations. *Behaviour Research and Therapy* 10: 85–91.

Slade, P.D. (1974) The external control of auditory hallucinations: an information theory analysis. *British Journal of Social and Clinical Psychology* 13: 73–9.

Slade, P.D. (1976a) Towards a theory of auditory hallucinations: outline of a hypothetical 4-factor model. *British Journal of Social and Clinical Psychology* 15: 415–24.

Slade, P.D. (1976b) An investigation of psychological factors involved in the predisposition to auditory hallucinations. *Psychological Medicine* 6: 123–32.

Slade, P.D. and Cooper, R. (1979) Some difficulties with the term "schizophrenia": an alternative model. *British Journal of Social and Clinical Psychology* 18: 309–17.

Slater, E. (1953) *Psychotic and Neurotic Illnesses in Twins*. London: HMSO.

Spaulding, W.D. and Cole, J.K. (eds) (1984) *Theories of Schizophrenia and Psychosis*. Lincoln: University of Nebraska Press.

Spitzer, R.L. and Endicott, J. (1978) Medical and mental disorder: proposed definition and criteria. In R.L. Spitzer and D.F. Klein (eds) *Critical Issues in Psychiatric Diagnosis*. New York: Raven Press.

Spitzer, R.L. and Fleiss, J.L. (1974) Reanalysis of the reliability of psychiatric diagnosis. *British Journal of Psychiatry* 125: 341–7.

Spitzer, R.L. and Wilson, J.B.N. (1983) The revision of DSM-III. *Psychiatric Annals* 13: 808–11.

Spitzer, R.L., Andreasen, N.C. and Endicott, J. (1978a) Schizophrenia and other psychotic disorders in DSM-III. *Schizophrenia Bulletin* 4: 489–94.

Spitzer, R.L., Endicott, J. and Robins, E. (1978b) Research diagnostic criteria: rationale and reliability. *Archives of General Psychiatry* 35: 773–82.

Spivak, G., Shure, B. and Platt, M. (1976) *The Problem Solving Approach to Adjustment*. San Francisco: Jossey Bass.

Stengel, E. (1959) Classification of mental disorders. *Bulletin of the World Health Organisation* 21: 601–63.

Stephens, J.H. (1970) Long-term course and prognosis in schizophrenia. *Seminars in Psychiatry* 2: 464–85.

Stephens, J.H. (1978) Long-term prognosis and follow-up in schizophrenia. *Schizophrenia Bulletin* 4: 25–47.

Stevenson, C.L. (1944) *Ethics and Language*. New Haven: Yale University Press.

Strauss, J.S. (1975) A comprehensive approach to psychiatric diagnosis. *American Journal of Psychiatry* 132: 1193–7.

Strauss, J.S. and Carpenter, W.T. (1974) The prediction of outcome in schizophrenia. II. The relationship between predictor and outcome variables. *Archives of General Psychiatry* 31: 37–42.

Strauss, J.S. and Carpenter, W.T. (1977) Prediction of outcome in schizophrenia: III. Five-year outcome and its predictors. *Archives of General Psychiatry* 34: 159–63.

Strauss, J.S. and Carpenter, W.T. (1978) The prognosis of schizophrenia: rationale for a multidimensional concept. *Schizophrenia Bulletin* 4: 56–66.

Strauss, J.S. and Carpenter, W.T. (1981) *Schizophrenia*. New York: Plenum Medical.

Strauss, J.S. and Gift, T.E. (1977) Choosing an approach for diagnosing schizophrenia. *Archives of General Psychiatry* 34: 1248–53.

Strauss, J.S., Bartko, J.J. and Carpenter, W.T. (1973) The use of clustering techniques for the classification of psychiatric patients. *British Journal of Psychiatry* 122: 531–40.

Szasz, T. (1976) *Schizophrenia: The Sacred Symbol of Psychiatry*. Oxford: Oxford University Press.

Szasz, T. (1987) *Insanity: The Idea and its Consequences*. New York: Wiley.

Thouless, R.H. (1974) *Straight and Crooked Thinking*. London: Pan Books.

Tienari, P. (1963) Psychiatric illness in identical twins. *Acta Psychiatrica Scandinavica* Suppl. 171.

Tienari, P. (1975) Schizophrenia in Finnish male twins. In M.H. Lader (ed.) *Studies of Schizophrenia. British Journal of Psychiatry* Special Publication No. 10.

Tobias, L.L. and MacDonald, M.L. (1974) Withdrawal of maintenance drugs with long-term hospitalised mental patients: a critical review. *Psychological Bulletin* 81: 107–25.

Toon, P.D. (1976) Letter. *British Journal of Psychiatry* 128: 99.

Toon, P.D. (1981) Defining "disease": classification must be distinguished from evaluation. *Journal of Medical Ethics* 7: 197–201.

Toon, P.D. (1982) The Sutcliffe trial: some philosophical implications for psychology. *Bulletin of the British Psychological Society* 35: 265–6.

Torrey, E.F. and Peterson, M.R. (1973) Slow and latent viruses in schizophrenia. *Lancet* 7 July: 22–4.

Trouton, D.S. and Maxwell, A.E. (1956) The relation between neurosis and psychosis: an analysis of symptoms and past history of 819 psychotics and neurotics. *Journal of Mental Science* 102: 1–21.

Tsuang, M.T., Dempsey, M. and Raucher, F. (1976) A study of "atypical schizophrenia": a comparison with schizophrenia and affective disorder by sex, age of admission, precipitant, outcome and family history. *Archives of General Psychiatry* 33: 1157–60.

Tuke, S. (1813) *A Description of the Retreat*. York: W. Alexander.

Turner, W.J. (1979) Genetic markers for schizotaxia. *Biological Psychiatry* 14: 177–206.

Tyrrell, D.A.J., Crow, J.J., Parry, R.P., Johnstone, E. and Ferrier, I.N. (1979) Possible virus in schizophrenia and some neurological disorders. *Lancet* 21 April: 839–41.

Ullman, L.P. and Krasner, L. (1969) *A Psychological Approach to Abnormal Behaviour*. Englewood Cliffs, New Jersey: Prentice-Hall.

Vaillant, G.E. (1964) Prospective prediction of schizophrenic remission. *Archives of General Psychiatry* 11: 509–18.

Vaillant, G. (1978) A 10-year follow-up of remitting schizophrenics. *Schizophrenia Bulletin* 4: 78–84.

Vaughn, C. and Leff, J. (1976) The measurement of expressed emotion in the families of psychiatric patients. *British Journal of Social and Clinical Psychology* 15: 157–65.

Von Economo, C. (1931) *Encephalitis Lethargica: Its Sequelae and Treatment*. Oxford: Oxford University Press.

Wallace, A.F.C. (1959) Cultural determinants of response to hallucinatory experience. *Archives of General Psychiatry* 1: 58–69.

Warburton, D.M. (1985) Addiction, dependence and habitual substance use. *Bulletin of the British Psychological Society* 38: 285–8.

Ward, C.H., Beck, A.T., Mendelson, M., Mock, J.E. and Erbaugh, J.K. (1962) The psychiatric nomenclature. *Archives of General Psychiatry* 7: 198–205.

Warren, M. and Gregory, R.L. (1958) The auditory analogue of the visual reversible figure. *American Journal of Psychology* 71: 612–13.

Watt, A.D.C., Gillespie, C. and Chapel, H. (1987) A study of genetic linkage in schizophrenia. *Psychological Medicine* 17: 363–70.

Watts, F., Powell, G.E. and Austen, S.V. (1973) The modification of abnormal beliefs. *British Journal of Medical Psychology* 46: 359–63.

Wender, P.H. (1963) Dementia praecox: the development of the concept. *American Journal of Psychiatry* 119: 1143–51.

Wender, P.H., Rosenthal, D., Kety, S.S., Schulsinger, F. and Welner, J. (1973) Social class and psychopathology in adoptees: a natural experimental method for separating the roles of genetic and experimental factors. *Archives of General Psychiatry* 28: 318–25.

Wender, P.H., Rosenthal, D., Kety, S.S., Schulsinger, F. and Welner, J. (1974) Cross-fostering: a research strategy for clarifying the role of genetic and experiential factors in the etiology of schizophrenia. *Archives of General Psychiatry* 30: 121–8.

Wing, J.K. (1978a) Clinical concepts of schizophrenia. In J.K. Wing (ed.) *Schizophrenia: Toward a New Synthesis*. London: Academic Press.

Wing, J.K. (1978b) *Reasoning about Madness*. Oxford: Oxford University Press.

Wing, J.K. (1988) Abandoning What? *British Journal of Clinical Psychology* 27: 325–8.

Wing, J.K., Cooper, J.E. and Sartorius, N. (1974) *Description and Classification of Psychiatric Symptoms*. Cambridge: Cambridge University Press.

Wing, L. (1970) Observations on the psychiatric section of the International Classification of Diseases and the British Glossary of Mental Disorders. *Psychological Medicine* 1: 79–85.

Wingate, P. (ed.) (1976) *Medical Encyclopaedia*. Harmondsworth: Penguin.

Witelson, S.F. (1986) Man's changing hypotheses of his internal universe. *Canadian Psychology* 27: 123–7.

Wong, D.F., Wagner, H.N., Tune, L.E., Dannals, R.F., Pearlson, G.D., Links, J.M., Tamminga, C.A., Broussolle, E.P., Ravert, H.T., Wilson, A.A., Toung, J.K.T., Malat, J., Williams, J.A., O'Tuama, L.A., Snyder, S.H., Kuhar, M.J. and Gjedde, A. (1986) Positron emission tomography reveals elevated D_2 dopamine receptors in drug-naive schizophrenics. *Science* 234: 1558–63.

World Health Organisation (1948) *Manual of the International Statistical Classification of Diseases, Injuries and Causes of Death*, 6th Revision. *Bulletin of The World Health Organisation*, Suppl. 1. Geneva: WHO.

World Health Organisation (1965) *Report of the First Seminar on Psychiatric*

Diagnosis. Classification and Statistics. Functional Psychosis, with Emphasis on Schizophrenia. London/Geneva: WHO.

World Health Organisation (1967) *Manual of the International Statistical Classification of Diseases, Injuries and Causes of Death*, 8th Revision. Geneva: WHO

World Health Organisation (1973) *The International Pilot Study of Schizophrenia.* Geneva: WHO.

World Health Organisation (1974) *Glossary of Mental Disorders and Guide to their Classification for use in Conjunction with the ICD*, 8th Revision. Geneva: WHO.

World Health Organisation (1977) *Manual of the International Statistical Classification of Diseases, Injuries and Causes of Death*, 9th Revision. Geneva: WHO.

World Health Organisation (1978) *Mental Disorders: Glossary and Guide to Their Classification in Accordance with the 9th Revision of the International Classification of Diseases.* Geneva: WHO.

World Health Organisation (1979) *Schizophrenia: An International Follow-up Study.* Chichester: Wiley.

Young, J.Z. (1951) *Doubt and Certainty in Science.* Oxford: Oxford University Press.

Zilboorg, G. (1941) *A History of Medical Psychology.* New York: Norton.

Name index

Subject index